MW01244115

The Way of Peace

The Way of Peace

A. J. Muste's Writings for the Church

Edited by
Jeffrey D. Meyers

Thanks for your interest and help!
Jeff Meyers

CASCADE *Books* • Eugene, Oregon

THE WAY OF PEACE
A. J. Muste's Writings for the Church

Cascade Books
An Imprint of Wipf and Stock Publishers
199 W. 8th Ave., Suite 3
Eugene, OR 97401

www.wipfandstock.com

PAPERBACK ISBN 13: 978-1-4982-2837-4
HARDCOVER ISBN 13: 978-1-4982-2839-8

Cataloguing-in-Publication Data

Muste, A. J., 1885–1967.

The way of peace : A. J. Muste's writings for the church / A. J. Muste, edited by Jeffrey D. Meyers.

xiv + 316 p. ; 23 cm. Includes bibliographical references and indexes.

ISBN: 978-1-4982-2837-4 (paperback) | ISBN: 978-1-4982-2839-8 (hardback)

1. Pacifism. 2. Peace Religious aspects Christianity. 3. Radicalism. I. Jeffrey D. Meyers. II. Title.

JX 1963 .M8457 2016

Manufactured in the U.S.A. 04/04/2016

"Fellowship and Class Struggle," "Unwilling and Unable to Conform," "What the Bible Teaches About Freedom," "Theology of Despair," "Pacifism and Perfectionism," "I Believe," "Jesus and the Way to Peace," and "The Sound of the Trumpet" are used by permission of the Fellowship of Reconciliation.

"Return to Pacifism," "The True International," and "The Way of the Cross," are used by permission of the *Christian Century*.

"Fragment of Autobiography" is used by permission of World Council of Churches Publications.

"Evangelism and the Industrial Workers," "The Knowledge of God," "Admonitions for War Time," and "Unity in Crisis" are printed here for the first time with the permission of A. J. Muste's heirs.

The poem "Saint Thomas" by William Hard is quoted with the permission of his heirs.

Contents

Acknowledgements

Each work in this collection has a long history. Thanks is due to all those who touched them along the way, including the secretaries who typed Muste's handwritten drafts, the editors who helped perfect and publish them, and the librarians and archivists who preserved them.

Although my research led me to many libraries and archives across the country, I would especially like to thank Wendy Chmielewski and the staff of the Swarthmore College Peace Collection and Geoffrey Reynolds and the staff of the Joint Archives of Holland, Michigan for their expert assistance. A number of the pieces in this collection exist only in a few copies. Without the dedication of these and other archives, many of them would have been lost.

I would also like to thank my master's thesis advisors, Lonnie Valentine of Earlham School of Religion and Scott Holland of Bethany Theological Seminary, for their help and support while I was doing the research that led me to many of the works in this collection.

Many friends and colleagues contributed to making this collection a reality. Gary Benson typed many of the selections. Gary, Kayla Fik, and Alina Kanaski helped me with research in libraries too far away for me to visit. When I did travel, Amy and Mark Kornelis hosted me in their home on numerous occasions. Marc Baer, Steven Bouma-Prediger, Leilah Danielson, Bridger Hamilton, Alina Kanaski, Samantha Miller, Olivia Myers, Michael Oellig, Iren Raye, and Rob Worley looked over parts of the manuscript, helping me improve my writing and saving me the embarrassment of numerous typographical errors.

Of course, no book comes to print without the hard work of the staff of its publisher. All of the staff at Wipf and Stock, especially my editor Rodney Clapp, deserve thanks for all of their work on this project.

Introduction

Late on a Friday night about a year after his brother was assassinated, a staffer brought US Attorney General Robert Kennedy some urgent papers from the White House to sign. After asking what they were about, Kennedy exclaimed, "Let me get this straight. You want me to sign that letter so that an eighty year old man can't walk eight hundred miles?"[1] Kennedy refused to sign the injunction, which was meant to prevent the protestors an aging A. J. Muste was working with from getting on a boat in Florida in order to sail to Cuba. The protest, known as the Quebec-Washington-Guantánamo walk, had drawn the attention of the Johnson Administration for its criticism of US Cold War policies, its challenge of segregation in the South, and the international press it generated.

Georgia proved the hardest stretch of the walk. There, the racially diverse walkers were repeatedly beaten by police and arrested. The protestors spent months in jail for trying to walk down the street, African Americans and whites together.[2] They eventually reached Miami, but despite Kennedy's actions were unable to get permission to sail to Cuba. When five of the protestors set sail anyway, they were quickly stopped by the Coast Guard. A few days later, the US Attorney in Miami filed a case to seize their boat, which, after much consideration, the walkers had named "The Spirit of Freedom."[3]

1. Adam Walinsky, interview by Thomas F. Johnston, November 29, 1969, transcript RFKOH-AW-01, p. 3, Robert F. Kennedy Oral History Program, John F. Kennedy Presidential Library, Boston. Muste was actually seventy-nine at the time. Kennedy was told, "The White House wants it signed." The walk was sponsored by the Committee for Nonviolent Action, an activist group primarily focused on opposing the nuclear arms race.

2. Marjorie Swann Edwin, "AJ, Kennedy and King: The Quebec to Guantanamo Walk in Georgia November 1963," *Muste Notes* 14, no. 3 (Spring 2007); "Nonviolence and Police Brutality: A Document," *Liberation* 8, no. 10 (December 1963), 9–13.

3. An untitled report mailed to a CNVA staffer in New York reveals that they also considered naming it after Muste. The report can be found in the Swarthmore College Peace Collection, Committee for Nonviolent Action Records, box 19. For information

The case, *The United States of America v. The Spirit of Freedom*, was taken on by the American Civil Liberties Union and the Florida Civil Liberties Union. They hoped the case could be used to challenge the ban on travel to Cuba.[4]

Leadership of creative nonviolent protests like the Quebec-Washington-Guantánamo walk was typical of Muste, a pastor turned activist well known for his devotion to the pursuit of peace and justice. His remarkable life as a pastor, labor leader, professor, and peace activist was shaped and informed by his Christian faith and deep theological reflection.

The Making of a Pacifist

Abraham Johannes Muste (1885–1967) immigrated to the United States as a small child and grew up in the strict Dutch Reformed tradition prevalent in western Michigan at the time. He went to schools run by his denomination through college and seminary.[5] His concern for peace and justice developed gradually, as he interacted with the wider Christian church and struggled to interpret Scripture in new ways. This process led him to oppose the United States' participation in the First World War. His early embrace of pacifism shaped the rest of his life.

Although he was an ordained minister, Muste did not limit himself to traditional forms of ministry. He first became famous for his work as a labor leader in the 1920s and 30s. At a time when strikes and other labor actions were often met with severe violence, he sought to keep union organizing largely nonviolent. His brand of union organizing is also notable for its insistence on racial equality and the inclusion of women and young people.[6]

---

on the stopping of the boat, see the October 30, 1964 press release in the CNVA records, box 3.

4. "Government Stops Five Pacifists En Route To Cuba In Small Boat," *Liberation* 9, no. 9 (December 1964), 30. Archival material held in the CNVA records at the Swarthmore College Peace Collection confirm this account, although I have not been able to find any information on the outcome of the court case.

5. At age thirteen, Muste's interest in going into ministry allowed him to obtain scholarships that made it possible for him to attend the Reformed Church in America's preparatory school at Hope College in Holland, Michigan and then Hope College itself, where he graduated as the valedictorian of the class of 1905. He earned his first seminary degree at New Brunswick Theological Seminary in 1909.

6. Jo Ann Robinson, *Abraham Went Out: A Biography of A. J. Muste* (Philadelphia: Temple University Press, 1981), 32–61, 109; Leilah Danielson, *American Gandhi: A. J. Muste and the History of Radicalism in the Twentieth Century* (Philadelphia: University of Pennsylvania Press, 2014), 90, 104, 128. The labor college he headed from 1921 to 1933 was notable for its equal enrollment of women and men, its full inclusion of

After he left the labor movement, he quickly made a name for himself in the peace movement during the Second World War and the Cold War. He advocated for nonviolent foreign policy and strongly opposed government restrictions on civil liberties. It was this work that truly made him famous, leading *Time* magazine to proclaim him "the No. 1 U.S. Pacifist" and pacifists in India to refer to him as the "American Gandhi."[7] He also played a significant role in laying the foundations for the civil rights movement.[8]

Muste was not just a capable leader and passionate activist; he was a pastor and theologian whose work for peace and justice was deeply rooted in his theology. This collection brings together a representative selection of Muste's works for Christian audiences, making it possible for the first time to easily study his theology. Although he frequently spoke to non-Christian audiences in purely secular terms, the works in this volume reveal the theological basis of his lifelong work for peace and justice.

This Collection

This collection is divided into four sections, each covering a major period of Muste's life. The first contains writings from Muste's early career as a pastor. In the first selection, Muste presents theological and practical arguments against US entry into the First World War. In the next two pieces, a sermon and a speech from 1918, Muste emphasizes Christianity's role in rebuilding a world devastated by war. In the final selection, an article written just before he joined the labor movement, Muste urges his audience to reject materialism and excessive consumption.

The second section addresses Muste's time as a leader in the labor movement from 1918 to 1936. In the first two selections, he argues that Christians need to become involved in work to help the poor and oppressed by joining in the struggle for fair labor practices. In three of the following pieces, those from 1936 and 1939, Muste gives three different perspectives on why he left the labor movement to return to work in the church. In the remaining selection, titled "Evangelism and the Industrial Workers," he issues a prophetic critique of the church's relationship with the working class.

African Americans, and its insistence on including all factions of the labor movement.

7. *Time* 34, no. 2 (July 10, 1939), 37; Danielson, *American Gandhi*, 15.

8. Muste had a lifelong concern for combating segregation and racial prejudice. He was the person who first introduced Rev. Dr. Martin Luther King Jr. to nonviolence and he greatly influenced the civil rights movement by mentoring key leaders including Bayard Rustin, James Farmer, George Houser, and James Lawson. See Martin Luther King Jr., *Stride toward Freedom: The Montgomery Story* (New York: Harper & Row, 1958), 95; Robinson, *Abraham Went Out*, 111, 117–18, 121.

When Muste returned to full-time ministry in 1937, he focused on combating communism as a false alternative to Christianity. He was also well aware that Europe was again headed toward a major war. Soon this became his main preoccupation, especially after he left his new pastorate in April 1940 to head the pacifist Fellowship of Reconciliation. The third section focuses on Muste's writings during this period. It begins with an evangelistic sermon where he argues that religion is the only hope for peace. In the next three pieces, Muste calls Christians to embrace the gospel of peace—the way of the cross—which rejects all war. Two sermons from 1940 and 1941 follow. In the first, Muste gives "admonitions for wartime." In the second, he details how the church might maintain unity between pacifist and non-pacifist Christians during a war. This section concludes with an article in which Muste discusses his refusal to register for the draft—despite the fact that as an ordained minister he could claim automatic exemption from service.

The final section reflects Muste's broad array of interests during the postwar period. It begins with a remarkable pamphlet from 1943 where Muste addresses racial inequality and how African Americans and whites alike might work against it. In the second selection, Muste responds to the Second World War and the use of the atomic bomb, arguing that Jesus showed humanity that there are better ways of confronting evil than resorting to evil in return. In the next two pieces, Muste argues against Reinhold Niebuhr's "Christian realism" and neo-orthodox thought. Following those selections are a short formal prayer Muste wrote for a conference on the church and war, a speech he gave at his sixty-fifth birthday party about what he believes and what has shaped him, and a pamphlet where he tries to convert Christians to pacifism by examining Jesus' life. Another critique of Niebuhr's thought follows, this time based on how its popularity has negatively affected Christians' thinking and behavior. The collection concludes with a lecture given to a Quaker audience in which Muste calls them to pursue the kingdom of God together, while not underestimating the difficulty of this calling.

I have added short introductions to each selection, footnotes to explain references to individuals and events that are no longer common knowledge, citations to allow the reader to find Muste's sources, and section headings within some of the longer pieces that did not already have them. I have also updated some outdated spelling and gendered language. Where multiple previously published versions differ, I have used my own judgment in harmonizing them. All footnotes are mine unless otherwise indicated.

My hope is that this collection will introduce A. J. Muste's genius to a new generation. Although educated and shaped in the Reformed tradition,

Muste fruitfully explored the great diversity of the Christian church. He devoted himself to calling his fellow Christians to live out their faith in radical ways. In this he was frequently ahead of the church, as one Quaker woman expressed when she wrote that "time and time again, when we Friends have weighed and considered the course our witness was to take we have seen far off down the road ahead of us the tall spare frame of A. J., already in the Way."[9]

9. Irene Koch, "Letter for the Society of Friends and the American Friends Service Committee to A.J. Muste," January 23, 1960; quoted in Jo Ann Robinson, *A.J. Muste, Pacifist & Prophet: His Relation to the Society of Friends* (Wallingford, PA: Pendle Hill Publications, 1981), 24.

The Pastor and the Great War

1

Of What Shall We Be Afraid? (1915)

In this tract Muste addresses the national debate over whether the United States should prepare to enter the First World War, which was already being fought in Europe. It is an important early piece that reveals his fledgling pacifism and, although written a few years prior to his work in the labor movement, shows he was already sympathetic to it. Muste contends that the focus should be first on the United States' own sins—its treatment of African Americans and Japanese immigrants, its industrial and social order, and the "liquor problem." He argues that by preparing for war, the US runs the risk of sacrificing its freedoms and embracing the very philosophies it seeks to defend itself against. Muste wrote this piece while in his second pastorate, a Congregational church near Boston. After graduating from the Reformed Church in America's New Brunswick Theological Seminary in 1909, he first pastored a church in that denomination in New York City. In 1913 he earned a second seminary degree, this time from Union Theological Seminary in New York City.

"Be not afraid of them that kill the body, and after that have no more that they can do: fear him who after he hath killed hath power to cast into hell."[1] The words suggest the attitude of Jesus toward outward, material trouble on the one hand and toward moral disaster on the other. The general principle on which he acted seems to be abundantly clear. He was firmly convinced that no amount of suffering inflicted on a person from without—loss of money, comfort, honor, reputation, life—could be compared with the inward moral and spiritual loss that one inflicts upon oneself by sin, by all living that is out of accord with God. I want to set forth the application of this principle to some of our larger national problems. What I wish more precisely to do is to mention three or four of the dangers that threaten us from without—dangers that you are reading about in every newspaper, hearing about from every platform—dangers that seem very real and terrible to many millions in America in these days when the lengthening shadows of European war-clouds ever and again leap for a moment across our pathway, yea, when the hand of violence is sometimes wantonly laid upon our own people. And then I want to set over against each of these dangers from without, as I mention it, a danger that threatens us from within, a wrong that we are doing which consequently affects the whole being of the nation; and I want you to ask yourselves which of these evils, the outward or the inward, the material or the moral, the one done to us or the one done by us, we have greater cause to fear and to defend ourselves against with all haste and thoroughness and patriotic fervor.

In the first place, we have been considerably exercised in recent years about the treatment accorded to our citizens in various parts of the world. I have seen formidable lists giving the names of American citizens badly treated, insulted, robbed, killed perhaps, in Mexico during its reign of revolution and terror.[2] Much indignation has been expressed because the offenders have not, so it is charged, been brought to justice and punished as summarily as they might have been. Many have told us that American honor has been lowered because we have not forcefully protested against mistreatment of American subjects, that the United States is in certain circles a by-word and a derision because it is believed that we are not prepared manfully to defend our citizens abroad. We have all heard during the past weeks demands that the most vigorous representations be made to Germany, hints more or less veiled that war be declared, if necessary, that the American name may be respected and the American citizen safe

1. Luke 12:4–5.

2. This piece was written during the Mexican Revolution, which had begun in 1910.

once more, after the "Gulflight" and "Lusitania" incidents.[3] I want to make absolutely no comment now on these demands, simply to note the existence of this feeling, this conviction, that being a citizen of the United States ought to stand for something large and fine, ought to make a person safe, free to do one's work, respected, everywhere on this broad earth, and that it is a grievous thing when such is not the case.

Very well. Now, one feels justified in drawing two conclusions regarding a nation of such high spirit as ours which desires its citizens to be safe and free and respected wherever they go. You would expect such a nation to treat its own citizens on its own soil honorably, and you would expect it to treat the people of other nationalities honorably. Do we? As to our treatment of our own citizens, what about the black? We have about ten million black people in this country. Our ancestors brought them here by force and for many years used them as slaves. Then we set them free, nominally, and made them citizens of this country, citizens. How honorably do we treat these fellow-citizens? How much is our pride hurt when they are not honorably treated? There are a number of states in the Union where these citizens never vote, never have a voice in national affairs nor even in their own local affairs. Every week or two one of these citizens is lynched, killed without an opportunity of defense, in many cases not even charged with a sexual crime, and in many cases disposed of though there is no reasonable proof of guilt. We call them inferior to us in mind and character. Suppose they are.[4] That means that mentally and morally they are still children. Are we in the habit of subjecting children, just because they are children, to all sorts of disadvantages? Do we think it wise to bring up our children in slums and vice-districts? Do we not deliberately seek to place them in the fairest and noblest surroundings? According to what philosophy of education, then, is it that we compel these black children of the nation to attain their

3. The *Gulflight* was a US merchant ship torpedoed by a German submarine prior to US entry into World War I. Three of the crew were killed. It had been under escort by British patrol vessels and had not been sufficiently marked as a US vessel, making it a legitimate target, a fact that was not publicized due to the desire to use the incident to increase support for US entry into the war. Six days after the *Gulflight* incident, on May 7, 1915, the *Lusitania*, a British passenger ship, was sunk during a trip from New York to Liverpool, killing just under 1,200 people. The sinking caused international outcry despite the fact that the German embassy in the United States had issued a statement that the *Lusitania* was liable to be attacked, which was printed next to advertisements for the voyage. It was classified as an auxiliary war ship and had been carrying a significant amount of munitions, only a portion of which were on the official manifest. President Woodrow Wilson used both incidents to increase support for US entry into the war, leading Secretary of State William Jennings Bryan to resign in protest.

4. Muste makes the following statements for the sake of argument. It seems clear that he did not think that racial minorities are inferior.

development under the severest handicaps? They are barred from many occupations. They have not the social and cultural advantages of white people. In many cities in this country they are virtually compelled to live in or on the edge of the vice-district, in houses that are poorer than those in which the lowest and most ignorant of our recent arrivals from Europe live, and in houses for which they have to pay exorbitant rents, because landlords know that black people can be kept out of better neighborhoods and have to take what they can get. They are inferior, these people. Oh, yes, dull and stupid, emotional, prey to passions, incapable of high notions and honesty, and so on, mere children in the realm of mind and character. And so we put them in precisely where the struggle for education and respectability and character will be the hardest, where they would be angels, and not human, if the majority of them came out clean and strong. Do you consider this fine, high-spirited treatment of our own citizens?

No one can feel more horrified than I at the loss of several hundred of our citizens recently in Mexico and in connection with the European war. But I wonder, my friends, if, in view of the treatment we accord every day to ten million of our own fellow-citizens, there is not something foolish, perhaps disproportionate, about the hue and cry about national honor in connection with the death of a few hundred people due to the carelessness or cruelty of others? The United States does not want to be insulted: why do we insult ourselves? Which do you think Jesus would like to have us toil and fight to correct, the wrong done to us or the wrong done by us? On the supposition that God is just, that for every wrong done by individual or nation the penalty is paid, which do you think is the bigger danger to the welfare of America, the little wrong done to us or the great, shameful injustice perpetrated by us everyday in every year upon the weak in our midst, upon those of whom the Word says, "We that are strong ought to bear the infirmities of the weak?"[5] Instead of that we say: "Let them that are weak bear the infirmities, the cruelty, the indifference, the desire for gain and power, of us the strong."

And what of our treatment of citizens of other nations? Quite a number of years ago Japanese coolie labor was imported into some of our western states; inducements to come were held out to these Japanese by American contractors. The newcomers were able to live on very little and willing to work terrifically hard. Presently American labor felt it was handicapped in competition with these people and sought relief. At about the same time Japan began to prove herself a first-rate nation in the Western sense, i.e., able to shoot down more people in a given time than her neighbors, and

5. Romans 15:1.

so the sense of uneasiness and prejudice against the presence of Japanese labor grew apace on the western coast. The matter was taken up with Japan by our State Department and during President Roosevelt's administration Japan made with us what is called a Gentleman's Agreement to see to it that no Japanese coolie labor should be sent to this country. I have never seen anywhere the least hint of any failure on Japan's part to live up to that agreement. However, there were, of course, some laborers in the West already, and each year there are a few Japanese desiring to come here to study and to do business, quite as missionaries and business people go from us to Japan to do their work there. I have not read in recent years a hint of unfair treatment by Japan of our missionaries and business people in Kobe, Tokyo, Yokohama. But we have kept right on passing discriminatory laws against Japanese in the West. Japan protests to our State Department that its citizens ought to receive here the same treatment as those of other nations, or at all events the same treatment as Americans get in Japan. Our State Department in Washington answers Japan that the anti-Japanese legislation was passed by a state and the federal government has no power to interfere. And there the matter rests. Japanese are insulted, discriminated against by laws on the statute-books of our states, and we say we cannot do anything about it. How long would we endure such treatment from Japan, from Germany, from Mexico? Is it enough for us to fill the newspapers with protests against wrongs done to a few of our citizens while we ignore the wrong we do to a high-spirited people who have done us no wrong? And in view of what some insist on saying about a coming conflict with Japan, I wonder what we had better devote ourselves to—even from the lowest, most selfish point of view—the righting of the wrong done to us or the righting of the wrong done by us?

In the second place, we are told that our peace is in danger of attack from without. We, a quiet, orderly, self-respecting nation, going about our own business, with no great desire to harm anyone, are now to be interrupted in our tranquility and repose. We are to be attacked; we shall have to live in a state of preparation for war. The old days of seclusion, peaceful development, and all that are past. One of the most talked of books at the moment is Professor Usher's work on "Pan-Americanism," in which he sets forth the extreme probability, from his point of view, that the victor in the present European conflict, whoever it may be, England or Germany, will pursue an aggressive and hostile policy against our peace and commerce.[6] I am not inclined to make light of this possibility. If history is to consist for

6. Roland Usher, *Pan-Americanism: A Forecast of the Inevitable Clash between the United States and Europe's Victor* (New York: Century, 1915).

some years to come, as it has consisted for some years back, of a gigantic effort on the part of the great nations to seize the markets of the world by whatever means may present themselves; if America is to take part in that scramble; and if our last resource for the settlement of the question who shall have and who shall not is to be the sword—then I think it altogether probable that we are to be involved in war within a few years. Let us admit that our peace may be disturbed from without.

Are we certain, however, that all the conditions that may disturb us in the even tenor of our way are outward? That some of them are not here in our own midst, conditions which perhaps we have helped bring to pass, for the remedying of which we have at least some responsibility? Let me remind you that within a very few years we have had most serious labor disturbances in Lawrence, in New York, in Paterson, in Little Falls, in West Virginia, in Northern Michigan, in Colorado. Nothing could be more superficial than to say that professional agitators are alone responsible for these troubles. Those agitators did not come to you and me to ask us to revolt, to carry red flags, and to commit acts of violence, did they? We were not the right kind of material. They did find people in such a condition that they were willing to strike, to starve, to fight, to kill, on the chance of making some change in the conditions of their life. Very well; let's find out what it is in the character and in the condition of these people that makes them inflammable material. That will be much more reasonable than merely to harangue against agitators who are only the match that set fire to a powder magazine that they had nothing to do with making. Personally I think our present industrial and social order is very far from being what Jesus would have it be. The great majority of people in the world spend practically all their time and energy in trying to make a living, to keep alive. But on those terms human life is not any better than a brute's, is it? Jesus Christ could not approve of slums, of the housing-conditions in many places, of child-labor, of sweat-shops. With his notions about the equality of people before God and the comparative unimportance of wealth and what wealth can buy, Jesus could not approve of our extremes of poverty and luxury, our haphazard method of distributing the products of our common toil. With his notions of democracy and service Jesus could not approve of an organization of industry in which those who work have almost no voice as to the conditions under which they work. Oh, we talk about socialists, anarchists, I. W. W.'s—revolutionaries, we call them.[7] The only trouble with them from Jesus' point of view is that they are not half revolutionary enough, for they are only tinkering away at the

7. The Industrial Workers of the World, an international union, endured severe resistance from business and the government. It opposed US entry into the First World War.

outward machinery of life; he would strike at the heart of humanity and take out of it the very desire for money, for ease, for power, for honor, which creates the outward order of industry and society. Now which do you think we ought to pay more attention to, possible aggression from without or the unjust and unChrist-like conditions eating at the nation's heart? On the very lowest plane, can a nation that is not sound within hope to withstand aggression from without, and would such a nation be worth saving if it could be saved? Louis XIV was busy defending himself against hostile nations and attacking them in turn, and all the time he was even busier creating the unjust and burdensome conditions that led to the French Revolution. How much wisdom did he show in his solicitude about attack from the outside when at home he was helping to prepare that flaming and fathomless cauldron of discontent into which all that he had battled for was presently flung? Oh, for a wise nation! Oh, for a nation that is not afraid of them that kill the body but fears the one who can destroy both soul and body in hell! If it were the last thing we did before every American was wiped off the earth by Germany, England, Japan, whoever it may be, would it not be worthwhile to clean our own house, to make a desperate, wholehearted effort to establish here a society in which the Christ-spirit of truth, of justice, and of brotherhood reigned supreme?

Again, we are told that our commercial prosperity may be endangered. If we do not enter into or remain in the race for markets and colonies, and do not for that purpose arm adequately, then we shall become a poor nation, our comfort and prosperity will be a thing of the past. And again I wonder whether all the foes of our material prosperity are out there somewhere across the Atlantic or the Pacific, coming presently with dreadnoughts and cruisers and submarines to take away our markets and drive our manufacturers off the seas, or whether perhaps we are not engaged on so grand a scale in robbing ourselves that we really are laughable when we howl so loudly about robbers from foreign shores. Take the liquor problem. We spend every year hundreds of millions of dollars in buying intoxicating liquor of various kinds. Does it do any good? Not to speak of. The people who buy it rob themselves of so many hundred million dollars yearly. To manufacture, distribute, and sell this product that does no good to the nation requires capital, extensive buildings, and machinery, and the labor of many. If that which they make in no sense enriches the nation, then this capital, equipment, and labor are wasted. Every year we rob ourselves of all that energy that might be used to enrich the nation, set it apart to make something that will rob us of hundreds of millions of dollars. Furthermore, not only does liquor do its consumers no good, it actually lowers the efficiency of the vast majority of them. They can produce less wealth: again we are robbed of what we might have. Then in many cases they lower the efficiency of their dependents, wives, children, and of their fellow-workers: so we are once more robbed of wealth-producing energy. Finally, many of the consumers of liquor and their descendants become vicious or else wholly incompetent, and we spend millions of dollars every year in maintaining prisons, police courts, asylums, poor-houses, to take care of them. Now here is an organized system by which we rob ourselves of capital, of labor, of machinery, buildings, land, of human efficiency and intelligence, of actual and potential wealth running into billions every year. Does it not sound just a little silly to object so strenuously to being robbed by others when we gayly attack, gag, and rob ourselves all the time?

If any other food for thought along this line is needed, consider how we rob ourselves consistently through our national vice of extravagance, extravagance as individuals and extravagance as communities and a nation. Millions of dollars are spent yearly in graft and in the inefficient management of our governmental departments. We have thought ourselves staggered on hearing the sums spent for war purposes by the nations of Europe. Professor Usher has this to say: "any one who will take the trouble to turn to the census and see the millions spent annually upon tobacco, beer, fine clothes, theaters, automobiles, will see that a small fraction of the total sum . . . would provide us with an armament sufficiently large to achieve every conceivable purpose the American people might ever have."[8] Think of that! In spite of what we know of the cost of militarism, we could go in for it and become the ruling military and naval power of the world, and never feel it, by using for the purpose a small fraction of what we spend yearly on luxuries! Does it not seem as if Jesus were right, as if we were disproportionately afraid of the wrong done to us and far too indifferent about the wrong done by us to ourselves?

Finally, we are told that our American ideals are threatened. We must arm ourselves as we have never done before, or other nations will come over here, conquer us, and impose their ideals upon us. Do you know of any clear case where a nation simply by military force and superiority has imposed its ideals, its attitude toward life, upon another? I do know many instances where the attempt has been made and failed. Babylonia, Persia, Greece, Rome, and most modern nations tried by force to impose their culture, religion, and so forth upon the Jews. Have the Jews become Babylonians, Persians, Greeks, Romans, Spaniards, Russians, to your knowledge? The inrush of Teutonic and other tribes into Europe drove the earlier Celtic inhabitants

8. Usher, *Pan-Americanism*, 349. This quotation differs insignificantly from the original.

back into the distant corners of France and over into Ireland. But during all these centuries the mental and spiritual temperament of the Celt has never been fundamentally altered by Teuton, Frank, or Saxon. The Irishman isn't an Englishman yet. Or has Germany made Alsace-Lorraine German? Has Prussia made Poland Prussian? Furthermore, there are clear cases of a conquered nation imposing its culture and ideals on the conqueror. Rome conquered Greece, but Greece was not Romanized; the Roman Empire was Grecianized, that's all. No, it has been shown that under some circumstances one nation or tribe can exterminate another, simply wipe it out absolutely—an overwhelmingly big power could do that to a very small one; a new, fresh, virile race can do that to an old and effete one. But not the most critical and cynical reading of human history can prove that you can shoot ideals either into or out of a people.

Our national character, temperament, idealism, are in our own hands. The dangers to them are in our own hearts mostly, and such dangers as may threaten from without will never hurt us until we have admitted them to our hearts. Do not let us yield to the puerile superstition that we have to fight in order to keep foreign ideals from being imposed upon us. If we do that, then by that time strange and false ideals will already have been imposed upon us. For consider: you say you do not want anyone to come here to take away our ideal of freedom. But if you saddle yourself with militarism and all that implies, out of fear for what other nations may do to you, then you are already robbed of freedom, are you not? Then you are won over to the side of autocracy, repression, militarism, before ever a gun has been fired upon you. You say you want to guard the idealism of America, we must not become sordid and materialistic, at least not any more so than we are. But if we permit ourselves to get tricked into this race for markets and colonies at any price, which has involved Europe in the pangs of hell, then have not greed and materialism already been imposed upon us? If we then arm ourselves to keep out strange ideals, is it not to keep out what we have already let in? We have expressed our abhorrence of the Nietzscheanism, the philosophy of force, might makes right, the strong person is the good person, which seems to have so completely hypnotized the rulers of Germany. And now people are telling us that we must arm ourselves or else this philosophy of force will be imposed upon us. But, blind idiots that we sometimes are, can't we see that if we admit that victory on the battlefield is the only way, ultimately, in which a nation can prove its worth and superiority, the only way in which it can defend and extend its ideals, that the last appeal always must be to the sword and the gun, then we have already yielded official Germany's point? That is all she contends, not that you need to be brutal, engaged in war, all the time, but simply this, that in the last analysis a nation must be prepared to defend and extend its *Kultur*, ideals, standard of living, attitude toward life, by force, and that the nation which can do that more successfully than any other is *ipso facto* the noblest, highest nation. And if we now increase our military establishment, then we say to Germany: "You are right. The only way we can prove that we are nobler than you is by fighting you some day, and so we are preparing ourselves." Now if someone comes to me and says we shall be killed off or be put out of the commercial race if we do not increase our military establishment, I think they might have some reason on their side. But if someone tells me we must defend ourselves by force against the ideal of force, then I say it cannot be done. You can't fight against a principle that you are yourself acting on.

And there, I become ever more firmly convinced, is our great danger, that fear, hysteria, failure to count the cost and think through our present problems, may lead us to adopt as basis of our own action those very ideals of autocracy, militarism, commercialism, materialism, brute force, against which we think we have to take up sword and gun. Is it not again a case of fearing that which kills the body and not dreading the evil which blasts the soul?

2

Glad to be Alive and a Christian in 1918

In this sermon given during the First World War, Muste asks whether it is good to be alive and a Christian. He argues that although there is much cause for depression, Christianity provides the resources to deal with a world torn apart by war.[1]

I remember that almost exactly three years ago I gave a talk on the subject, "I am Glad to be Alive and a Christian." Since then I have many times asked the question, "Do I still dare to say that?" As we stand at the beginning of another year, it may be helpful for us all to face for a moment this question, "Are we glad to be alive and Christians in 1918?"

One might be pardoned for expressing the wish that they were dead. Some of you will recall that strange fantasy which occurs in one of the works

1. Muste preached this sermon on January 10, 1918 at the ordination and installation of Harold Linson Stratton at Harvard Congregational Church in Dorchester, Massachusetts. Stratton earned his degree from Andover Newton Theological Seminary while also taking classes at Harvard Divinity School. He then served as a pastor at a few churches in the greater Boston area. His relationship to Muste, who had just resigned as pastor of another Congregational church in the area, is unknown.

of H. G. Wells, published soon after the outbreak of the war in Europe. Wells tells of walking down the road and seeing seated beside it a stranger evidently in much distress. He invites the stranger to accompany him home. When they arrive there, he asks his guest what he can serve him, and the guest orders, as I recall, a glass of brandy with plenty of red pepper in it. When his host returns, having filled this unusual prescription, he finds the stranger seated before the open fire with a great live coal between his hands, but still apparently shivering with the cold. Curiosity gets the better of Mr. Wells and he asks the stranger who he may be. The answer is, "I am the Herdsman of the Wild Asses of the Devil. For a long time I faithfully carried on my work in the lower regions, and none of my Master's wild asses ever escaped. But there came a day when a certain very distinguished orator from the earth made his appearance in our midst. Everyone ran to hear him make a speech, I among them. When I returned to my post, we found that the wild asses had all run away to the earth, and I was sent here to find them."[2]

Thereupon the stranger takes Mr. Wells out upon a plain, and in the distance shows him an immense horde of these wild asses. Poverty, Disease, War, Ignorance, Prejudice, all the evils that sorely afflict humankind. As they stand gazing, it becomes apparent that this horde is bearing down upon them, but the stranger says to his trembling host, "You need have no fear of these beasts. When they come near, you have but to take out your little cruet of Attic salt, the salt of humor, laughter, ridicule, and throw a pinch of it at them, and then they will flee from you." Meanwhile the horde of evil beasts draws nearer, the thunder of their hoofs grows louder, one may feel the waves of their hot breath coming closer. They are very near. Wells trembles with fear. "Hurry," says his guest, "take out your Attic salt and throw a pinch at them, or they will overwhelm you." "And then," says the author, "I felt for my cruet of Attic salt, and found that I had it by me, but I was powerless to take it out and use it. For other generations, our children, may be able to laugh again; but we shall never be able to laugh again."[3]

2. Wells published several versions of this story, but I have not found one that matches Muste's quotations. See H. G. Wells, "The Wild Asses of the Devil," in *Boon, The Mind of the Race, The Wild Asses of the Devil, and The Last Trump: Being a First Selection from the Literary Remains of George Boon, Appropriate to the Times* (New York: George H. Doran, 1915), 234–250; H. G. Wells, "The Wild Asses of the Devil," in *The Man with a Nose and Other Uncollected Short Stories of H. G. Wells*, ed. J. R. Hammon (London: Athlone, 1984), 142–150.

3. See Wells, "The Wild Asses of the Devil," in *Boon*, 298–99.

There must be many people in the world who feel that way. And if there is anyone among us who in recent months has never felt so, they have either been asleep or have a shallow soul indeed.

Abundant reason for depression we have, as we contemplate, for example, the amount of physical suffering in the world today; as we contemplate the breakdown of the agencies and movements upon which we had depended to prevent such a calamity as is upon us now; as we contemplate the utter failure of the churches to prevent the evil day; as we consider what may yet be if suicidal strife must go on indefinitely. We need not deliberately aim at pessimism, yet a facile optimism under the present conditions is one of our most serious dangers. There is a Latin work written about half a century before the fall of Rome. It represents a number of citizens of the imperial city meeting to discuss the state of affairs. The tone of their remarks is highly optimistic. They speak of evils that have been reformed, of wars that have been stopped, of better organization of the Empire's affairs that has been effected. They are agreed that an era of quiet, well-being and progress is before them. Within fifty years of that time Rome fell, the Empire collapsed, and the night of the Dark Ages descended upon Europe! Let us not be too certain that upon the walls of the house in which we dwell the moving finger has not already written the sentence: Weighed and Found Wanting!

Yet, when all reasons for discouragement and gloom have been faced, I am ready to stand here and say, "I am glad to be alive and a Christian in 1918!"

Glad to be alive and a Christian, in the first place, just because it is such a fateful, hard, and trying time. There are moments when we stand helpless and afraid in the presence of the mighty events that transpire about us. But there are also times when the red blood in us mounts to the challenge of such an age, and we sing:

It's great to be out where the fight is strong,
To be where the heaviest troops belong,
And to fight there for man and God.

O, it seams the face, and it tries the brain,
And it strains the arm till one's friend is pain,
In this battle for man and God.

But it's great to be out where the fight is strong,
To be where the heaviest troops belong,
And to fight there for man and God.[4]

4. This poem appears repeatedly in publications in the early 1900s. Both Cleland B. McAfee and Maltbie D. Babcock are commonly cited as its author. The original place of publication is unknown. It is cited as by Cleland B. McAfee in William Leslie King,

An immeasurable privilege to live, to think, to choose, to act, in a day of responsibilities and opportunities like ours! And then we involuntarily bow our heads and pray, "O God, make our little souls worthy of the great time in which thou hast summoned us to live."

In the second place, I am glad to be alive and a Christian in 1918, because, being a Christian, I know and believe in God. I know that in me is no wisdom and power adequate to the problems and tasks of our age. I know that other people are beings very much like myself, that a billion and a half weak links do not make a strong chain, that there is not in all humankind, unaided, wisdom or power equal to the need. But one cannot walk with Jesus Christ without presently apprehending the one who is beyond oneself, beyond humankind, who can come to our rescue when the last ounce of our strength is gone and the waters begin to wash over us—apprehending Eternal Love tirelessly active in one's own soul and in history.

> Hast thou not known? Hast thou not heard? The everlasting God, the Lord, the Creator of the ends of the earth, fainteth not, neither is weary. There is no searching of his understanding. He giveth power to the faint, and to him that hath no might he increases strength. Even the youths shall faint and be weary, and the young men shall utterly fall; but they that wait for the Lord shall renew their strength; they shall mount up with wings as eagles, they shall run and not be weary, they shall walk and not faint.[5]

O, my friends, if you know God thus, then of course you are glad and nothing shall make you afraid. If you do not yet know God thus, as a living, real presence, will you not drop everything else and diligently seek until you find him?

In the third place, I am glad to be alive and a Christian in 1918, because, being a Christian, I have what I call a philosophy of catastrophes. You recall the sayings of the Gospel:

> Nation shall rise against nation, and kingdom against kingdom. . . . Ye shall be hated of all men for my name's sake. . . . These are the days of vengeance, that all things that are written may be fulfilled. . . . There shall be signs in sun and moon and stars; and on the earth distress of nations, in perplexity for the

Investment and Achievement: A Study in Christian Progress (Cincinnati: Jennings and Graham, 1913), 16; and in *The American Missionary* 62, no. 8 (October, 1908), 257. It is cited as by Maltbie D. Babcock in *The Reform Bulletin* 2, no. 35 (September 1, 1911), 2; and in *The Christian Century* 37, no. 48 (Nov. 25, 1920), 16.

5. Isaiah 40:28–31.

> roaring of the sea and the billows thereof; men fainting for fear and expectation of the things that are coming upon the world, for the powers of the heavens shall be shaken. *And then*—then—shall they see the son of man coming in a cloud, with power and great glory. And when these things begin to come to pass, look up and lift up your heads, because your redemption draweth nigh.[6]

You see the evident suggestion that a time of upheaval in human history is the signal for a new entrance of Christ, of God, into the world. Now let us not fall into errors. There are multitudes today who believe that the literal, physical second coming of Christ is at hand; multitudes also who appear to believe that after this war is over, as a matter of course and without further effort on our part, a sort of millennium will be ushered in; things are so very bad now, there must be something very good coming next. In either case, the good is to come from without, it is to be bestowed on us as a gift of the gods. There is the dangerous error. Whatever may be the time or manner of Christ's coming, let us be assured that he never comes save as we become channels and instruments through which his spirit may flow and operate upon our fellows. And to say that this war is of itself to usher in a new world is like saying that the great fire made Chicago a new city. It did no such thing. It did give the people of Chicago an opportunity to build a finer city. The war will not make a new world. It will give you and me an opportunity to build a new world on more ideal lines than the old, an opportunity to bring the spirit of Jesus to bear upon history in a new way.

Shane Leslie says in the introduction to his book *The End of a Chapter* that we have "witnessed the suicide of the civilization called Christian and the travail of a new era to which none of the gods have been as yet rash enough to give their name."[7] No, I reply, this world-catastrophe is giving you and me an opportunity to record our vow: We have witnessed the suicide of a civilization that after all was Christian only in name, in some slight degree; we are witnessing now the travail of an age that, by the grace of God, we shall make in some real and high sense Christian.

Finally, I am glad to be alive and a Christian in 1918, because, being a Christian, I believe that we have in the vision and method of our Master the program which the world needs at this hour. Can we say in a brief word what sort of human order Jesus desired to have established on earth? I think we can.

6. Luke 21:10, 17, 22, 25–28.

7. Shane Leslie, *The End of a Chapter* (London: Constable, 1916), iii. This quotation differs insignificantly from the original.

For one thing, he saw in his vision the establishment of free, spiritual religion. Every person is a child of God, with the right of immediate access to their Father. Priest, church, dogma, may help people find the way to God; but they may not impose authority on people from without, may not come between them and God. Free, spiritual religion.

In the second place, Jesus saw the coming of freedom, democracy, in government, the abolition of government in so far as that term implies a despotic, external authority, saw the coming of self-government. "The rulers of the Gentiles lord it over them, and their great ones exercise authority over them. It shall not be so among you. He that is chief among you shall be your servant."[8] Rulers, the representatives and servants of the people, political democracy in the most thoroughgoing sense.

In the third place, Jesus taught that in the kingdom of God there were to be no rich and poor; men and women were to share according to their ability in life's tasks and according to their needs in life's goods; there was to be cooperation and not strife at the foundation of industry and society. And this not only because the present system works hardship on the poor, but quite as much because it is demoralizing to the rich, making it easier for a camel to go through the eye of a needle than for a rich person to enter the kingdom of God.[9]

To use current phraseology, then, Jesus' vision included free, spiritual religious political democracy, and industrial democracy or the cooperative commonwealth. But is it not a great thing for a Christian to be able to say to the world, "These goals after which you have been groping, which now at last are becoming somewhat clear to your eyes, Jesus eighteen centuries ago envisaged as being in the plan of God, as being, that is to say, the inevitable goals of human history?"

But here an important question emerges: Did Jesus have anything significant to say about the method by which these goals were to be achieved? I think he did. Again three points deserve mention.

In the first place, Jesus ruled out violence as a method of attaining the kingdom. He rejected the sword. He would not permit his followers to use it. Reason, love, and the willingness to die, not kill, for their ideal, were to constitute the weapons of their warfare.

Secondly, it was Jesus' conception, I think, that people touched by the divine spirit, seeing the vision, should straightway, without waiting for others or for a change in their environment, begin to live as children of the kingdom so far as possible, in utter obedience to the will of God, in

8. Matthew 20:25–27; see Luke 22:25–26.

9. Matthew 19:24, Mark 10:25, Luke 18:25.

absolute love to others and God, that then these people should win others to the divine way of life, until the whole world was leavened. In other words, regenerate people are to regenerate the world.

Thirdly, help from above, an outpouring of the Spirit, a new sense of God, was to be given in order to empower people to live as children of the kingdom and establish it on earth.

Now it is on the question of method that Jesus differs from many other reformers and radicals. They are willing, to say the least, that the revolution should be achieved by violence and terror. He rejects that method as devilish. Many of them are chiefly concerned about changing the system, often concerned, it is to be feared, with very superficial, external changes in government or the arrangements of society, changes that will put money out of John's pocket into William's. Jesus is chiefly concerned about the revolution in people's souls, satisfied that people whose souls have been renewed will quickly enough set about changing the world, and that only sons and daughters of God can either establish or live in a holy social order. Other revolutionists, again, depend on human strength. Jesus frankly contends that we must look to God; theirs is a secular, his a sacred revolution.

Thus it seems to me that the Christian, having the vision and method of Jesus, stands at the very center of the turmoil of our age, can interpret its meaning, has the means to speak to the world's condition. To all Power, Authority, Privilege, the Christian proclaims: "Free, spiritual religion, political and industrial democracy, the holy cooperative commonwealth, this is the plan of God, the inevitable goal of human history. You cannot hope to prevail against it. Yield obedience to the heavenly vision, or you will be crushed by it." And to the seething, restless, uprising masses of humanity the Christian proclaims: "Do not resort to violence, terror, hate, to effect your redemption. Against the idea, the ideal, love, naught can prevail. Your day has come. Do not seek to achieve by foul means the beautiful human order of your dream. Also, do not look to a mere change in the external arrangements of industry, politics, society, to bring in the new day. You must become new people, then you can make and inhabit a new world. And do not try to accomplish in your own might this superhuman task, but effect a new contract with God, that the Eternal Love may accomplish the impossible in you and through you."

Because, then, this is a great, trying, crucial time; because I know and believe in God; because the world-catastrophe will give the spirit of Christ a new opportunity to enter the world; because we have in the vision and method of Jesus the program which the age requires, I am glad to be alive and a Christian in 1918.

3

Christianity, the Only Hope of the World (1918)

Muste gave this speech to a group of young Quakers in Westtown, Pennsylvania in June 1918.[1] *An indispensable source of his early theology, it was later published as a pamphlet. Muste examines three responses to the great needs of the world: seeking a major change in the economic system, trying to use military force to set up a new order, and despairing of human ability to bring change while hoping solely in the second coming of Jesus. He rejects all three and argues that Jesus pointed to a different way, the way of love, which he expected his followers to begin to follow immediately. Muste concludes with a call for bold experimentation in this way of living. It is this way of love that makes Christianity the world's hope.*

Between the time in which we are living and the age when Jesus lived on earth, there are startling and suggestive parallels.

The world in Jesus' day felt itself dissatisfied, in great need. There was a strong hope in many places that the need was to be met, a new day was dawning. But people differed as to the way in which the kingdom should

1. A Quaker meeting in Rhode Island had recently employed Muste after he resigned from his previous pastorate in December 1917 because his newfound pacifism was splitting the church.

come and in their conception of what it should be. There were those who said, "It's a question of bread. See that people are fed, clothed, and housed decently, and the rest will follow. The economic system must be changed first." Others said, "Human beings can't do anything to establish the kingdom. God or his heavenly representative must come and do it for us. We can only stand and wait." Others said, "In a great politico-military leader who will first conquer the world by his good sword and then set it straight, is our one hope."

Jesus said to such people—if I may venture the difficult role of interpreter—"What you need is new hearts, a new spirit, a new attitude toward life, a new way of living. Repent, become as little children. Begin all over again, for as it is you are all wrong. Love is the royal way, the losing of self in others—so to find one's self. You have been seeking power over others—seek instead to become their humble servants."

Start Now

Now it seems to me that there can be no question that Jesus expected his followers at once to begin to live the life of love as he set it forth, to live as citizens of a divine society, without waiting for anyone else to come round to their point of view, certainly without waiting for the world generally to come round to it. And in his mind the kingdom, the divine society, was in existence on earth so soon as a group, however small, undertook to live as its citizens.

Thus Jesus responded to the need and hope of his day, not by inaugurating an economic or a political revolution, nor by miraculous intervention from above in the course of human events, but by inaugurating a spiritual revolution, giving people a new spiritual basis and power for living—that of love—and establishing on this basis of love a new order of society.

The means by which Jesus achieved this result is very simple. He did it by himself living the life of love even unto death. That life taught people the meaning of love, it imparted to others the impulse of love, it was the foundation of the new society.

Now let us come to our own time and situation. We have referred to the spiritual unrest and seeking found among us, and to the prevalent expectation that a new world is being or about to be born. Do we not find that again people are looking in three directions mainly for the fulfillment of their hope? There are those who say that it's a question of bread primarily, that we must have an industrial or economic revolution. There are those who say that the new order can only be established from above, miraculously, by the literal second coming of the Messiah on the clouds of heaven. There are those who believe that through political changes, made possible by the use of the sword, a new order of things will be established.

My proposition is, my friends, that we must refuse, as Jesus did, to be led astray by such expectations, that the one hope of the world is in a spiritual revolution, in the Christianity of Jesus, in the rediscovery of his attitude toward life, the actual practice of his way of living, the re-realization and re-founding of the divine society based on love and not on force, the citizens of which are those who here and at once will try the way of love to the utmost.

Economic Revolution

Take the contention that the economic basis must first be attended to, that people must be decently fed, clothed, and housed, and that then the way will be clear for a nobler and more beautiful social order. You are aware how very general this conviction is among us, how you meet it not only among labor people who are now exercising so much influence in many countries, but among intellectuals (largely committed now to what is termed the economic interpretation of history), among liberals and progressives in politics, and among those in the churches who have espoused the social interpretation of the gospel. For that matter, even conservatives are perfectly willing at present to countenance a large measure of economic readjustment, since that seems to be the way to get all the elements in the nation to working harmoniously to push the war now and to pile up an immense volume of business after the war. I will confess to having been very much influenced by this trend of thought, though never finding a conclusion in which I could rest satisfied as to the attitude that as followers of Jesus we ought to assume toward the industrial revolution, the working class movement, or whatever one may term it.

It seems clear to me now that in fixing their hope upon the economic revolution, centering their energies upon getting the economic basis right first, the oppressed of earth may be following a false light. When I say that, I wish to do no injustice to the idealism associated with this movement. I am criticizing its underlying philosophy and method. Jesus preached the Sermon on the Mount to an audience composed mainly of common people, who had always to be asking anxiously, "What shall we eat?" We know that he was keenly alive to their sufferings, and that he could say very severe things about the rich and the mighty who oppressed them or at best were indifferent to their needs. He came to establish the kingdom in which people should not want. Nevertheless, he did not preach economic revolution to these people. He did not tell them to organize, strike, fight, and to obtain food and their rights. He intimated that if their lot was in many respects wretched, they were yet blessed in comparison with the rich and powerful, and would be very foolish to try to usurp the places or to practice the way of life of the latter. He said the bread question was not primary and fundamental, that the trouble with the world was precisely that people thought it was. "After all these things do the Gentiles seek," and there's the mischief, for there is implied here an absolutely wrong view of human nature.[2] It is implied that a person is first body and then spirit, and that therefore people must look out for food first, consult their material needs, and then attend to the wants of the soul. But this is a false view. A person is a spirit manifesting itself for the time being in a body. The spirit must therefore always be in control, and if people would only let it be, the needs of the body would be supplied as a matter of course. Therefore Jesus set these peasants and fishermen and tax-gatherers to organizing, not a society whose first care should be the economic basis of life, but a society in which the economic question should be pushed far into the background. His was not the slogan of modern social Christianity: "Get people food and clothing and shelter, and then you will have a people that can establish the kingdom of God." His was the command: "Seek ye first the Kingdom of God and all these things shall be added unto you."[3] Of course this sounds ridiculous to many. "The world in its wisdom" has never believed in this way.[4] But I wonder if here is not the light that we seek.

How to get "all these things" *has* been the chief concern of the multitudes of humanity through the centuries. And through all these centuries people have by their own confession failed to attain satisfaction; and the world has not begun to be freed from the rich who ruin body and soul with excess of earthly goods and the poor who are ruined body and soul by want of them, nor from periodical desolating calamities such as the present, which result in the last analysis from this very preoccupation with the material, and which by a singular irony carry down to destruction the multitude of things that people so feverishly toil to gather and build. And now come hosts of our leaders who tell the masses that the method which has produced such results is exactly the right one, that our one hope is in pursuing this method more ardently and unitedly than ever, that the bread question is the primary one, that having concentrated our energies upon it for many centuries and reached only hell, we must now concentrate our

2. Matthew 6:32.

3. Matthew 6:33.

4. See 1 Corinthians 3:19.

energies upon it more fiercely for a few years and—presto—we shall enter heaven! I ask you whether you think the hope of the world is indeed in these voices, or in that voice which long ago cried: "Lay not up for yourselves treasures upon earth, seek ye first the kingdom of God"?[5]

Let us put ourselves another question. Suppose we teach the masses to fix their attention more closely than ever upon material well-being, assuring them that along this way is the path to the highest. What will be the result? Well, they will not be satisfied. People cannot live by bread alone.[6] They will not find the highest along this road. They were made for God, and their hearts will be restless till they find their rest in him.[7] But they will not find God by pursuing Mammon. So, unless they are called back in time, you will have multitudes with unrest and discontent gnawing at their hearts, demanding ever more in the way of material goods and comforts, failing to find true happiness, degenerating morally, again madly reaching out for more material goods, persuaded that therein is satisfaction, and at last revolution, anarchy, the complete breakdown of our civilization as utter as that which has prevailed for centuries in the lands where once ancient civilization flourished. Are there not alarming indications that we have already entered upon this descent?

Again, the masses are being told that this battle for economic freedom that they are now waging is the last great conflict humanity will need to wage. Let us establish a new industrial and social system, and heaven is here. Is that so? Change the system, but neglect to change people's hearts, and will you have achieved your end? Does anyone suppose that any system will keep the strong and capable and clever from exploiting the weak and poor and slow, so long as the will to possess and rule abides in the former? Has not this dream, too, been pursued through the centuries? And have not people found themselves abolishing oppression and slavery in one form only to have them spring up in another? Must it not always be so until people are born again into the life of love?

This is preaching a revolution far more complete than your Bolshevists have ever proposed, for it is advocating not a new order that shall, after all, be based on the old spirit of materialism, selfishness, strife, but a new order based on the new spirit of love and sacrifice, achieved not by changing the outward system, but by renewing people's hearts. And when that is done, we shall have democracy, because we shall have the thing that will make democracy both safe and possible and inevitable, namely, love, fellowship.

5. Matthew 6:19, 33.

6. Deuteronomy 8:3, Matthew 4:4, Luke 4:4.

7. Augustine, *Confessions*, 1.1.1.

Violence

Having dwelt at such length upon the problem, we shall be able to deal much more briefly with the other two methods by which people today think the New World may be established. To change the order, let me refer in the first place to those who look to politico-military methods to establish the League of Nations and presently a new world. There are some of us who believe they have a divine witness in their hearts teaching them that the sword may not be used by the children of God and cannot possibly achieve his purposes. And does not that witness find support in human experience and reason? Through all these centuries people have been fighting to achieve a free and righteous and happy world. Does it look as though they had succeeded? Is it not true that they have obtained release from one form of slavery only to find themselves involved in another? That freedom and right when apparently won by the sword have speedily again been taken away by the sword? After all these wars of freedom, have oppressions ceased on the earth? If it seems unreasonable to suppose that a change in the economic system will keep the strong from exploiting the weak, is it reasonable to suppose that a political change will have that happy result? Will anything but a new love in human hearts suffice? Do we really believe that the modern state based on force will evolve, is evolving, into a society based on love? Evolution is a name to conjure with now, but do things evolve into their opposites?

The Second Coming

In the third place, there are the multitudes to whose numbers recruits seem to be added daily, who believe that miraculous intervention from without, power above, the second coming of Christ on the clouds, is speedily to wipe the wicked from the earth and to set up the heavenly reign among those who have believed in Christ. Now undoubtedly there are passages in the Bible that seem to give express warrant for such an expectation. But firstly, all that many of these passages prove is that the first disciples of Jesus expected Jesus to come back to earth in that way during their lifetime—and of course that expectation proved a mistake. Secondly, just what Jesus thought about the ultimate triumph of the kingdom, his own return, and similar matters, is by no means easy to determine. We cannot really determine at this late day how much that is attributed to him he really taught, how much was read into his sayings by the disciples; how much is to be taken literally and how much figuratively. Thirdly, people misuse Scripture, commit the same mistake that people have committed over and over again, when they think they find detailed signs indicating the course of the last events of history, the date and the place of the second coming, and so on. Anything can be made out of the Bible by this method, and pretty much everything has been made for centuries. Fourthly, in every such period of upheaval as ours these apocalyptic hopes are revived. They are really in great measure born of despair: we cannot do the thing, we give up the effort to establish the kingdom; therefore God will come and do it for us. But in so far as this is the basis for these hopes, we are surely on very unsafe ground. If people have failed hitherto, shall we conclude to fold our hands and let God do the work, or shall we seek divine wisdom and power and try again? Fifthly, people did not recognize the Christ when he was on earth, because they were looking for a being who should come suddenly on the clouds. They could not see him in the man from Nazareth, whose father and mother they knew, whose development they had witnessed, who did not seek by miracle to set up the reign of God over them, but by love to set up the reign of God in them and through them. Now does it not sometimes occur to those who set so great store by the doctrine of the second coming on the clouds, that if God is coming in some great new way into the world today, as I, too, most firmly believe, he may come again in some such way as he came before, that people who now insist that he must come directly from heaven in such and such a way may be as much mistaken as those who thought similarly nineteen hundred years ago, may as a result of their mistake crucify whatever messenger or messengers of God come to us today, even as those people crucified Jesus? If we may argue from our conception of the character of God to his probable method, have we not every reason for thinking that whenever he undertakes to establish or advance his kingdom, he will do it for people indeed, only not over them and outside them, but in them and through them? And sixthly, our immediate duty at any rate is perfectly clear. If we are Christ's, love will reign in our hearts, and we shall at once begin to live as citizens of the kingdom. Wherever a group so live, the kingdom will already be established, and *necessarily* the love in their hearts will set them to work to try to extend the kingdom in all the earth. However, the final triumph will come, and how love—God—can really triumph save through love-filled people, I for one do not see; but however the final triumph will come, no one who has love in their soul can possibly help beginning to work for it at once, can possibly think of waiting for God to come to set up his reign, since God is already in their own soul. Some such thought as this, I suppose, George Fox had in mind when he said to the Fifth-Monarchy Men of his time: "Christ is come, and hath already set up his Kingdom."[8]

8. George Fox was one of the founders of Quakerism. The Fifth Monarchists were a

Christianity: The Hope of the World

And so, my friends, we come back to our proposition that the primary and fundamental need of our age is spiritual. People's hearts must be touched and transfigured. We need God, the living God. We need open heavens, and God coming down upon us irresistibly to purge us and heal us and lift us out of ourselves, and make us swift and shining instruments to do his will. We need a fresh inner experience that shall cause us to see Jesus' vision of the meaning of life and to adopt his way of living. That is what I mean when I speak of Christianity as the only hope of the world. I do not have in mind the old theological formulations of the gospel. I think we can afford to set as little value upon calling Jesus, "Lord, Lord," correctly, as Jesus himself did.[9] But Jesus had a vision of God as Father, of love as the central and eternal and inescapable fact of the universe. He had a way of living—in absolute obedience to the demands of love. He had a conception of humanity organized into a divine society on the basis of brotherhood, of love, not of force. He had a method for bringing about this divine society, making love triumphant, the method of non-resistance, of not using violence against violence, on the negative side, and on the positive side the method of reason, of service, of self-sacrifice. This vision of God, this way of living, this conception of society, this method, all set forth not alone in words, but in a life of unutterable beauty and heroism and power; this is the contribution of Jesus to the race. This is Christianity. This is the hope of the world. Everything else has been tried. This has never been tried on a considerable scale. There is a witness in our hearts that if it were—if it were—there would be breaking up of swords, and wiping away of tears, and ringing of laughter, and release of human energies, and extension of human experience, far beyond the present imagination of any of us. Whenever some individual like St. Francis has arisen and honestly, passionately sought to relive that Christ-life, how beautiful and mighty the result has been; what a benediction to those who came in contact with it. Is it to be given to us, to thee and thee and me, to relive that Christ-life and to make his vision of God, his way of living, his conception of society, his method of progress, operative on a larger scale than ever before? Are we to witness a new Pentecost, a new coming of the divine to earth? A great creative spiritual era that shall set people actually

---

revolutionary group during the interregnum in 1600s England. They believed, drawing on prophecies in Daniel 2, that four empires had already come and that Jesus was about to return and establish the fifth. If this is a direct quotation, its source cannot be found. Fox expresses similar sentiments in ed. Rufus M. Jones, *George Fox: An Autobiography* (Philadelphia: Ferris & Leach, 1919), 264, 384–85.

9. See Matthew 7:21.

to working out the dream that was dreamed in Nazareth of Galilee nineteen hundred years ago?

I believe that we are, and that by far the most important service we can render to the world is to be preparing ourselves to receive the outpouring of the Spirit that is about to come. Behind this war is an inhuman and ungodly social order. Behind that social order is the weak and corrupt heart of humanity. With that we must deal if we are in earnest about getting at the root of things. Therefore we are driven back upon fresh spiritual experience to meet the world's need.

How, then, shall we prepare for this new entrance of God into our lives? First of all, we shall need faith, faith that God is, and that he will come to us. Jesus was born into a circle of people who believed God's anointed one was coming, and kept right on believing in the face of all discouragement. According to our faith it will be done unto us.[10]

Secondly, if we would have God, we must desire him. He will not come until our souls desire him more than anything else. They that ask shall receive. They that seek shall find.[11]

My friends, how often in spiritual things we achieve but little because we desire little. O yes, we wish to be of some service, hope that a little good may be done. But that God should seize us, as he seized the apostles, and impose fearful burdens and battles upon us, and set us to turning the world upside down; do we really want as much as that? Are not many of us, in the secret depths of our hearts, often a little anxious that God will carry things too far; that the Spirit will indeed lead us to fearful wildernesses and crosses? How many of us burn with passionate desire for the world such as possessed Savonarola when he cried, "O Florence, Florence, that I might present thee with spotless garments to thy King!"[12] or John Knox, when he cried, "God, give me Scotland, or I die"?[13]

All which leads directly into the third point, upon which I do not need to dwell, namely, that if God is really to come to us in some great new way and we are to be his instruments, we must wholly surrender ourselves to

10. See Matthew 9:29.

11. Matthew 7:7, Luke 11:9.

12. Girolamo Savonarola was a Dominican Friar who participated in the overthrow of the Medici government and in the establishment of a republic in Florence, Italy in the 1400s. He hoped that the city would become a New Jerusalem, the center of Christianity. He was excommunicated by the pope and later hanged after the people of Florence turned against him.

13. John Knox was ordained as a Catholic priest in 1536. He later became an important leader of the Protestant Reformation in Scotland and was prominent in the Catholic/Protestant political struggles of that era. According to legend, he prayed these words while rowing as a prisoner on a French ship.

him. As was said to us the other night, he must move in, we must move out. We must abandon ourselves to God. The great saints and inspirers have always done that. "I live, yet no longer I, but Christ liveth in me."[14]

Experiment

So, finally, I suggest that you and I must go forth in this spirit of faith, desire, self-abandonment, to experiment in the Christian way of living, actually to live up at once to all the light along this line that we have. There is fearful danger in talking and talking, and never doing.

Now it is true that we still need to do much by way of thinking out the Christian position, but I am much mistaken if one of our great troubles—if the thing that keeps God's new day waiting—is not that we already know so much more than we do, and talk so much more than we do. I plead with you, my young friends, to go out and experiment. Live the Christian life right up to the limit in the place where you are. Do the absolutely most Christian thing that you know in every situation that arises, utterly regardless of the cost. Face every question squarely as it arises, seek to learn God's will regarding it, and then do it without evasion.

But I must draw to a close. You see my point. Let us go forth and try our Christianity out. I think some of us should do it in communities that shall, as communities, be built on absolutely Christian foundations, instead of only as individuals in half-Christian communities. In spite of all the dangers and difficulties involved, I believe the holy experiment toward a Christian state or society made here in Pennsylvania by early Friends, must be made again, made many times, perhaps, before we succeed. At any rate, we are living in a time of upheaval, when the world is to undergo changes much more radical than most of us as yet imagine, and when every such experiment as I suggest will have peculiar value.

I see that many things will happen as we go forth on the great adventure of living by Christ's principles to the utmost limit. I see that we shall be misunderstood, ridiculed, persecuted. I see that it is not long before some of us shall lay down our lives. And I see that out of this experience we shall gain a joy that is beyond all words, that as we do the will our insight into the truth of God will become mightily clear, that a new day of God will then dawn upon the earth, that the heavens will be opened once more to people.

"Mine eyes have seen the glory of the coming of the Lord—Oh, be swift, my soul, to answer Him; be jubilant, my feet."[15]

14. Galatians 2:20.

15. Julia Ward Howe, "Battle Hymn of the Republic," 1861.

4

Surfeit and Famine (1918)

In this article, which was published in October 1918, Muste looks forward to life after the end of the Great War. Worried about a return to the economic status quo of the prewar years, he urges his audience to reject materialism and avoid affluent lifestyles. He argues that Christians should embrace a disciplined form of voluntary poverty so that they might avoid complicity in the economic inequality that lets some go hungry while others live in luxury. Soon after this article was written, the war ended and Muste's solidarity with poor and oppressed people led him into the labor movement.[1]

Those who have the cause of true Christianity at heart have good reason today for preaching and practicing a more disciplined and self-denying life. The history of religions and the lives of the saints of all times and of all faiths make it abundantly clear that the highest reaches of spiritual experience and power are not attained by those who deal over-gently with their

1. Around the time this article was written, Muste moved back to Boston from Providence, Rhode Island, although he remained employed by a Quaker meeting there until early 1919. In Rhode Island, he had established a reading room in the basement of the meetinghouse that attracted Christian pacifists, socialists, Trotskyists, and other

bodies. The well fed, well clothed, always comfortable body may become a weight upon the spirit, even though innocent of any gross sin; while those who endure physical hardships often achieve spiritual insight and courage far beyond their fellows.

Though we have reacted, and rightly enough, from many of the principles and practices of monasticism, we may recognize in that ancient philosophy lessons which we in these days greatly need to learn. How can we explain the practically universal instinct in the saints to deny themselves sensual pleasures? Why do the New Testament and the early church couple fasting with prayer? When Paul feared that he might himself miss the goal, in spite of having taught others how to reach it, it was his body that he regarded as likely to cheat him of his prize: "I bruise my body and bring it into bondage; lest by any means after I have preached to others, I myself should be rejected."[2]

It may be written down as an undoubted law of the spiritual life that the purest Christian joy is only for those who are willing to lead frugal lives, to endure some degree of physical hardship, and to limit the amount of sensuous pleasure in which they indulge. The pagan life, which many of those who call themselves Christians lead in these days, has in it some measure of beauty and dignity and joy. It is a cardinal principle of the natural life that the body is equal partner with the mind and soul, that its right to expression and happiness must ever be recognized. Not so in the Christian view. To the Christian the body is the bondservant of the spirit, even as the spirit is the bondservant of God, albeit freer and happier in such divine bondage than in its natural freedom. The Gospel lays the law of sacrifice upon the body. "Present your bodies as a living sacrifice."[3]

All this greatly needs to be said and said again in these days. If it is hard to be religious on an empty stomach, as we are so often told (all the ascetics to the contrary notwithstanding), it is at least equally true that it is as impossible to be religious on an overfull stomach.

radicals. In Boston, where he had helped found the local chapter of the pacifist Fellowship of Reconciliation in 1916, Muste and his wife moved into an intentional community affiliated with the organization. There he spent hours each day poring over the New Testament with other pacifist ministers who had lost their jobs during the war. It was as a part of this group that Muste first became involved in the labor movement. The war came to an end the month after this article was published, on November 11, 1918.

2. 1 Corinthians 9:27.

3. Romans 12:1.

The Unnecessary Labor of the Poor

But another and no less important aspect of this question is whether our indulgence in numerous comforts and luxuries of modern life is socially defensible under existing circumstances. John Woolman said in "A Word of Remembrance and Caution to the Rich": "Every degree of luxury of what kind soever, and every demand for money inconsistent with divine order, hath some connection with unnecessary labor."[4] And he was careful to point out that luxury had "connection" usually with the "unnecessary labor" not of the one who enjoyed the luxury, but of someone else who with difficulty procured even the necessaries of life. And this is still the case. The time may come when all can have such a share of material things as some have now, but that time is not yet. Today some of us eat cake, because others have no bread. Some of us have luxuries, the production of which draws labor away from necessary work. The war is teaching us this lesson. We all realize now clearly enough that the maintenance of "non-essential industries" means the withdrawing of labor from the essential; that if one person has too much, another has too little. This fact was just as true before the war. The draining of workers into industrial centers to busy themselves with the making of luxuries for the few was, even before 1914, bringing the Western world near to the edge of famine. It is a plain fact, far too little known, that even in those days of the armed peace millions of people in every country were living under famine conditions.

This being so, must we not ruthlessly cut ourselves off from "non-essentials" and luxuries? How can we eat our cake and know that somewhere one of our sisters or brothers lacks bread? We are inextricably bound up with the social order. But we need not be coward enough to take only its benefits. We can elect to suffer under it. It is the hero who remains behind when the ship sinks. "If any must die, let it be me," the hero cries. Can there be no such heroism in industrial life? Why should we not say, "We will starve for others rather than others should starve for us." Are there no Christian captains of industry who will deny themselves and live under the same conditions as those under which their workers are compelled to live?

To be definite, can we any longer continue to live in fine houses, eat in expensive restaurants, habitually use automobiles for pleasure, so long as all these things are types and symbols of the dispossession of the few by the many and have a close and inevitable "connection" with the "unnecessary labor" of the poor?

4. John Woolman, "A Plea for the Poor: A Word of Remembrance and Caution to the Rich," in *The Journal and Major Essays of John Woolman*, ed. Phillips P. Moulton, (New York: Oxford University Press, 1971), 246.

It cannot be said that such self-denial would be of little effect, that it would not mean more food for the hungry. In any case we cannot continue in wrongdoing simply because ceasing from it may produce no obviously good results in others. Thoreau has trenchantly stated the case for us: "What I have to do is to see, at any rate, that I do not lend myself to the wrong which I condemn. . . . A man has not everything to do, but something; and because he cannot do *everything*, it is not necessary that he should do *something* wrong."[5]

But secondly, if the call to a simpler basis of living were heeded by any considerable portion of those who profess and call themselves Christians or consider themselves to be socially enlightened, the economic result would be far from negligible. The voluntary saving of food by the American people is today making possible the feeding of thousands of our Allies. The voluntary abstention of many of us from "non-essentials" would strike a body blow at one of the main causes of much of the world's misery—at that which compels the many to minister to the whims of the few instead of to satisfy their own desperate needs.

The Vision of John Woolman

Thirdly, there is the moral reason. The redemptive power of the example of even a single individual who honestly seeks self-identification with the oppressed is incalculable. History is full of such cases. To take a modern instance, who can estimate the value for this hour of what the Englishman, Stephen Hobhouse, has done for humanity? There is no forgetting the story as Gilbert Murray tells it in the January number of *The Hibbert Journal*.[6] Or to go back again to John Woolman's *Journal*:

> In a time of sickness, a little more than two years and a half ago, I was brought so near the gates of death that I forgot my name. Being then desirous to know who I was, I saw a mass of matter

5. Henry David Thoreau, "Civil Disobedience," in *Walden and Civil Disobedience* (New York: Signet Classics, 2012), 284. The ellipsis has been added where Muste omits material.

6. Murray reports that Hobhouse, born into a wealthy family, renounced his inheritance and pursued "self-identification with the oppressed" by moving into a flat in Hoxton, a working class area of London, and doing social work there. He also worked with Muslim refugees in Constantinople during the Balkan Wars of 1912–13. A Quaker, he sought exemption from military service during the First World War but was instead drafted and repeatedly imprisoned under harsh circumstances for refusing to obey orders. Gilbert Murray, "The Soul As It Is, and How to Deal With It," *Hibbert Journal* 16, no. 2 (January 1918), 202–4.

> of a dull gloomy color between the South and the East, and was informed that this mass was human beings in as great misery as they could be, and live, and that I was mixed with them, and that henceforth I might not consider myself a distinct or separate being.[7]

Yea, when we seek voluntarily to make our lot one with that of the hungry and oppressed, are we not following the supreme example of him who took "the form of a servant"?[8] Can we have any doubt of the efficacy of the redemptive method?

Finally, the question arises whether we can ever have peace on earth until all people are won to a simple life, comparatively freed from dependence on, or of desire for, material goods. The catastrophe in which we are involved today is in the last analysis due to human greed. No nation, no class in society, is guiltless. There are no indications that the pursuit of wealth is to cease when the war is over. On the contrary, one hears on every hand talk about the "drives" for new business that are to be made when the soldiers return, of the economic war after the war. Some actually propose to compete for the wealth of the world against the Central Powers. Others hope to have all nations, friend and foe alike, included in a League of Nations, so that all together may be free to pursue riches. And it must in fairness be said that the revolutionary movements in various countries center not a little of their attention upon these material things; that all should have as much of what money can buy as some have now seems to be in the forefront of the minds of the workers of the world. Multitudes in all classes in all countries are guilty of such preoccupation with the material issues of this war that it behooves them to take to heart the reproach which an English soldier flung at the business class recently: "You calculate the profits to be derived from 'war after the war,' as though the unspeakable agonies of the Somme were an item in a commercial transaction?"[9]

In writing thus I do not mean to imply that we must not have economic changes, a fairer system of distribution, decent food, clothing, and shelter for all, equality of opportunity. But as I see it there is grave danger in cultivating in people an obsession with the economic problem, a concentration of attention on material things. In a society where all are eager for as much as they can get, it is impossible that any should be satisfied, and it is certain

7. Woolman, *The Journal and Major Essays of John Woolman*, 185.

8. Philippians 2:7.

9. "Some Reflections of a Soldier"; quoted in Willard L. Sperry, "The Gulf," *The Atlantic Monthly* 121 (June 1918), 741.

that there will always be those who consider themselves unjustly treated. No system of distribution can bring contentment to selfish human beings.

Whatever economic system we devise, it is not to be supposed that the strong and clever will cease to exploit the weak and dull, so long as the will to possess and to exploit remains. If I read the Sermon on the Mount right, Jesus, at any rate, did not believe that our hope lay in getting all people decently fed, clothed, and housed first, and then organizing them into the kingdom of God. These things, he said, were what the nations have always sought after first, and people who enter upon that pursuit have never got beyond it. His hope lay in people who had a lofty contempt for material things, who did not seek to lay up treasure on earth, who could be rash enough to think that if they cared supremely for higher things, the problems of food and clothing and housing would somehow take care of themselves!

If it be a truth that we must not forget, that without a certain amount of food and shelter human life is impossible, it is an even more important truth that until people quit caring for these things supremely, they will never get them—the many will starve while the few surfeit as from time immemorial—nor will people ever achieve that society of love without which no amount of wealth will ever satisfy the human spirit.

But to breed in people a contempt for the material, a courage to live for unseen and eternal things, we must have this contempt and courage in our own souls and show them forth in our own lives. Here lies the highest service we can render to the world. Certainly those Christians whose social conscience has been stirred by present conditions will render but an ill service to the workers of the world if they encourage them to lapse into materialism or to become absorbed in the pursuit of phantom luxury.

It is the idealism and spirituality of the masses that must be brought forth in the new day. Now when the worker seems to be near release from their chains of involuntary poverty, they must be shown the beauty and worth of voluntary poverty, of the disciplined, self-denying, spiritual life, lest they should become like the rich and powerful of the world and their last state be worse than the first.

The Labor Movement

5

Questions from the Left (1929)

In this essay from an anthology of works by labor leaders about religion, Muste argues that Christians should commit to helping the more radical elements of the labor movement. At the time, he was the director of Brookwood Labor College in Katonah, New York.[1] *He emphasizes Christianity's revolutionary implications and criticizes the church's failure to think through how the modern "industrialist and imperialist civilization" contradicts Christian values. He calls other Christians to join him in his radical work for justice for workers.*

Christianity has revolutionary implications for a system that stresses the acquisitive rather than the social motive, and that proceeds largely by the method of strife rather than that of education, persuasion, and love. In their pronouncements on political, social, and economic questions, the churches quite frequently refer, though in guarded language, to these im-

1. At the beginning of 1919, Muste and a few of his pacifist friends heard of an impending strike in Lawrence, Massachusetts, the site of a famously violent strike in 1912. They traveled there and persuaded the strikers to use nonviolent methods. The strike was eventually successful and in the process Muste's leadership skills became apparent to the workers, who asked him to lead the strike. Before the strike was over,

plications. In practice however, the churches that interest themselves at all in labor and industrial questions confine themselves, in a great majority of instances, to advocating moderate reforms rather than insisting upon drastic changes of motive, aim, and method. Such measures as abolition of child labor, extension of educational opportunity, gradual increase of wages and reduction of hours, old-age compensation and unemployment insurance, the rights of employees to organize, and the settlement of industrial disputes by conciliation and arbitration, are advocated by "advanced" ministers and churches who feel that they are putting the social message of Christianity into practice.

It happens that in taking this line, they are in close accord with the main body of the American labor movement at the present time; with the leadership, for example, of the A. F. of L. and most of the great independent unions, such as the Railroad Brotherhoods.[2] These also are definitely non-revolutionary in temper. They have no serious quarrel with the economic or ethical foundations of the present system. They want to get ahead and improve their own position in the scheme of things. There are abuses, of course, which must be corrected. The benefits that accrue from the operation of industry must be more widely spread. Prosperity must be made universal. But prosperity is very emphatically what we are after, and that involves a strong disposition against disturbing the status quo, of looking too narrowly into its fundamental assumptions.

On the whole, therefore, there is a decidedly friendly feeling at present between the official labor movement and the official church. Each party lays the flattering unction to its soul that this is highly significant; that it indicates that we are moving toward a realization of Christian ideals in industry; that the church has become practical and progressive, the labor movement constructive and an agency for the advancement of Christianity.

It is the purpose of this paper, without for a moment denying that certain advances have been made, to probe into these assumptions, to inquire whether religious leaders and institutions, instead of confining themselves largely, when it comes down to it, to advocating the moderate immediate demands of the labor movement, should not busy themselves with a more fearless and thorough analysis of the motives, the spirit, the ultimate fruits of modern industrialism.

---

he was appointed the head of a union. His unique method of union organizing became known as "Musteism" and was notable for its use of nonviolence and concern for racial equality. The gap in this collection from 1918 to 1929 is partially a result of the fact that during his involvement in the labor movement, Muste rarely addressed specifically Christian audiences.

2. The American Federation of Labor was a large federation of unions.

> I am a revolutionist [says Henry de Man, former president of the Belgian Labor College, in his important work, *The Psychology of Socialism*, now fortunately available in an English translation (be it observed, in order to prevent misunderstanding, that the book is largely a criticism of dogmatic socialism and Bolshevism)]. I am a revolutionist: this means that the transition from a capitalist system to a socialist system is for me a spiritual motive which can only enter my mind as the conception of an antagonism between two incompatible moral principles. The detestation of social injustice, of the degradation of human dignity, of bourgeois selfishness, of philistine greed, of conventional hypocrisy, and of the degeneration of taste, which led me in early youth to revolt against the outlooks of my social environment, has become intensified as the years have passed. I find the cultural atmosphere of contemporary bourgeois society irrespirable. I cannot go on living unless I withdraw from it at intervals in a more direct way than by mere activities on behalf of socialism—either by refreshing myself through contact with unsophisticated nature, or else by delighting in the beauties handed down to us from earlier ages.[3]

I quote this passage not so much in order to indicate agreement or disagreement with it, as because it is typical. It is, as has already been suggested, the kind of utterance that is not made in any but very radical labor circles in the United States today, and that is not made either in the churches, save in exceptional cases. It is the kind of utterance that was quite common, however, in labor circles before the war. It is the kind of thing that Walter Rauschenbusch used to say.[4] It is the kind of thing we can readily imagine Jesus saying, and many of the great prophetic and mystic figures. The reason why such things are not said in respectable church and labor circles today is the same as the one that accounts for the election of Harding and Coolidge by an overwhelming majority—"Prosperity." America has come into her own. She sits on top of the world. We are well fed. Why should we revolute, why be so childish and impractical as to bite the hand that feeds us?

Consider for a moment, however, some of the points at which it would appear Christians must meet the present system with an absolute rejection, where their "spiritual motive" can express itself only in "the conception of an antagonism between two incompatible moral principles." In the old days,

3. Hendrik de Man, *The Psychology of Socialism*, trans. Eden and Cedar Paul (New York: Henry Holt, 1928), 500. Muste follows this and other early editions in spelling the author's name "Henry."

4. Walter Rauschenbusch was a pastor and professor who became famous for his book *Christianity and the Social Crisis* (1907), a key text in the social gospel movement.

as it has been said, "The handicraftsman worked because it was his duty as a Christian, and because he took pleasure in his occupation . . . and although his children had little hope of bettering their station."[5] In a country like the United States, no one can any longer live in this spirit of moderation, contentment, of loyalty to "the moral ties connecting the laborer with the land, and the worker with the work shop."[6] If they do, they are hopelessly left behind in the struggle. They cannot make a modest livelihood. They become down-and-out farmers or migratory workers. The great aim in life is "to get on in the world," to "get ahead." Capitalism frankly depends upon this motive to develop the drive for production that it needs in the masses, and the qualities of energy, push, intense application, greed for success that it requires in its leaders. The masses are pretty well imbued with this psychology now. The labor movement is not offering much resistance to it anymore. Can the church respect it? Is keeping up with the Joneses, or getting ahead of them, a motive with which it can compromise in any measure?

A closely related problem is presented by the stimulation of the acquisitive motive by capitalism. Capitalism must stimulate wants in people, ever more wants, in order that its intense production may be absorbed, the wheels of industry kept turning, the competition for profits maintained. The person who walked today must ride in a Ford tomorrow, in a Dodge next year, a Cadillac the year after, and so on ad infinitum. The churches inveigh occasionally against the individual who yields to the temptation to acquire things, especially if they permit themselves to be over-persuaded by high-pressure salesmanship and buy something on which they cannot keep up the payments. That is extravagance. But what is the good of scolding the individual when the institution of high-pressure salesmanship is kept up; when it is indeed indispensable for keeping the system in operation; when its practitioners are the people who put pep into our men's clubs, and by their contributions keep the churches going?

Here in America especially, conditions have conspired to develop in great numbers of people the gambler's instinct. The country has been so rich, its development so rapid, so many have become wealthy by "striking oil" rather than by the practice of the copybook maxims of sobriety, industry, and thrift, that our whole nation is imbued with the get-rich-quick, the get-something-for-nothing, the get-results-and-don't-bother-too-much-about-the-methods psychology. That, I think, is one of the great reasons why we have graft in our political life. Americans are not inherently low-down creatures as compared with Englishmen, Germans, and Frenchmen, among

5. de Man, *The Psychology of Socialism*, 61.

6. Ibid.

whom this evil is much less prevalent. We simply gamble—in politics as elsewhere. The same thing applies to the labor movement. In our American unions, we have graft on a scale unknown in the movement in England, Germany, or France, and for the same reason. If Brindell or "Umbrella Mike" get the "results" for their followers, what more can you ask?[7] The followers also have the gambler's instinct and admire the fellow who "gets away with it." But can the churches tolerate such a psychology? They can, of course, because they do; but should they? In tolerating it, are they not sacrificing a chance to stimulate and really help labor itself?

On the technical side—with certain reservations, to be sure—there continues the tendency to which Frederick W. Taylor referred as the ideal of simplifying the work to such a degree that it can be done by a trained gorilla. As someone else has put it, the physical load is taken off the worker and put on the machine; the mental load is taken off the worker and put into the office. What position has the church, with its doctrine of the infinite worth of the individual soul, its insistence on the importance of spontaneity and creativity, to take over against such a tendency as this? The labor movement has opposed it in the interests of craftsmanship when it could, but it is well-nigh helpless at present, especially in the highly mechanized industries where the tendency is at its height.

Many more such problems might be mentioned if space permitted. They would seem to be pretty fundamental for anyone who has the Christian philosophy of life and who is concerned about making the living of such a life possible on earth. It does not seem plausible, on the face of it, that they can be adequately dealt with by church or labor forces that are themselves so complacent toward our modern industrial system and civilization. Those Christian thinkers who are interested in a radical change in our industrialism, and who are skeptical about the possibility of solving the spiritual and ethical problems, which have been suggested, by respectable reforms which leave the system as a whole pretty much unaltered, will naturally look about them to see if there are other forces in the modern world that challenge with some degree of thoroughness and energy the dominant tendency. When they do so, they find at work the forces of radical labor, having their extreme expression, of course, in the communist or Bolshevist movement. For the most part radicalism, however, is to both labor and the

7. Robert Brindell, a union leader, gained extensive control over the New York City construction industry in the early 1900s through systematic extortion and racketeering. He went to prison after the Lockwood investigation of 1920–22 exposed his actions. "Umbrella" Mike Boyle, a local-level Electrical Workers Union official, was convicted of conspiracy in 1917 and 1919 for threatening employers with strikes unless they paid him off by placing money in his umbrella.

church today the very incarnation of the evil one, or is at best regarded as an unscientific, clumsy, and visionary way to achieve what in certain instances may be desirable aims.

I am not here concerned to argue that this view is wrong, but simply to suggest that the serious-minded in the church need to think the matter through more seriously than they have yet done. If modern industrialist and imperialist civilization is as direct and flagrant a challenge to the Christian view of life as the church has ever been called upon to meet—and that is a position for which a very strong case can be made out—then the church is truly confronted with an overwhelming task, and can perhaps hardly afford to ignore, and even in some measure to work at cross-purposes with, the only major force that is openly and energetically combating the prevailing trend.

It may be said that when we see the reds, there is "no comeliness that we should desire them."[8] There is truly much in their method and manner that is offensive; often it seems unnecessarily so, to the sensibilities of those brought up in a middle-class atmosphere and on traditional Christian morals. Still this complaint of being uncouth, assertive, impolite, breakers of the accepted rules of the game, has frequently been made. People made it about Jesus, for example. The squeamishness that some people manifest toward the Bolsheviks today may be another manifestation of that tendency to be overparticular about "the outside of the cup and the platter" but careless about their contents, of which Jesus complained, in the good, respectable church people of his own day.[9] Assuming, for the sake of argument, that the spirit and practice of Bolshevism, for example, need Christianization, may it not be the business of the church to tackle precisely that job, instead of busying itself with dispensing comfort to the beneficiaries of the existing system, or inspiring those who would reform it, but at no cost to themselves?

Historically speaking, may it not perhaps be said that the genuine test in critical times comes in one's attitude toward those dubbed extremists? In England in the seventeenth century, the important question at a certain point came to be whether you were with Cromwell or against him; not whether you held the opinion, more or less academically, that it might be desirable to limit somewhat the powers of the king. In America in the eighteenth century, the real question came to whether you were with Samuel Adams, John Hancock, and George Washington, or against them; not whether you agreed with some of the Tories that George the Third had been impolite and unwise about certain matters.

8. See Isaiah 53:2.

9. See Matthew 23:25–26; Luke 11:37–41.

It may be observed in closing that when it comes to friendly relations between the churches and the radical elements in the world labor movement, it is precisely those in the church who are most definitely revolutionist in tendency, in revolt against the prevailing standards and ideals, who find themselves confronted with a great difficulty as to the method of procedure. They are pacifistic, whereas the radical labor movement is militant and to no slight degree militaristic. Here is a serious problem indeed. No adequate statement of it, not to speak of a solution, can be attempted here. We may, however, make three important observations of a preliminary nature.

Firstly, there is danger of crying "violence" when no external force is being applied at all; or, to put it the other way about, of thinking that there is really "peace" when there is no disturbance; that everything is running smoothly, when nobody is registering any complaints. The moment something is said that arouses deeper emotions, that makes people question, that disturbs the status quo and shakes the powers-that-be out of their complacency and lethargy, then "disturbers of the peace" are at work, "the world is being turned upside-down," and so on. If pacifically inclined Christians shy away from economic radicalism because it is performing that function in the modern world, it can only be because they attach more importance to superficial good manners than to honesty; and, quite possibly, because they cannot bear to be close to people who are doing in some fashion what they, the Christian pacifists, ought to be doing, and are not doing at all.

Secondly, there is often the greatest blindness as to just where the violence and the roots of violence are. Jesus and the disciples were turning the world upside down in the estimation of the estimable people of their day. That the Pharisees, for example, or the Roman armies, had turned it upside down, did not occur to them. The nationalists are the people who are said to be "making a revolution" in China today. What of the Powers during the past hundred years? "We deplore class struggle, and declare against all class domination . . . sympathizing with labor's desire for a better day, and an equitable share in the profits and management of industry, we stand for orderly and progressive social construction instead of revolution by violence."[10] Thus says the statement of the Social Ideals of the Church. The assumption appears to be that it is the radical elements that threaten a revolution by violence. But is not the régime against which they are in revolution itself founded upon violence and deceit? Does it not daily extend its power over the lives of women and men, in backward countries, for example, by violence and deceit? Carrying on, in other words, a "revolution by violence"?

10. Federal Council of Churches, "Federal Council's Declaration on Industrial Justice," *Christian Century* 36, no. 24 (June 12, 1919), 17. The original text has "reconstruction" where Muste has "construction."

If moral judgment is to pass upon realities and not appearances, then here is a problem that requires more careful thinking through than has yet been given it, lest in their anxiety to wash their hands of some manifestations of violence Christian pacifists be supporting much more horrible forms of the same evil.

Lastly, Christian pacifists are presumably revolutionists. We, too, are in revolt against the world as it is and would bring in a new order. Only we have a more efficient way for bringing in the rule of truth and brotherhood than the violent revolutionists. There are two ways of abolishing monarchy: the people may put the king away, or the king may abdicate. Christian pacifists feel that by nonviolent methods we can persuade the powers-that-be to abdicate. If in the long run we fail, we will find ourselves abandoned in practice, if not discredited in theory. However, anyone may fail, and the charge of futility and vanity is one that can be made against many things in this world. But Christian pacifists are not only futile, but hypocrites and liars, if we do not stick to our job, make an honest effort to bring about the revolution in our own way, concentrate some ninety percent of our energies on working to make the holders of power and privilege abdicate, rather than preaching to revolutionists to postpone their violence. We must deal with disease, not with symptoms, if we are to gain any respect.

6

Fellowship and Class Struggle (1930)

This speech addresses the importance of the labor movement to the establishment of the kingdom of God. It was originally delivered to the 1929 annual conference of the Fellowship of Reconciliation just over a month before the stock market crash that marks the beginning of the Great Depression. Muste proposes that the establishment of fellowship, defined in part as a classless society, is a key foundation for the good life and the kingdom of God. Like many theologians of the time, he explores the similarities between Marx's thinking and that of Jesus. He criticizes materialism and the violent system that maintains it, points out that Jesus set aside national and racial consciousness (Israel v. Rome, Jew v. Gentile) for class consciousness (poor v. rich), and argues that Christians should give up privileged positions and identify with the poor and oppressed.

The Fellowship of Reconciliation envisages as the goal of history the kingdom of God, an order of society in which there shall be no master and slave, no exploiter and no exploited; where all human beings shall be regarded as ends in themselves; where each shall contribute according to their ability; and each shall share according to their need; an order of society based on cooperation, not on competition and strife; where fellowship shall be a reality and not a lovely dream or a pious wish.

The Fellowship believes that we cannot divorce the end from the means, cannot divide the human mind into compartments, in one of which we keep an ideal of brotherhood some day to be realized, and in another of which are methods of hate, ill will, and bitterness by which this fair ideal is to be achieved. The one who has glimpsed the vision of fellowship and brotherhood must, we feel, seek to live in a spirit of fellowship and brotherhood now.

We live, however, in a world that is one of strife, contending groups, and conflicting interests. We speak sometimes of the worldwide human brotherhood, but such a brotherhood is still an ideal and not a reality. Our problem is, then, how in such a world of conflicting interests to live the life of goodwill, particularly how we may do it in view of the conflict between economic classes, capital and labor, which characterizes the modern world. The Epistle of the Romans is addressed in a memorable phrase: "To all that are in Rome, beloved of God, called to be saints."[1] How the beloved of God are to be saints in Rome and not in Heaven or Utopia is the problem.

At the outset it must be clear that in the world as it is now, the Fellowship member must be a revolutionist. We live in a social and industrial order that emphasizes the acquisitive rather than the creative side of human nature; that arouses the spirit of competition rather than that of cooperation; that offers its highest rewards to the speculator rather than to the laborer; that by methods of high-pressure salesmanship and other devices constantly encourages the piling-up of material goods rather than an inward culture; an order of industry and society which was established by violence, as for example, in the English, French and the American revolutions, and that to this day is maintained and extended by violence. It is an order of society that brings with it inevitably such evils as unemployment, child labor, the sweat shop, imperialism and war. Against such an order those who hold the Christian ideal cannot but be revolutionists. They must desire a radical transformation to a cooperative commonwealth.

A number of things follow from this fundamental proposition. If under this system you belong to those who are privileged, who live in whole or in part upon unearned income, who exercise power over others, you have to repent of the corporate guilt involved in the oppression, robbing, and degradation of your fellows. In practice this means that you must abandon your privileged position, must get out of the exploiting group, must identify

1. Romans 1:7.

yourself with those who hunger and thirst, and "weep now."[2] That is the first and essential step in the atonement you must make, the at-one-ment, the reconciliation you must achieve. You must join in the sacrament of eating bread and drinking wine with the unprivileged and oppressed. As we have said, we cannot wait to live the life of love, to be at one with our fellows, until the kingdom of love has been established.

What concretely does this identification with the oppressed mean? It is impossible here to go into great detail. Besides, no one can answer for others what they are to do in a thousand and one concrete situations. We may, however, suggest three lines for consideration. For one thing, this identification with the oppressed is a psychological matter. It means that we must experience a change of mind (*metanoia*), of focus, attitude and approach. You who have enjoyed wealth and privilege and been happy about it, must become uncomfortable about it. You who have felt at one, at home with the cultured, the well-to-do, the respectable, despite all their shortcomings and vices, must become at one and at home with the uncultured, the poor, the oppressed, the unrespectable, despite all their shortcomings and vices. And while there is always the subtle danger of deceiving ourselves, in the main it is possible for us to search our hearts and see whether at bottom we are with the forces which maintain the status quo, or whether we are with those that are working for a new day in which "the hungry shall be satisfied with good things and the rich sent away empty."[3]

In the second place, this identification with the oppressed may well involve personal renunciation of a certain amount of luxury and comfort. Asceticism has its dangers. Certainly, personal habits cannot be regulated by laws, nor can any individual sit in judgment over another in matters of this kind. Nevertheless, there are limits to the indulgence, the comfort, the laughter that we may allow ourselves in a world where millions go hungry, and where rebel saints are persecuted and jailed. We do well to remember also that it is possible, though difficult, to pray on an empty stomach but impossible to pray on an overloaded stomach.

In the third place, and this is of the utmost importance, identification with the unprivileged means practical activity for the cause of labor, for the establishment of social justice. When we are speaking of what is, and not of what ought to be, we face the fact that violence and oppression inevitably beget violence. If, therefore, we genuinely abhor violence, our chief concern must be to do away with the conditions that inevitably create violence. There are numerous ways in which those who are not themselves manual

2. Luke 6:21.

3. Luke 1:53.

laborers may cooperate to that end. There is still child labor in this country. In most states there is utterly inadequate legislation for safety and sanitation in mills, mines, and factories. The compensation paid to those who suffer in industrial accidents is still utterly inadequate, and it is well for us to remember that the number of American soldiers who died in the great war is no greater than the number of those who perish in every similar period from the injuries received in industry. Hours of labor for women and children are still inordinately long. Night work is permitted in many occupations and for many individuals where it constitutes a menace to society. We can all work for legislation to remove such evils, and to be of assistance in securing adequate enforcement of such legislation.

The Cause of Labor

There is more violence in this country in connection with an ordinary strike of a few hundred workers than occurred in the general strike of Great Britain a few years ago, which involved several million workers and tied up the essential industries of the country. Why is this? Is it because Americans are naturally more violent and bloodthirsty beings than our British fellow-workers? Not at all. We suffer in this country from two evils which constantly provoke to violence in industrial disputes. The one is the evil of injunctions, the usurpation of law-making powers by our judges. When, as happens practically every day, injunctions are issued forbidding workers to organize or to remain away from work in a plant where the employees are striking against bad conditions; when by such extra-legal means protection is withdrawn from workers seeking to conserve human values, while the fullest protection is extended to the property of the employer, workers have no recourse save to sullen submission or to violence.

In the second place, ours is the only important industrial country that supports the evil of private detective agencies, sending thugs and spies into areas of actual or potential industrial conflict. The ostensible task of the labor spy is to report to the employer about the activities of the employees. Theoretically, this may be justified, though obviously it betrays an attitude of distrust on the part of the employer that is only too likely to create distrust among the workers. In the nature of the case, however, labor spies are not likely to confine themselves merely to reporting what they find workers saying and doing. If they report that these workers are for the most part ordinary sensible human beings, and are not about any subversive or revolutionary business, then it will presently appear, of course, that there is not much use for their activity, and they will be discharged. If this were to happen in many instances, the agency that employs them would naturally lose a great amount of business. Therefore, both the agency and the individual spy are under constant temptation to invent stories that seem to justify their existence. There is abundant proof that this is constantly being done.

The process, however, does not end here. If the labor spy constantly makes up stories for which there are no foundation, that also will presently come to light, and once again the business of the spies and the agency which employs them is likely to suffer. Consequently, spies will provoke violence in order to justify their existence. I have seen this done repeatedly in my own experience in labor organization work. In the great Lawrence textile strike of 1919 I heard a man urge the strikers to seize the machine guns that had been brought into Lawrence and turn them upon the police. Within two weeks I was in the city hall of Lawrence confronting this individual and the police department of the city with conclusive evidence that he had actually been employed by the police themselves. Another individual engaged in similar activities was proved to have been in the employ of the largest textile company involved in that strike.

If we honestly desire to minimize violence in industrial disputes in this country, we can take a tremendous step in this direction by seeing to it that there is federal and state legislation to put an end to the judicial abuse of injunctions, and to put an end to the operations of private detective agencies in industrial disputes.

We might go on and suggest other ways in which without any participation in violence one may advance the cause of labor and social justice, and so bring nearer the realization of brotherhood, as, for example, support of the movement for labor education. Members of the Fellowship, however, will hardly be satisfied with activities of this kind, which involve no personal risk and may be carried on in the midst of the utmost comfort and respectability—activities, furthermore, which involve an intellectual rather than an emotional and spiritual identification with the cause of labor. They will wish to engage in the feeding of strikers and their families. When workers are thrown in jail for exercising their civil liberties, they will wish to mount the rostrum to assert those liberties in order that they may have an opportunity to visit their brothers and sisters in prison. When workers are being clubbed on the picket line, they will wish to take their place on that picket line in order that by the application of the policeman's club they may be made at one with their sisters and brothers struggling in defense of their rights. They will wish, in other words, to be "tagged," to be known as one of those queer people who are always on the "wrong" side.

It needs to be emphasized that our allegiance to the forces that are standing against the status quo, our identification with the unprivileged, must be thoroughgoing and uncompromising. I fear that we sometimes get confused by the use of such expressions as that "there is good in everybody"; that there is "right on both sides"; that "we ought to have a balanced mind"; and that "if we only understood each other" everything would be all right. I do not wish to underestimate the importance of the truth that is sometimes expressed in these phrases, but I think that sometimes they serve rather to conceal muddled thinking and sentimentality.

Sometimes, as the columnist put it, people are opposed to each other not because they misunderstand each other, but because they understand each other only too well. We can't be for the right and for the wrong at the same time. If a person comes with a balanced mind to view the existing organization of society and industry, they will be against it. It is the unbalanced mind that results from our personal comfort under the status quo, from being drugged with propaganda, from being unable to break away from habit and custom, which prevents us from seeing that. Of course, there is a vast amount of good in the world under the existing system. Fortunately, the need for mutual aid and the urge for fellowship is so strong that these things are found even under an order that appeals more exclusively to the economic or acquisitive motive than probably any other in history. But these things exist not because of capitalism, but in spite of it. In itself, this regime of capitalism, militarism, and imperialism is anti-Christ. Precisely, if we look at it with a balanced mind, we shall see that just as under chattel slavery there was often much happiness and beautiful personal relations between certain slaveholders and their slaves, but that essentially the slave system begot pride, contempt, laziness, and lust for power in the owners, and ignorance, fear and superstition and hate in the slaves, and eventually brought war and misery upon all, so capitalism despite all the good that exists under it, and the kindly personal relationships that obtain here and there, is in its essence uneconomic, unjust, inhumane, and un-Christian.

Similarly, the assertion frequently made that there is always right on both sides in an industrial conflict needs to be analyzed with some care. If by rights are meant prerogatives that can be enforced by the power of the state or by public opinion, it is quite true that there are rights on both sides, most of them on the side of capital. It follows that it is expedient for all the interests involved in any particular industrial conflict to take these things into consideration. If one is speaking, however, of rights in some more absolute sense—rights from the standpoint of Christian morality—the case may be different. Is there such a thing as a right to murder? To steal? To gamble? To own another human being? Nevertheless, all these things are involved in the capitalist system of industry—the murder, for example, of little children, of miners in mines inadequately equipped with safety devices, in violation of law. What of those who are responsible for such things, who condone them, who are beneficiaries of them?

Recall the parable of Dives and Lazarus, and that in that parable Jesus does not accord Dives, the rich man, so much as the right to a drop of cold water from the tip of Lazarus's finger as he suffers the torments of hell, does not accord him so much as the right to ask that Lazarus be sent to warn his brothers lest they come into the same torment.[1]

If this seems shocking, it is said precisely because we need to be shocked into thinking anew and very earnestly on these things. The Fellowship has no reason for existence unless there is clearness in our thinking and downrightness in our action. We cannot afford to be like the person of whom it was said that he mounted his horse and rode off in all directions.

Preaching Repentance

Having taken steps to identify ourselves with the unprivileged, with the forces making for a new social order, we have also the task of preaching repentance to our fellow-sinners, seeking to persuade them to be reconciled with the great mass of their brothers and sisters.

The question is bound to arise whether this means that we must preach to individual capitalists that they must renounce their business and their unearned income. It may well be that more individuals ought to follow this course than some of us suppose. Very few church members would doubt that bootleggers ought to give up their business if they profess religion. It may be questioned whether there are not other businesses regarded as more respectable by the world that are not really on any higher moral plane. We must not forget either that Jesus advised at least one rich young man to sell all that he had and give it to the poor.[2]

Fundamentally, however, the problem is a social one and is not likely to be solved by action however unselfish and dramatic on the part of this or that individual. It would mean a great deal, however, for example, if employers generally were to cease offering constant resistance to every attempt on the part of their workers at self-organization. Violent revolution comes at last because the legitimate peaceful efforts on the part of workers to organize in order to advance their rights and to improve their status are met by opposition. Encourage such efforts, and labor organization will certainly become more powerful, but it will also become more responsible, and having no occasion for violence, will eschew it.

1. Luke 16:19–31. The traditional name "Dives" is simply the Latin for "rich."

2. Matthew 19:16–22, Mark 10:17–22.

The same point can be put in a somewhat different way. Necessary and fundamental social changes occur not only because there is pressure from beneath, but because opposition from above is weakened and eventually broken down. Now, no social system will yield to pressure so long as those who enjoy power and privilege under it are thoroughly confident of the rightness of their position. Feudalism in France was broken down eventually because in their subconscious, if not in their conscious minds, the circles of the Court, the higher nobility and the higher clergy knew that their position was morally untenable. Thus, when we subject the ideals and the practices of capitalism to the light of Christian ethics and idealism and thus undermine the moral foundations of capitalism, the morale of the privileged and respectable, we are making an important contribution toward the establishment of a new social order.

All of this would seem to mean that it is our task to diminish and to break down the class-consciousness of the privileged and ruling group. That is true, for class-consciousness in these groups is that in their psychology that enables them to exploit and to oppress without suffering the pangs of conscience. Thus, to take a very simple illustration, every effort toward the abolition of child labor in this country has had to be carried on in the face of the most determined and bitter opposition from the employers of child labor. Most of these employers unquestionably were kind and indulgent fathers toward their own children. Very few of them, as individuals, would willingly have injured or neglected a little child. When it came to a question, however, of the abolition of child labor in their factories, they opposed it, because it was to the interest of their class to do so, and because the propaganda agencies of their class drew up all sorts of defenses around their minds and consciences—rationalizations that identified the abolition of child labor with communism or socialism or interference with states' rights, and thus there was developed in them a class-consciousness that bound them to the service of their class, and in doing so enabled them to commit crimes that, as individuals, they would have shunned. Unquestionably, it is the duty of the Fellowship constantly to diminish, and ultimately to break down, such class-consciousness.

Class Consciousness Among Workers

Having indicated that it is our task to break down the class-consciousness of the privileged and ruling groups, I now venture the paradoxical suggestion that it is our task to develop class-consciousness among the workers. Class-consciousness among the workers is that in their psychology that makes them cease thinking of themselves as individuals, and seeking advancement as individuals; that attaches them to the most inclusive fellowship possible, namely, the fellowship of all those who contribute by hand or brain to the common tasks of humankind; that gives them the sense of the oneness of labor throughout the world, regardless of distinctions of nationality, race, creed or color, and a sense of the mission of labor, not merely to improve the material conditions of any number of individuals, but to bring in a new world in which life for all shall be as beautiful and dazzling and rich as the colors on the autumn foliage outside my window as I write.

It is sometimes taken for granted that the worker who is not class-conscious occupies some broader and more inclusive viewpoint. In an overwhelming majority of instances, the facts do not bear out such an assumption. Workers who have not achieved the consciousness of the solidarity of labor will be found in one of three groups. Some of them are simply ignorant of what has happened in the world. They accept the status quo uncomplainingly. There may be, and often is, something noble about their industry and their faithfulness to their tasks. Because they are ignorant, however, they help to perpetuate the status quo with all its evils of child labor, unemployment, industrial accident, and war. Still others sullenly submit as long as possible to what they regard as inevitable. There is nothing noble about this sullen acquiescence in a cramped life or mere submission to superior force. There is as vast a difference between such submission of the masses and the glad acceptance of pain by the saint, as there is between the sodden poverty of the urban or rural slum and the voluntary poverty of St. Francis "that walks with God upon the Umbrian hills."[3] No one who has ever inwardly experienced the spiritual exaltation and the intense brotherhood created by a strike on the one hand, and the sullen submission of hopeless poverty or the dull contentment and "respectability" of those who are too fat and lazy to struggle for freedom on the other hand, will hesitate for a moment to choose the former, even though it involve a measure of violence. Still other workers who are devoid of class-consciousness are merely capitalist-minded. They have succumbed to the prevailing psychology and are out "to get theirs."

As with individuals, so with groups. The American Federation of Labor, for example, does not have for the most part a class-conscious philosophy. This does not mean that it occupies a broader standpoint, but rather that it is organized on the narrow basis of craft, and is primarily concerned

3. If this is a direct quotation, its source cannot be found. Umbria is the region in Italy where Assisi, St. Francis's hometown, is located. The "Umbrian hills" frequently feature in accounts about him. It is also possible that this is a reference to the poem "The Lady Poverty" by Evelyn Underhill.

with immediate material gains such as higher wages, shorter hours and improved conditions of work. On nearly every important issue in which the Fellowship is deeply interested, the A. F. of L. tends to take the unidealistic attitude. Many of its unions discriminate against black people. It becomes increasingly nationalistic rather than international in its spirit. President Green makes a ceremonial visit to West Point, and accepts the chairmanship of a Citizens' Committee to raise emergency funds for Citizens' Military Training Camps, at the same time that the A. F. of L. fails to provide relief for starving strikers in Southern cotton mills, and counsels these workers against laying down their tools rather than submit any longer to intolerable degradation, because it is not assured that relief can be provided. This is the result of the absence of class-consciousness in the A. F. of L. It is much less class-conscious than the British labor movement, for example, but obviously this does not mean that it is more idealistic than the latter. It seems natural, for example, for church people such as Bishop Gore and Archbishop Temple to be prominent members of the Labor Party in Great Britain.[4] It is difficult to conceive of them as definitely and prominently identified with the A. F. of L.

Jesus, Marx, and Nonviolence

So far I have been stating fairly good Marxian doctrine, and also, I think, fairly good Christianity according to Jesus. In other words, the answer to the question how we are to reconcile the philosophies of Marx and Jesus is that at many fundamental points there isn't anything to be reconciled.

Let us glance for a moment at the role that Jesus played in the world of his day. He, too, cut himself off from, set himself in definite opposition to the dominant imperialism of his day. It is recorded that Satan took him to a high mountain and showed him all the kingdoms of the world and the glory of them.[5] Actually, that meant the Roman imperialism of his day, the dictatorship of the Roman bankers expressing itself politically in the dictatorship of the Roman Caesars, which was giving to the ancient world two centuries of unexampled culture, prosperity, and magnificence. For a little bowing of the knee, a little compromise, Jesus might have become one of the rulers of that world. What was his reply? Not that this world which lay before him was very magnificent; that it was bringing prosperity and culture to great masses

4. Charles Gore had retired after serving successively as the bishop of Worcester, Birmingham, and Oxford. William Temple was the archbishop of York and would later become the archbishop of Canterbury.

5. Matthew 4:1–11, Luke 4:1–13.

of people; that it might need to be improved at this little point or that, but on the whole represented a great triumph of the human spirit. He regarded this Roman imperialism as Satan, anti-Christ. He set himself positively and unmistakably over against it. Jesus was a revolutionist. He set himself the task of building a new social order—the kingdom of God (in the terminology of that day)—in which there should be no arbitrary distinctions between people, and justice and brotherhood should be realized on earth.

Furthermore, Jesus shifted the spirit of revolt among his people from a nationalistic or racial to what may quite fittingly be described as a class basis. Nowhere in his teachings do you find him pronouncing woe upon the Romans and blessings upon the children of Israel, woe upon the Gentiles and blessings upon the Jews. Nowhere do you find him pronouncing woe upon the ignorant and unlearned and blessings upon the learned, or woe upon the harlots and the publicans and blessings upon the chaste and respectable. There is one distinction, however, which is written in the teachings of Jesus and runs pretty clearly throughout the entire New Testament and other writings of the early church. He did say: "Blessed are the poor, blessed are the persecuted, blessed are those that weep now, and woe to you that are rich, woe to you that laugh now."[6] There is the parable of Dives and Lazarus to which reference has already been made. It was surely not an accident that it was precisely the money-changers who were driven out of the temple.[7] Under the circumstances it was logical that the rulers both among the Jews and among the Romans should have been suspicious of him. The early church undoubtedly practiced a large measure of communism. Christians were anti-militaristic. They were regarded, and doubtless rightly so, as a danger to the imperial Roman government. The rich, it is true, could also enter into the new order, but only provided that they disowned their own class and their class privileges. Nor will it be easy to find in the most lurid denunciatory literature of modern revolutionists anything to surpass the denunciation of the ancient imperial world order and the rejoicing over its impending downfall presented in the eighteenth chapter of the book of Revelation.

By what method, however, was the kingdom of the world to be overthrown and the new order to be brought in? Surely by the process of love and goodwill. Those who do not understand how Jesus could pray for the forgiveness of those who crucified him are probably as far from comprehending his real character and mission as those who do not see that he

6. See Luke 6:20–25.

7. Matthew 21:12–13, Mark 11:15–17, Luke 19:45–46, John 2:14–16.

was distinctly a revolutionist as over against the imperialism of the Roman bankers and the Roman Caesars of his time.

In this connection, it is important to emphasize again that he cut himself off definitely from the nationalistic and terrorist movement among the Jews of his day. Incidentally, is there not here an interesting analogy with the way in which Karl Marx struggled to free the socialist labor movement of his time from the influence of Bakunin's brand of Terrorist Anarchism?[8] It seems to me sufficiently clear that Jesus did not believe that a violent revolt against Roman imperialism was feasible or desirable under the circumstances with which he found himself confronted. Whether, however, this means that he would never under any circumstances have countenanced the use of violence against the oppressor, does not seem to me susceptible of a conclusive answer. When he told people to turn the other cheek rather than to retaliate, it is quite conceivable that he was not primarily trying to lay down a rule of universal application, but was trying to persuade the lowly and the oppressed of his time not to waste their energies in personal quarrels with each other. Just as when he told people not to be concerned about what they ate or drank, he probably did not mean to suggest that the material foundation of life is not important, but rather that the material foundation of life could never be secured so long as people engaged in bitter individualistic strife with each other, whereas if they were to seek first the kingdom of God, that is to say, establish a human order based on justice and brotherhood, it would be a comparatively simple thing for all to obtain food and clothing and shelter from the natural resources provided by the earth. In making these suggestions I do not have in mind suggesting the slightest doubt as to the primacy of the attitude of love, the spirit of brotherhood, and respect for human personality in the soul of Jesus.

Positively, it seems to me that when Jesus built the foundations for the Christian church, what he was trying to do was to develop a worldwide fellowship of the lowly, the oppressed, the toilers, who were to be bound together in solidarity and affection for each other, and to devote themselves to the bringing in of a new social order. It is possible that he believed that if the oppressed would shed their individualism and overcome the petty differences constantly separating them, they would not need to use violence in overthrowing the powers that held them in thrall.

Those who desire to work for the kingdom of heaven in the world today will certainly therefore build a worldwide labor movement, aiming to bring together all those who toil by hand or brain, in a great fellowship that

8. Mikhail Bakunin was a rival of Karl Marx who sought the establishment of socialism through abolishing the state.

shall aim to establish a social and industrial order based on the motives of service and cooperation instead of exploitation and strife.

Not a Perfect Movement

When, however, one undertakes to work in some practical way to this end, one finds that the labor movement also is composed of human beings, not angels, and that there is much about it that is out of accord with the ideals of Jesus. The same can be said, of course, about every institution and organization, including the church. Those, however, who hold up the labor movement as the great idealistic movement of our time, in spite of its shortcomings, may not lightly evade the problem created by those shortcomings. The following observations may be made in the brief space at our disposal.

For one thing, those who experience a certain shock and disillusionment on first coming into practical contact with the world of labor, should ask themselves whether this arises from a fundamental defect in that world or from superficial external characteristics. It is desirable to have both the inside and the outside of the cup and the platter clean, but we cannot always have it that way. Some of us have long tolerated a social and industrial order which was "full of dead men's bones" within because it was outwardly pleasant and agreeable.[9] We shall be more nearly in accord with the Christian spirit if we learn to overlook certain crude and unpleasant outward marks of a movement that is fundamentally sound.

We must beware also of being led astray by words. There is the parable of the son who said he would do his father's will and did not, and of the other son who said he would not do it but nevertheless did.[10] Many things sound Christian and are not; others are Christian though they don't sound like it. In both labor and employer circles, for example, there is a considerable amount of talk these days about conciliation and reconciliation, which does not mean these things at all, but rather a compromise between labor or certain sections of it, and the employing class, which leaves the underlying social situation as vicious as ever or perhaps worse, because it means that certain sections of the workers also become obsessed with the capitalistic get-rich-quick psychology.

It must be borne in mind, when reports of violence on the part of labor in industrial disputes are made, that these are almost invariably grossly exaggerated, and that much of it is provoked by industrial spies to whom we have already referred. The basic fact furthermore is that the economic,

9. Matthew 23:27.

10. This parable is found in Matthew 21:28–32.

social, political order in which we live was built up largely by violence, is now being extended by violence, and is maintained only by violence. Our foremost task certainly must be to seek to persuade those who, directly or indirectly, are the beneficiaries of that situation, to relinquish every attempt to hold on to wealth, position and power by force, to give up the instruments of violence on which they annually spend billions of dollars of wealth produced by the sweat and anguish of the toilers. So long as we are not dealing honestly and adequately with this 90 percent or more of our problem, there is something ludicrous, and perhaps hypocritical, about our concern about the small percentage of violence that may be employed by rebels against oppression. "Cast out first the beam which is in thine own eye."[11]

In general, while we may believe that a particular industrial dispute is unnecessary or inexpedient, we shall take care not to fight against the workers, even if they use violence. This does not mean that we have to approve the violence. We may do all we can to prevent it, but we shall be careful not to put ourselves in the position where we oppose the fundamental things for which they are striving, for in that case we should simply be helping to perpetuate a system of violence and oppression of which we happen to be the beneficiaries.

For the most part, workers today are like such groups have always been, prone to endure suffering and injustice passively, until they become thoroughly intolerable. When then, in their despair, they use violence, it is begotten by the violence systematically used against them for years and generations. They who have sown the wind reap the whirlwind at last.[12] Perhaps few of us have earned any moral right in such circumstances to stand before workers and preach to them against the use of violence. In Marion, North Carolina, I have seen children ten or eleven years of age, who have been working in the cotton mills; men and women dying in their prime from diseases contracted because of the unsanitary conditions in those mills and the near-starvation induced by an average wage of $11.00 for a sixty-seven hour week. What have we ever done to root out these conditions? If violence should be used by workers in the attempt to banish them, what right should we have to protest?

In that same mill village six workers engaged in peaceful picketing were recently killed by "officers of the law," killed by being shot in the back after having been blinded with tear gas. The sheriff in charge of those who did the killing is not only going scot free, but he is still the chief officer of the law in that county. There was "not enough evidence to hold him for

11. Matthew 7:5, Luke 6:42.

12. See Hosea 8:8.

trial." There has been no gesture of violence against that sheriff and against others involved in this unspeakable outrage. If workers were to rise up and make such a gesture, what right would any of us have to protest? What have we done to make a tragedy such as this impossible in North Carolina or in other states? The fact is that they are occurring incessantly. If it is not the cotton mill workers in North Carolina, then it is a miner beaten to death in Pennsylvania, or Sacco and Vanzetti murdered in Massachusetts, or Mooney and Billings imprisoned in California.[13]

Yet all this does not mean that evil does not beget evil when used by labor as a method, as well as by any other group in the community, nor that the labor movement is not confronted with a serious problem regarding the means to which it will resort to advance its aims.

The labor movement in New York City not long ago gave a striking illustration of the law upon which the pacifist so often insists that the means one uses inevitably incorporate themselves into the ends and, if evil, lead to one's own defeat. Some years ago employers in the garment trades resorted to the practice of employing armed gangsters to attack peaceful picketers. It seemed impossible to send men and women on the picket line to meet such brutal attacks, so the union also resorted to hiring gangsters. Once you started the practice, you had to hire gangsters in every strike, of course. Thus a group of gangsters came to be a permanent part of the union machinery. Next it was easy for officers who had employed the gangsters in strikes to use these same gangsters, who were on the payroll anyway, in union elections to ensure continued tenure to the "machine." The next step in the "descent to Avernus"[14] was for the gangsters on whom the administration depended for its tenure of office to make themselves the administration, the union "machine."

In the meantime, the union gangsters naturally came to a gentleman's agreement with those hired by the employer, so that both sides were paying out large sums of money to gangsters no longer doing any decisive work in strikes or lockouts; both sides had likewise to pay graft to the police so that they would not interfere with their private armies; and the rank and file of

13. Nicola Sacco and Bartolomeo Vanzetti were Italian-born anarchists convicted in Massachusetts in 1921 of murdering two men during a robbery. Many people considered their trial unfair and their case became an international cause. They were executed in 1927 despite significant evidence of their innocence, leading to widespread protests. Thomas Mooney and Warren Billings were labor leaders convicted of bombing a San Francisco parade in 1916. Widely believed to be innocent, both were sentenced to death and spent over two decades in prison before being released. Mooney was pardoned in 1939 and Billings in 1961.

14. This is part of a famous proverb by Virgil roughly translated, "the descent to hell (*avernus*) is easy."

union members, having come to look to gangsters to do the real picketing, no longer had the desire, courage, or morale to picket peacefully, appeal to strikebreakers to join them, and so on. The whole process, working itself out so fatally and from the aesthetic viewpoint so beautifully, had not a little to do with the deterioration undergone by these unions of which the bitter left-right fractional strife was rather a symptom than a cause.

The Dilemma

Those who can bring themselves to renounce wealth, position, and power accruing from a social system based on violence and putting a premium on acquisitiveness, and to identify themselves in some real fashion with the struggle of the masses toward the light, may help in a measure, more doubtless by life than by words, to devise a more excellent way, a technique of social progress less crude, brutal, costly, and slow than humankind has yet evolved.

It would appear then that in practice we are caught in a cruel dilemma. If we function in some ordinary capacity in a capitalist, imperialist, militarist system, we share in the corporate sin; we are beneficiaries of corporate injustice, oppression, and violence. If we throw ourselves into the struggle to supplant such a system, we find that the forces actually working to this end are also far from being perfectly angelic, and employ methods that we may be unable to reconcile with the spirit of love that we seek to enthrone in our lives. I do not think that there is any complete and final escape from this dilemma. No more than the body can jump out of its own skin can the spirit jump out of, extricate itself from the social system in which it lives and moves and has its being.

Furthermore, it seems that this is what theoretically we might have expected to find. If we were indeed made for fellowship and if the good life is possible only on that basis, then there can be no good life until the means for the expression of fellowship are established. In other words, until we have realized a classless society. There is no escape from sin for anyone save as escape is provided for all.

It follows also that we achieve accord with "the Father's will" not by the negative process of refraining from this and not doing that, of withdrawing from this temptation and the other, but by the positive process of keeping our inner integrity, keeping the soul poised, keen, alert, striving ever as straight as possible toward the light that it sees. Thus we achieve the only perfection that is possible in this world, not the perfection of the Pharisee who has broken no rules, but the perfection which is still clothed in the garments of humility, saying "Why callest thou me good?"[15]

In conclusion, humankind has many times developed an imposing civilization such as that in the midst of which we live, and invariably the imposing structure has again crumbled into dust. If we ask ourselves what forces exist in the modern world that humankind has not previously possessed, and that might conceivably enable us to maintain and constantly to enrich, ennoble and extend our civilization, the answer is that there are two such forces: namely, modern science and the organized labor movement. Now, ordinarily, when new forces have emerged in history, they have been met with suspicion and opposition, not least from the good, the respectable, the supposedly religious elements of their day. When Jesus came "there was no comeliness that we should desire him."[16] The result has been not the destruction of the new elements, though their progress was often slowed up, but rather the destruction eventually of the institutions and persons that stood in their way. "There shall not be left here one stone upon another which shall not be torn down."[17] If the elements in our modern world that seek to conserve moral and spiritual traditions that have come down from the past, now meet the new force of science with obscurantism, and of labor with suspicion and hostility, shall we not have a repetition of the age-old tragedy?

On the other hand, if the various agencies that exist to pass down to us the heritage of moral and spiritual idealism out of the past, were to take these new forces by the hand and spiritualize them, then indeed we might hope, with more reason than people have ever had before, that in the years ahead the fellowship of all those who toil might replace class control, that an intelligent and classless society would be developed, and that so we might build in America and England and "every green and pleasant land," the city which hath the foundations whose builder and maker is God.[18]

15. Matthew 19:17, Mark 10:18, Luke 18:19.

16. Isaiah 53:2.

17. Matthew 24:2, Luke 21:6.

18. The quoted phrase is probably an allusion to William Blake's poem "Jerusalem," originally titled "And Did Those Feet." The last part of the sentence comes from Hebrews 11:10.

7

Return to Pacifism (1936)

In this article for the Christian Century, *Muste expresses his dissatisfaction with the Marxist-Leninist position he had embraced for a short time and explains why he left the labor movement to return to ministry within the church. The ominous signs of another world war forced Muste to recognize that the labor movement was no longer capable of or interested in opposing war. He cites the internal deterioration of most unions and the deplorable situation in the Soviet Union as evidence of the movement's abandonment of its principles and need for moral grounding. What is missing, Muste argues, is religion. The individual must be won not to a political movement, but to the kingdom of God, which affects all parts of life—including political activity.*

In recent years, I have been a part of the labor movement and of its left wing. I have accepted fully the Marxist-Leninist position and metaphysics. I have regarded the working class movement as the one effective agency to bring in a finer social order. I have believed that it was the most dependable, indeed the one really dependable, force to maintain world peace, or at least to abolish war—since it would abolish capitalism which begets war. It has seemed to me the expression of practical idealism, the "religion" that was able to call forth in its members the devotion and self-sacrifice which characterized the early Christians, for example. I have said to those who claimed that they desired to obey the teachings of Jesus in our time *that they must*, in spite of all its shortcomings, identify themselves with this movement or at least wholeheartedly support it. I do not now repudiate all this. But, in addition to rejecting some of it, there are a number of things that I would put in a different way and some things that I would add.

Take first the issue of war and peace. No one can spend a few weeks in Europe, as I did this summer, without feeling the overpowering urgency of this issue, and without being appalled by the nightmare of whole populations living day after day under the threat of the outbreak of a general war, a threat that hangs over them like a sword suspended on a single gossamer thread. If we are to be realistic, we must say, as so many who are not ordinarily alarmists have said, that unless a dynamic and methods hitherto not widely employed be found, war will come, possibly before many months, certainly before many years, and that when it comes it will be of an unimaginable horror and will wreak incalculable destruction. It seems to me now that one must be a romanticist capable of flying in the face of all the evidence to believe that such a war, under modern conditions, will be the portal to socialism or higher civilization or whatever one may prefer to call it. Rather it must set back the clock for generations, if, indeed, it does not involve the total eclipse of Western civilization.

Labor Cannot Stop War

If we are to continue being realistic, then we must state next that the labor movement by itself, using the approach and the methods that it has hitherto used, is not a dependable agency to prevent or abolish wars. That applies to all wings and tendencies of the movement.

So far as the reformist wing, trade union and socialist, is concerned, in 1914 it became an instrument of the respective warring imperialist powers, recruiting the workers for slaughter on the plea that a distinction had to be made between (relatively) "good" and (relatively) "bad" imperialist nations, and by other such specious arguments. In the post-war period, and particularly in recent years, it has failed to put up an effective resistance against the armament programs of the capitalist governments, and where it has been in office, as today in France, it continues or even exceeds the military preparations of its predecessors in office. Trade unions everywhere are still entangled in the contradiction of being "against war" but not scorning, often welcoming and avidly seeking, jobs for their members in war industries.

Nor is there any ground for looking to the Soviet Union and the Communist International under existing policies and leadership. These vociferously propagate the conception that there are two kinds of capitalist powers and that it may be quite all right for revolutionists and peace lovers and Christians to fight in the army of the better kind—fight just one more war to end war, one more war for "democracy," one more war against fascism. They have openly endorsed and supported, moreover, the war preparations of certain powers, such as France, and this not only now when there is an administration which has some title to be called democratic in its sympathies, but also under a Laval.[1] They hold that if a war should break out in which the government of the United States happens to be on the same side as the government of the Soviet Union, it will be your duty and mine loyally to support "our" government in that war.

Revolutionary Defeatism

Nor can I see that those who adhere to a thoroughgoing Marxist-Leninist position on war—that, as the lesser evil, the workers in each country must strive for the defeat of their own government in a war—give us any more dependable agency for preventing war. The Marxist-Leninists, of whom the Trotskyists, with whom I was until recently connected, constitute the main force, have in the first place what amounts to a fatalistic position—another war will certainly come, as capitalist collapse proceeds. They support rather than combat the psychological attitude that leads to war by espousing and acting on the view that violence is the only way to achieve fundamental social changes.

Such radicals are involved in the contradiction of abhorring war as the ugliest fruit of an outworn economic order and yet "welcoming" that war as giving them the opportunity to hasten the collapse of capitalism. Their formula for putting an end to war is to "transform the imperialist war into civil war"—which seems pretty much like saying that by this road, as by the one the governments of the great powers are traveling, we come to that war that will indeed be both international and civil, fought not merely along certain

1. Pierre Laval was prime minister of France from January 1931 to February 1932 and June 1935 to January 1936. Originally a member of the Socialist Party, he moved to the right after the Great War. He remained in politics during the Nazi occupation and was later executed after a controversial trial for his role in the Vichy government and complicity in the Holocaust.

clearly defined national boundary lines, but inside every nation—in every city, every hamlet, every street—that war that can hardly mean anything except collective suicide.

If we turn away for a moment from the question of war and peace, in its restricted sense, we are confronted by the fact that the movement has, since about 1924, suffered an uninterrupted series of defeats. The defeats of the Chinese revolution, the smashing of the Chinese Communist party by its one-time ally, Chiang Kai-shek, and the triumph of Hitler in Germany, followed by the total annihilation of the labor movement in the classic land of Marxism, constitute the great landmarks, in the East and West respectively, in this history of retreat and disillusionment. Nor can the reformist wing of the movement, when you take a broad worldview and mark the trend of the period as a whole, point to decisive progress and triumphs. Daily also it becomes more obvious that the Soviet Union itself, "the homeland of the working class," is in a serious plight. The Russian state has in recent years come to depend for the safety of its frontiers upon these very weapons—military forces and military alliances—that have so often proved to be nothing but preludes to war and agencies of insecurity.

A Time for Restudy

The devoted members of any movement, among other reasons because they have experience of what is fine and true in the movement, are apt to rationalize away its defeats as merely superficial and temporary. Personally, I have had to conclude that it is inexcusable, after all that has taken place in the labor movement since 1914, not to be willing to study the whole situation afresh, and as deeply and thoroughly as possible. There is reason to believe that this attitude is becoming more common.

One who has lived within the labor movement is compelled, it seems to me, to admit that it has not only suffered external delays or setbacks, something that might be of little or no significance for a great movement, but that there has also been a declension from basic principles and an internal deterioration. Consider, for example, the evidence of internal collapse presented by the external collapse, without one gesture of resistance, of the mighty German labor movement, in all its branches, at the advent of Hitler. No sane mind can believe that if that movement had meant one-tenth of what it once meant and was still thought to mean to its millions of members, this could possibly have happened. Consider the divisions that mark and so often gravely weaken the movement; the bitterness and virulence with which internal controversy is carried on; the methods used in dealing with opponents within the movement that are often devoid of any shred of honor, decency or fair play, which do not differ in any essential respect—be it said with shame—from the methods employed by militarists and Fascists. Or look again for a moment at the supposedly revolutionary wing of the movement, those who sit in the seat of Lenin.

Leninism Abandoned

The basic Leninist concept of world revolution they have abandoned, "for the time being," it is sometimes said. But it does not take a very profound mind or an extensive knowledge of history and Marxism to realize that such an idea cannot be put away in a drawer for a few months or years and then be taken out, dusted and put to work where it left off. The Leninist concept of fighting against war has been abandoned. Obviously the Leninist concept of party democracy can by no stretching of words be said to obtain in a party which, wielding the machinery of a totalitarian state and in a situation where expulsion from party membership means subjection to grave economic penalties, expels not less than 300,000 members in one operation, puts tens of thousands of political opponents into jail or concentration camps, and executes the remaining outstanding leaders of the October Revolution after a "trial" to which representatives of the socialist and trade union movement are refused admission.

If one looks squarely at these and many other such facts touching all organizations in the labor movement, then I think one is driven to the conclusion that the root of the difficulty is moral and spiritual, not primarily political or economic or organizational. Inextricably mingled with and in the end corrupting, thwarting, largely defeating all that is fine, idealistic, courageous, self-sacrificing in the proletarian movement is the philosophy of power, the will to power, the desire to humiliate and dominate over or destroy the opponent, the acceptance of the methods of violence and deceit, the theory that "the end justifies the means." There is a succumbing to the spirit that so largely dominates the existing social and political order and an acceptance of the methods of capitalism at its worst.

And wherever one turns, on a large scale or small, in greater or less (usually greater) degree, one sees the working out of the judgment that the Christian conscience would pronounce upon such motives and methods.

The Warning to the Soviet Union

Take the development in the Soviet Union during and after the great October Revolution—not in order to single it out for criticism or condemnation, but precisely because it is the most significant event in our own epoch and must be understood in more than a superficial manner both by the church and by the working class movement. You achieve a revolution by violence, though admittedly by a relatively small amount of it. You proceed to build the defenses of violence around your revolution. You create a great machine for war, repression and terrorism. You develop a Cheka, a system of espionage, numerous revolutionary tribunals.[2] You exalt ruthlessness into a major virtue. You deliberately become—temporarily, you tell yourself, of course—callous about the individual human life. What do you get? Certainly, something that is as yet far removed from socialism. And no one can deny that the machinery for repression that has persisted now gives evidence of becoming, like every machine, a vested interest.

Take another illustration from a common experience in trade unions. The employer uses violence against peaceful picketers in a strike. They fear to go on the picket line and so the union engages strong-arm men in its turn. Having done so in one strike, it feels compelled to do so in the next, and the next. The appropriation for gangsters becomes a regular and a big item in the union's budget—a steadily mounting one because, among other things, the employers' gangsters and the unions' strong-arm men are very apt to come to an understanding, in businesslike fashion, to do as little work for as much pay as possible, thus necessitating higher and higher pay in order to get them to do anything. Presently, the union's gangsters, sensing another avenue for gain, assert themselves in the union's internal affairs, in elections of officers, for example—unless, indeed, some group in the union, possibly the "machine" in office, has already bought their services for internal purposes. The next step is that the gangsters may dispense with intermediaries and simply make themselves the officers of the union. In any case, the union has become corrupted, its members demoralized, its effectiveness for advancing the cause of the workers destroyed.

To cite one more illustration: under the "end justifies the means" theory, "anything goes" in dealing with the "class enemy"; but those whom you regard as reactionaries in the labor movement you deem to be, in effect, "agents of the bourgeoisie" and "tools of the class enemy." Therefore they also must be ruthlessly crushed, and by any means. Thus the methods,

2. The Cheka was the first Soviet security organization. Founded in 1917, it had virtually unchecked power to arrest, torture, and imprison anyone deemed an enemy of the people.

standards and motivations of war are introduced inside the labor movement, with consequent divisions and weakening. Presently, within your own party, within your own faction of the party, and so on, almost *ad infinitum*, the view arises that other parties and other factions are "objectively considered" simply agents of the enemy. The necessary saving conclusion that a moral and religious spirit must be infused into this, as into every relation of life, is not drawn. Until it is, I believe that the movement will be cheated of its goal.

Peace Is Indivisible

Let no one think that I am standing outside of all this, observing and passing judgment. I was judged. Begin by assuming that in some degree, in some situations, you must forswear the way of love, of truth, must accept the method of domination, deceit, violence—and on that road there is no stopping place. Take the way of war and there is war—not only between nations, classes, individuals—but war, division and consequent frustration within your own soul. Thus, it seems to me that we have to say and practice, much more devotedly and consistently than we have yet begun to do, that peace is indivisible and that pacifism must be, is, religious—is religion!—or it will prove to be but a broken reed when the moment of crisis arrives when we have to lean upon it.

"Peace is indivisible," not only in the geographical and diplomatic sense in which Litvinov has so often and justly used the expression, but in the sense that the way of peace is really a seamless garment that must cover the whole of life and must be applied in all its relationships.[3]

Every pseudo and partial pacifism breaks down. Is it the pacifism of those who are against international war but who would, and do, use every form of coercion and violence in order to hang on to their own property and prestige and the system that gives them comfort? Lenin was absolutely right when he said that this pacifism simply served as a cover for war preparations. The pacifism of those who are against all wars except just one more war for what they regard as an absolute end? The pacifism of the unions, which are against wars but build battleships and guns in the unexpressed hope that they will somehow be smashed or rust away before they are used? The pacifism of those who are against international war but idealize and glorify class war? The pacifism of those who are against war but who are motivated by prejudice, fear, contempt in their relations with people of other races? All of these, I can see as plainly as my own hand under my eyes

3. Maxim Litvinov was a top Soviet official.

as I write, are either utterly invalid or have the most temporary and limited validity and in any case survive no real crisis.

God Is Love!

Pacifism—life—is built upon a central truth and the experience of that truth, its apprehension not by the mind alone but by the entire being in an act of faith and surrender. That truth is: God is love, love is of God. Love is the central thing in the universe. Humankind is one in an ultimate spiritual reality. Now, either such an affirmation is a mere form of words or it represents an essentially religious insight and experience—though its validity is verified in every form of human association, even that of thieves, where there must be "honor," some shred of trust, of each taking the other as an end and not a means, if the group is to "function" for a brief moment.

Such an affirmation one must accept and make, first in one's own soul. If it is not there, it exists only in formulas and abstractions. The individual must therefore be won and saved. But since it is precisely to love, to the apprehension of our unity with humankind, to the kingdom of God, that we are won, we must carry this dynamic and method into every relationship—into family life, into race relations, into work in the labor movement, political activity, international relations.

Surely no one can have visualized, in even one brief instant of insight, the abyss to which we are being carried by the dynamics and methods we have been employing, without agreeing that at least nothing could be lost by trying Christ's way of love.

The Church Comes to Judgement

I believe that people who hold such views as I have described must live and work in fellowship with those who hold like views in such an organization as the Fellowship of Reconciliation. They must also, I am convinced, work in and with the church. For the religious person can, less than anyone, live as an isolated atom. Nor can each of us go about organizing little private churches. That, too, expresses division and not unity. It may be indeed that the church everywhere will finally identify itself with the status quo, but that day is not yet. Even if it is to come, we must, after the example of Jesus, work from within and not without, though it lead to crucifixion. We must fulfill rather than destroy.

But let there be no mistake. Since the issue is finally and fundamentally religious, the church failing to meet it will receive the most terrible judgment of all. Of how many church buildings and organizations, in our day, has not the prophecy uttered by Jesus about the institutions of another day already been fulfilled: "There shall not be left here one stone upon another that shall not be torn down."[4] When we contemplate what has happened, must we not bow our heads and acknowledge once again that "the judgments of the Lord are true and righteous altogether"?[5]

On the other hand, if the church, or any substantial minority in it, will take seriously the gospel of the Lord whom it professes to serve and apply it persistently and in love, we can, in all soberness and calm, assert that never since the early Christian centuries has such a door been opened as now when, for the first time since that epoch, humankind is struggling to achieve a world civilization and waits, as never before in its history, for leadership possessed of dynamic and power adequate to such a task.

4. Matthew 24:2, Mark 13:2, Luke 21:6.

5. Psalm 19:9. Abraham Lincoln famously quoted this verse in his second inaugural address.

8

Evangelism and the Industrial Workers (c. 1937–39)

In this previously unpublished manuscript, Muste addresses reasons why the working class has little interest in Christianity. He presents a scathing and prophetic assessment of the church, arguing, among other things, that it is compromised by too close an alliance with the powers that be. At the same time, he also develops a strong critique of the labor movement.

In that very suggestive and perceptive "Oxford Conference Book" by W. A. Visser 'T Hooft and J. H. Oldham, *The Church and Its Function in Society*, Dr. Oldham opens his contribution with a chapter on "The Predicament of the Church."[1] He quotes an English critic to the effect that modern unbelief results from a widespread conviction that "the creeds of the churches cannot command a total act of the whole moral being."[2] Dr. Oldham continues:

1. The 1937 Oxford Conference on Life and Work, which focused on the theme "Church, Community, and State," was a major event in the history of the ecumenical movement.

2. Hugh Fausset, *The Modern Dilemma* (New York: E. P. Dutton, 1930), 19; quoted in W. A. Visser 'T Hooft and J. H. Oldham, *The Church and Its Function in Society*

"The cardinal fact with which we have to reckon, when we propose to take the church seriously, is that for large sections of the population in what was formerly known as Christendom . . . the traditional Christian ideas have ceased to have any living meaning. It is not so much that men disbelieve in Christianity as that they feel it to be entirely irrelevant to their actual experience of life." He cites one group of which this is true, "the working classes in all western countries which have broken consciously, and to all appearances irrevocably, with the Christian tradition because its assumptions and values have no recognizable relevance to the realities of their lives. Between their way of regarding life and what is uttered in the pulpit there is a gulf which in many instances seems to be unbridgeable."[3]

This analysis in its main outline is still applicable to the American scene also. It is true that there are still considerable numbers of workers who are in the church and consider themselves Christians; but they are either outside the organized labor movement, or of little influence in it, and for the most part they tend to keep their "Christian life" and their life as industrial workers in separate compartments. There are instances of labor leaders who are devout practicing Christians, and the bitter hostility toward the church and religion that has characterized the working class movement in some European countries is as yet a rare phenomenon in the United States. Nevertheless, it is true that for the decisive elements in the labor world in this country also there is no relevant and vital connection between the things in which they are absorbed and "what the preacher talks about on Sunday."

To observe the masses indifferent to or alienated from the church, and indeed joining in many lands in persecuting it, comes as a shock to those who recall that the Christian gospel was in the first instance largely directed to those "that labor and are heavy laden," that it was said of the early church that not many of the mighty and wise and noble were called, and that the people pressed into that church in the very face of persecution during the early centuries.[4] There is no doubt that the Christian message was once gospel—good news—to the poor. It seems not to be now. The contrast inevitably suggests going back to the fountainhead of the Christian movement for light on our problem, on this question of evangelism in the world of industry and among the working classes.

The gospel as it was preached by the one who is the Master of all true gospellers, was, as we need constantly to remind ourselves, primarily good news. Not theory, not argument, not manifesto or program, but good news

(London: George Allen & Unwin, 1937), 105.

3. Visser 'T Hooft and Oldham, *The Church and Its Function in Society*, 107, 110.

4. Matthew 11:28.

spoken and lived. It was addressed to the whole person and was such as could "command a total act of the whole moral being." It made sense out of life in all its aspects.

It was not addressed to an abstract individual who somehow existed apart from their environment and their relationships and who had a "soul" floating about inside them that had to be and could be "saved" by some process that stilled its unrest and enabled it to live "in eternity," in the sense of living in a trance insulated against and indifferent to most of what was going on in the world. On the other hand, the gospel was not the manifesto of a social, economic, or political system that took little or no account of the inner life of the individual and the spiritual and ethical adjustment that each soul must in the end make for itself with the source of its being—a perfect "system" that by some magic would solve humankind's ills without having anything important happen in people's souls. The gospel was not personal or social, not even personal and social; it was one indivisible personal-social, social-personal gospel.

True, in our halting thought and faltering speech we have to approach the matter more or less from one angle at a time. The gospel, then, was the fact that the Father of humanity is the creator and ruler of all. Love is the central and final fact and power in the universe. People are spiritual; we are not essentially of the natural order, to which we are now enslaved. God redeems us from that slavery by a love that is infinite and will not be denied, as the cross eternally and gloriously symbolizes. Clearly, however, such a gospel also involves "judgment." People have to "repent" in order to believe this good news. Sin becomes real and terrible in the light of the cross—not a mere defect that evolving humanity has not yet outgrown; not a failure to "live up to your best self"; not an irritant in relationships among a higher order of animals, but an insane refusal to accept life's highest gifts, a bestial trampling upon freely offered love. Moreover, the ethical standard proper to the children of God stands over the one who has heard the good news that they are a child of God and pronounces judgment upon them. You have to get a new mental apparatus, you have to become a child, to receive such a gospel!

The gospel, since it is the revelation that God is and that God is love, implies the announcement of the kingdom of God, the reign of love. The kingdom is here, since nothing that is not built on love can endure, since Jesus the Christ is here, since the community of those who love God and their fellows through Christ has come into being. The kingdom is to come, as all things are brought under Christ's feet, and this is the task in which people are to work together with God, namely, to establish fully the reign of righteousness and fellowship.

Differences of opinion as to whether the kingdom of heaven will be realized "in time" and similar theological questions do not, I think, vitally affect the main point we are making here. It is clear that in proclaiming the gospel of the kingdom Jesus stands in the succession of the Jewish prophets. He is the Messiah "that was to come."[5] The kingdom in that tradition had very definitely to do with affairs of people on this earth. Jesus addressed himself not to disembodied spirits, but to people in a concrete historical situation, functioning as members of social groups: Pharisees, Sadducees, Roman governors, tax collectors, fishermen, farmers. To people who hungered, who had overly heavy burdens laid on them, who were oppressed by native and foreign oppressors, Jesus spoke and held forth a way of deliverance from the real and concrete ills that afflicted them. They were foolish indeed to be personally worried and preoccupied with a grasping after food and raiment. God in his bounty supplied these things, and they would be "added unto" those who sought the kingdom of righteousness first and thus arranged human relationships in such a way that these did not cheat people of the gifts which nature proffered.[6] The early Christian churches, for all their expectation that "the end of the world" was at hand, understood Jesus in this sense and were not merely societies for ritual exercises or mystic communion but greatly concerned about the physical needs of their members and other needy ones: they were indeed communities built on other foundations than those of the world.

The gospel in this phase also was "judgment" as well as good news. Judgment is again spoken, as so often by the prophets of Israel, upon all oppressors, upon the hypocrisy underlying so much so-called religion and wisdom and statecraft, upon the complacent rich: a camel can more readily go through the eye of a needle than one of them enter into the new order of things which the Messiah heralds.[7] There is judgment upon the lust for domination and the violence of Caesar, and all the Caesars big and little in church, community, and state.

But, what is closer to our present purpose, the good news of the reign of justice and brotherhood presented itself as "judgment" also to those multitudes of the common people to whom the carpenter of Nazareth proclaimed his message. Many of them in their hearts were arrogant and full of hatred for their oppressors, just as the oppressors were arrogant and hateful, and in the sight of God these things became the one no more than the other. What the poor wanted in many cases was the same shabby regime as already

5. See Luke 7:19–20, John 6:14.

6. See Matthew 6:33, Luke 12:31.

7. See Matthew 19:24, Mark 10:25, Luke 18:25.

existed, only with themselves on top. Many were as fixed in national and racial prejudice as their rulers. If the Messiah would but put himself at their head as they were and lead them to the slaughter of their class or national foes, that would be all that was needed to establish the kingdom. That was all they desired. They did not really want to be changed; they wanted to see a change. They did not really want Jesus and his profound revolution and his rule; they wanted Barabbas and his pseudo-revolution and the reign of domination and violence in some new form—wanted one of those messiahs who in the words Maxwell Anderson puts in the mouth of one of his characters are "fools like myself / who rush themselves to power to set men free / and hold themselves in power by killing men."[8]

The Church's Difficulty

Do these essentials of the gospel as we have outlined them have any significance for the working masses and for the labor movement today? Is Christ, thus understood, an irrelevance? There is not the slightest question that there is still today no other name given among humanity whereby people may be saved.[9] How then shall we, to use Dr. Oldham's words once more, give "to the tremendous and startling affirmations of the historic Christian faith a meaning and expression which makes a living challenge to the thought and life of the ordinary man"?[10] What is it that causes our evangelism among industrial workers to be ineffective?

The difficulty is two-fold. On the one hand, the church misrepresents, or at any rate fails to adequately represent Christ; and it is too much compromised with Caesar, with the powers that be and the status quo in society and the state. On the other hand, modern workers and the organized labor movement are tempted to choose the way of Barabbas instead of Christ's. The church cannot win the masses away from Barabbas, save in the degree that its own alliance with or subservience to Caesar is broken and it gives whole-hearted allegiance to Christ. Let us deal with this issue first.

In part, the church's difficulty in approaching the urban masses springs from the same source as its difficulty in reaching the intellectuals who, like the former, are under the influence of modern thought and the modern "spirit." To say that these elements are irreligious and not open to the appeal of religion may have been true at one time, but if so the observation no

8. Maxwell Anderson, *The Masque of Kings: A Play in Three Acts* (New York: Anderson House, 1936), 140.

9. See Acts 4:12.

10. Visser 'T Hooft and Oldham, *The Church and Its Function in Society*, 108.

longer applies to them. They are turning in large numbers to communism and fascism. As has frequently been pointed out, but still needs to be borne home to the consciousness both of the church as a whole and of modern workers and intellectuals, these movements are not merely economic or political systems: they are life-views and they are religions. They do not seek control merely of certain outward actions of men and women, certain restricted spheres of life. They demand the absolute allegiance of the whole person.

It is of course true that these movements in part win allegiance by methods of compulsion, physical and psychological, which Christianity in so far as it is true to itself will not use. Where they have achieved a degree of influence and prestige, not a few join them for the vulgar and base reasons that characterize all those in whatever movement who play the role of politicians. The impoverished and oppressed are attracted frequently by the promise of "loaves and fishes." Yet when all such considerations have been advanced, it remains true that fascism and communism (I am not inferring in this argument that they are one and the same thing) have for multitudes filled the need of lifting them out of themselves, giving them a faith in something beyond themselves, providing them in their own eyes with a justification for living—and hence command religious, fanatical if you please, devotion.

The Church's Impotence

Over against them, the churches have largely stood impotent. The so-called orthodox sections, though they had grasped certain truths and sought to conserve certain values that the church in coming days must certainly retain, made the grievous mistake of acting on the unconscious assumption that proclaiming to people a form of words, with hallowed associations, was the same as preaching the gospel and mediating the experience of redemption in Christ to them. Nor were they in this by any means free from an attitude of arrogance and self-righteousness toward "sinners" and "unbelievers" and from identifying intellectual laziness with orthodoxy and spiritual faithfulness. The result at any rate is that their preaching is utterly unintelligible to great multitudes today. Moreover, as we shall indicate presently, the orthodox sections of the church in large degree shared with the rest of the Christian body in being entangled with Caesar, serving as conservators of a far from Christian status quo in the economic and political spheres, inculcating meekness before the rich and mighty of the earth as identical with meekness before the Eternal God.

The liberal and modernist sections of the church sought indeed to speak a language understood by the modern person and in a measure succeeded. But they were stricken with the malady of skepticism. The gospel in their hands was no longer authentic revelation of God, springing out of the unique and decisive intervention of God in history through Christ. People were no longer confronted in the preaching of this section of the church with good news verified in the experience of the preacher and the congregation, facts of the spiritual order in view of which they were called upon to make veritable and momentous decisions. Instead people heard speculations, essays—charming or boring as the case might be—comments on current events by commentators usually not too well qualified for the task.

There never has been and is not now any challenge or appeal in such "religion." It cannot even offer a decent battle against communism and fascism. Christianity will have to come before people again, not with an apologetic and shame-faced petition for a few moments' attention, but with gospel and judgment, with a claim deeply felt by Christians that they are bearers of a saving revelation about the ultimate truth of life and with a challenge to a daring and absolute allegiance. Then the masses will listen, as they listen to communism and fascism, and they will have to make a decision about the church and Christianity that will have genuine consequences for them, since it will not be a decision about joining a club or attending a tea-party.

But, as we have already suggested, this inability of the church and Christians today to speak with authority to the inner person of the inner experience of God is only one aspect of the difficulty. Communism and fascism do not speak to people as disembodied spirits for whom "salvation" consists in having a philosophy and some inner emotional experience that will make them indifferent to the fact that they are hungry and naked and humiliated by social discriminations and ground under the heel of oppressors and slaughtered in wars not of their making. These systems address themselves to people as to concrete human beings, total personalities, who cannot indeed be satisfied with fodder and a stall like domestic animals, who require a philosophy of life and an integrating sense of belonging to something greater than themselves, but to whom no philosophy appears to make sense and no god to merit a passing glance that seeks to justify or is indifferent to those tangible and terrible ills that afflict humanity and that verily make it impossible for them to realize themselves as human beings.

The same thing is true of Jesus and the early church. With what blunt sarcasm James in his Epistle speaks of the church that would put "a man with a gold ring, in goodly apparel," in the best pew and seat "a poor man in vile raiment" on a footstool; and of the "spiritual-mindedness" that would say to naked and hungry brothers and sisters: "Depart in peace, be warmed and filled" but not give them food and clothing![11]

The following things are indubitably true of Jesus and his gospel and the early Christian movement. First, they are in no sense identified with, the bulwarks of, the rich and the rulers in any sphere of life. They were the foes of tyranny of every sort, against everything that limited the freedom and development of the human being made in the image of God. In the eyes of the beneficiaries of the status quo in church, state and society, they were dangerous and revolutionary. Second, the early Christian movement addressed itself primarily to the poor and was mainly a movement of the poor and oppressed. Third, Jesus was tremendously concerned about the fact that people went hungry, particularly in view of the fact that others lived in luxury; and though he rejected as futile and self-defeating the methods by which nationalist and class revolutionaries sought to establish a new order, he made it clear that the old order of inequality and injustice would be overthrown, that he was leading people to a kingdom of God, a set of social relationships, which would mean among other things that the standard by which in the end he judged people was whether they gave a cup of cold water to some humble person and had visited the kind of people who get themselves in jail!

Fourth, within the church itself there was no discrimination on the ground of nationality, race, color, or social standing. If any such tendency appeared, it was severely condemned. And as the reference to James' Epistle and other references have already suggested, the church was not merely a society for ritual observances, still less a mere social club: it was a community in which the law of the kingdom of love and mutual aid in all relationships was practiced. "See how these Christians love one another," their neighbors exclaimed.[12] Fifth, Christians had renounced the way of violence and war. They would not bear the sword either on behalf of the kingdom of their Christ or on behalf of any earthly kingdom.

Contrast this with the situation in the church today. I do not wish to exaggerate here and I am anxious not to be misunderstood. For a number of years I renounced all religion as mere "opiate of the people" and the church as nothing but a bulwark of an iniquitous status quo.[13] I think I was wrong,

11. See James 2:1–7, 15.

12. Tertullian, "Apology," in *Tertullian: Apologetical Works and Minucius Felix: Octavious*, trans. Rudolph Arbesmann, Emily Joseph Daly, and Edwin Quain, Fathers of the Church, A New Translation, vol. 10 (New York: Fathers of the Church, 1950), 99. Muste paraphrases this quotation.

13. See Karl Marx, "Contribution to the Critique of Hegel's Philosophy of Law," in *Karl Marx, Frederick Engels: Collected Works* (New York: International Publishers,

dead wrong, and so are all those today who abandon the church. And while I have come back into the church primarily for my own soul's salvation, I have to be there where Jesus Christ is confessed as Lord and the sacrifices of praise and prayer are offered to the One God and Father of our Lord Jesus Christ, and while I certainly do not think of the church primarily as an agency to advance this or that good social "cause," I am firmly convinced that in this realm of social action that we are now discussing our Protestant churches have made immense advances in the past twenty or even ten years. Nevertheless, fidelity to our Master requires that we be honest and realistic in this matter. When we try to be and then compare the situation in the church today with the standard set by Jesus and his early followers, we have to confess that the church has still a long way to go and that unless it does so it will continue to meet hostility, suspicion, or utter indifference in its efforts at evangelism among industrial workers.

How can a church that is indifferent to the fact that people are hungry, unconcerned about the conditions that deprive them of the things required for the good life, which indeed in large degree justifies and protects these inequalities and injustices, expect to be listened to when it purports to bring them eternal life? James knew the answer, as did Jesus! Nay, the indictment against the church is really much more awful than this. The church has often run away from the areas where the most exploited, the least of the little ones for whom Christ died, were living because snobbish church people did not "like the neighborhood" and because, whether it put the matter into plain words or not, the church knew very well that if it were really to seek to evangelize these masses it would have to say and do something about the political, economic, and social conditions under which they lived. Churches that never supposed that being concerned about "spiritual" things and about "bringing souls to Christ" justified indifference to the liquor traffic did remain indifferent to the traffic in the bodies and souls of men, women and children implied in a regime of starvation wages, sweat shops, slum housing, and war.

It is fact that in our northern cities the churches have thus run away from the working masses because they were running away from economic and social problems. Figures compiled by the Methodist Episcopal Church South revealed that in the southern section of the United States about half the urban and more than half the rural population had to be classified as unchurched! What was behind those startling figures? Chiefly the fact that the economic condition of the masses in urban and rural slums in the south was such that their life was only slightly above the animal level and they

---

1975), 3:175.

were consequently incapable of what we think of as religious life and experience, susceptible only to the appeal of voodooism or occasional orgies of extremely emotional "religion." Any church that undertook seriously to win these souls for Christ and for eternal life would have to concern itself with their social and economic conditions, as our missionaries in such countries as China and India have of course realized. But too often the church is so involved with the status quo, with the Caesars in economic and political life, that its hands are tied in social and economic matters and hence it becomes impotent for the work of personal evangelism also.

To put the matter in another way, if the church in fidelity to the essentials of its own Christian philosophy, without at all meddling in things that are outside its province or where it is incompetent, were to take a clear and fearless position on certain critical issues of our day, it would be able to speak with genuine authority to the masses in industry. Wherever indeed some section of the church has made a beginning along this line, this has already been demonstrated. Ask any person of standing in the organized labor movement whether the Society of Friends, the Quakers, and their spokespeople are more respected than the general run of preachers and church people.

Take the issue of liberty. A church is no longer Christian that recognizes that any secular authority may in the final analysis dictate to the church or to the conscience of the individual. The concepts of the sacredness of personality, the infinite worth of the individual soul, are of the very essence of the Christian view of life. The church must be in the forefront of the struggle to maintain the civil liberties of speech, press, assemblage, teaching and worship. Liberty under modern conditions must include the right of workers to organize and bargain collectively, for obviously the individual worker has no real freedom in making a labor contract with a huge corporation. There can be genuine negotiation only when there is collective negotiation. The church and Christian people should identify themselves in suffering with those whose liberties are violated. Its own existence is indeed at stake here. Post-war history has made it clear that where other liberties go, freedom of worship presently also disappears. It is significant that where under dictatorships of the Right or Left there are no free trade unions, there are presently no free churches either.

The issue of violence furnishes another illustration of our point. Rejection of the way of the sword and faith in the way of the cross, of suffering love, is of the essence of the Christian position. When people think of violence in industrial disputes they are apt to think first and perhaps only of violence on the part of striking workers. That is, to put it conservatively, a very one-sided view. The police and other agencies of government in this country do not make it a practice in strike situations strictly to maintain the public peace, to isolate those actually engaged in violence from others, to use a minimum of violence themselves, and to impose the ordinary penalties on those who may have committed a breach of the peace. On the contrary, if there is a disturbance (quite possibly provoked by labor spies or by the police themselves) an entire picket line will be ruthlessly broken up and many individuals injured, unusually severe sentences will probably be imposed upon those who are arrested (by some strange coincidence these are almost invariably the strikers and not the non-strikers who were involved in the disturbance) and very likely an injunction will then be issued against the union seriously handicapping all of its activities, no matter how peaceful and legal they may be. Nearly a score of persons have been killed in strikes during the present summer in the United States. Surely it must give us pause that all of them were strikers engaged in efforts to establish collective bargaining that is presumably the law of the land, that none of those killed were non-striking workers or employers or police, and that a considerable percentage of the slain were shot in the back, in other words at a time when they were obviously seeking to escape and were not attacking anyone.

There is also the violence of employers, for example, who according to their own testimony have spent millions of dollars in recent years on labor spy services. Putting aside the question as to whether the employment of spies at all is Christian or can be expected to promote good labor relationships, as a general rule labor spies can never confine themselves to reporting what is actually said and done among the workers. That would hardly be worth millions of dollars. Labor spies go on, therefore, to give exaggerated and alarming reports of what is going to happen; and then they cannot run the chance that their predictions may not be verified and so they go on to provoke violence.

When the church pronounces Christ's judgment upon such practices, then it is in a moral position to rebuke violence on the part of the workers also, and it would at least be listened to with respect when it sought to evangelize them, to confront them with the eternal issues of sin and salvation.

Problems with the Labor Movement

This brings us to our final point. There is a tendency among some of the exponents of "the social gospel" to make the church's chief or even sole function that of giving a blanket endorsement to the labor movement and all its activities. The labor movement, in their view, is significant, is accomplishing things, is the Messiah leading our civilization to the Promised Land. It has little or nothing to learn from the church. The church had better "get behind the labor movement" or it will be doomed. That is, I think, an inadequate and distorted picture of the situation that in the end will benefit neither labor nor the church.

A realistic appraisal of recent years reveals that the history of the post-war period is far from constituting a clear and conclusive triumph for the working-class movement or a complete validation of Marxism. In Italy, Germany, and a number of other countries the labor movement was crushed. In France it is for the moment at a stalemate, leaning heavily on an alliance with a once despised middle class party, hoping to conserve its gains rather than aiming at power, and collaborating in the French armament program, thus reversing completely the traditional anti-militarism of the French syndicalist movement.

The labor movement in Great Britain certainly lacks the *élan* which marked 1918 and the succeeding years. It has difficulty in developing an effective opposition to the conservative government because at important points as, for example, in foreign policy it offers no clear alternative and with regard to rearmament it too has reversed its traditional policy and is cooperating with the conservative government.

In Spain, along with some other elements, the movement is waging a war marked by magnificent heroism against Fascist forces, but is there any assurance that it will be a victorious struggle? And, most tragic and significant of all, in the very midst of this struggle a fierce internal conflict rages in the movement, workers and peasants killing workers and peasants, revolutionists murdering revolutionists. In the Soviet Union gains have been made at certain points. No one who takes Marx and Lenin seriously, however, can argue that the foundations of socialism have been securely laid. At the moment the tendency is in fact the other way, toward the formation of privileged groups in the Communist Party, the Red Army, the Stakhanovites, and some of the collective farmers, on which the present regime bases itself.[14] Whatever one's interpretation of the executions that have marked recent years, no one can plausibly argue that they indicate that the regime is or feels itself to be secure. It looks for the "security" of the Soviet Union today to conventional military forces and military alliances, which all too plainly have always in the end proved to be factors of insecurity, not of security.

The fact that in the United States the labor movement in the past few years has made substantial and steady gains does not seriously affect the

14. The Stakhanovite movement glorified hard work and encouraged workplace competition in an attempt to boost productivity.

argument, for we are only accomplishing what the British working class, for example, accomplished several decades ago. There are no indications that, unless new factors enter, our labor movement will not in due time encounter the same problems and arrive at the same impasse. Indeed confusion is already the outstanding characteristic of the traditional radical parties in this country, the socialist and communist.

For any thoughtful person belonging to or interested in the labor movement, recent history emphasizes the need for re-evaluating the whole philosophy and strategy of the movement and the utter futility of parroting Marxian or pseudo-Marxian formulas.

It is at this point that Christians who have some understanding of and faith in the distinctly Christian viewpoint and who are not content to be mere endorsers of the labor movement any more than to be lackeys of capitalism, or to make a bargain with fascism, have a revealing and saving word to say.

What Christianity says to the modern labor movement is something like this, that the startling thing about it, especially in its more thoroughly Marxist phases, is not its anti-capitalism, but precisely that, in spite of surface differences, its underlying assumptions are so similar to those of our industrialist capitalist civilization at its worst, and that unless the labor movement is purified, deepened and spiritualized, it too will contribute to the dissolution rather than the redemption of our civilization.

Among the devotees of Marx and Lenin as among those to whom our industrial capitalist economy is god, one encounters:

- The same preoccupation with material abundance as the master key to all human problems.
- The same faith in the efficacy and sufficiency of external conditions or changes. Keep this capitalist system, which has worked such miracles, going and humankind will progress automatically and indefinitely, was the naive faith of pre-war capitalism. Smash all this and set up a different kind of economic system, and by that means alone, humankind will enter Utopia, is the similar and equally naive faith of Marxism. There is no place for a doctrine or a living sense of sin in our middle-class civilization, any more than in Marxism-Leninism.
- The same worship of the machine, of technology, and the same tendency to think of all problems as technological, to look at them from outside rather than inside the human soul.
- The same indifference to or contempt for the inner life of the soul—all that is sentimentalism, "escape from reality," to both systems.

- The same subordination of cultural and spiritual life to economics. For capitalism, religion tended to be merely an instrument to keep workers sober and submissive. For communism, the realms of culture are mere reflections of economic processes.
- The same contempt for democracy and democratic processes, as a rule camouflaged in capitalism and open in communism. The same falling back on dictatorship, and mystical justifications of it in Nietzsche and fascism on the one hand, and in communism on the other.
- The same contempt for the individual, treating people as cogs in someone's cruel machine, though ironically, both systems put humanity in place of God, capitalism claiming to be based on individualism and liking to speak of its "religion" as scientific and humanist, and communism claiming to be the deliverer of people from the inhumanity of industrialism.
- The same reliance upon power, domination, violence; the same lapse into ruthlessness in critical times; the same contempt for gentleness, humility, love, and fellowship.
- The same degradation of morality into expediency and easy resort to the doctrine that the end justifies the means.
- The same inability to break with war and presently the rationalization of war into the supreme and final means of the victory of the good.
- The same confining of life exclusively to this world—the secularization of all life.

Why should we believe that if such tendencies and convictions prevail in the labor movement, if it is not Christianized, it can lead to aught but disaster?

Still as of old, there is no other name given among humanity than the name of Jesus whereby individuals and society may be saved.[15] The church that achieves the authority and the grace to speak to the working masses and to the labor movement, because it is utterly faithful to its Lord, because it organizes its own life on his teachings and spirit, because it breaks all compromising ties with Caesar, because it is genuinely concerned about the ills from which the oppressed suffer—that church will be able to preach the gospel of the redeeming love of the Father to poor as well as rich and it will be able to call upon the labor movement to follow Christ and not Barabbas.

15. See Acts 4:12.

That will be effective evangelism, the everlasting gospel in terms understood by the people. If he be thus lifted up, shall he not draw all people unto him?[16]

16. See John 12:32.

9

The True International (1939)

Asked by the Christian Century *to explain his reconversion to pacifist Christianity from Marxist-Leninism in more depth, Muste responds by arguing that the church is the "true international." He recounts the changes in his life from 1919 to 1939 and details his thought process upon returning to the church. He then argues that "The Party" and the church are in fact very similar. People are attracted to communism and fascism in part because those ideologies pretend to be what the church is supposed to be. While the church may have its failings, communism is a false alternative. God is the only true source of the salvation and redemption of the world.*

At the beginning of 1919 I was a devout Christian pacifist. I had been compelled to resign from my pulpit a year or so before, because I could not give up or agree to keep silent about my convictions for the duration of the war. I considered myself, however, a faithful member of the Christian church and fervently hoped that its eyes might be opened to the sin that it had in my opinion committed in blessing war. As one of a group of Christian pacifists, a comradeship within the Fellowship of Reconciliation seeking by study and prayer to learn how to apply the spirit of Jesus in all relationships of life, I was involved in the Lawrence textile strike of that year. Our leadership at critical moments in that sixteen weeks' strike, involving thirty thousand people in the tense and turbulent months immediately following upon the armistice, was uncompromisingly pacifist. The power that carried me, with no previous experience in labor or strike activity whatever, through the severe labors and the nerve-wracking crises of that strike had been generated during the preceding weeks when Harold Rotzel and I got up on cold mornings in a drab house in a rooming-house section of Boston to pray and study the Sermon on the Mount together verse by verse.[1]

Ten years later, at the beginning of 1929, I was in my eighth year as director of Brookwood Labor College, then probably at the height of its prestige and usefulness, although (or perhaps because) the American Federation of Labor had the previous fall warned its unions against giving any support to this "communist institution" and also against the wiles of one John Dewey of Columbia University whom it designated as the principal agent of the Bolshevik International in this country! Brookwood was not at that time in any sense a communist institution, but personally I was moving rapidly along the road which made me a few months later an inwardly convinced Marxist-Leninist—though critical of the official Communist party's course—and a few years later a leader of the Trotskyist movement. I no longer considered myself in any sense a member of the church. It was to me nothing but a peculiarly pernicious bulwark of a reactionary status quo. I rejected the Christian worldview utterly.

Today, at the beginning of 1939, I am again a Christian pacifist. Though in my own thinking and feeling there is no separating these two terms as I define them, nevertheless I am first and foremost and altogether not a member of a secular anti-war movement but a member of the church of those who trust for redemption in the love of God in Christ.

An Ineffective Method

When, in obedience to the counsel of the editor of the *Christian Century*, I searched my "intellectual experience to discover if possible a single fundamental insight which comprehends and explains" my changed outlook, I thought of a number of answers to that question that one might to good purpose state and explain. For example, I was self-sufficient in 1929. Now

1. Rotzel, another pacifist minister, lived with his family above Muste's family in an intentional community organized by the Boston branch of the Fellowship of Reconciliation.

I know that I was not and am not: that I live by the grace of God and stand straightest when I am on my knees.

In 1929 I believed that the way to bring in a new world was basically, virtually exclusively, a matter of "social engineering," changing "the system"—economic, political, social. Today I recognize that we neglected too much the problem of what happens inside the human being. Whether there can be a democratic society, for example, depends in the final analysis upon what human beings are, whether they are capable of making moral decisions and therefore of building and maintaining a free society.

Still another clue to my changed outlook occurred to me. It has to do with the question of ends and means, whether or not evil can overcome evil. In the years from 1916 to 1919, for example, I was deeply and joyously convinced that only love, only good, can overcome evil. In those days our group of Christian pacifists was in all matters of economics, politics, international affairs, unsophisticated and poorly informed. But on all important issues—the real causes of the war, what led the United States into the war, the unreliability of propaganda, the kind of peace which would follow the war—we sensed the correct positions! Nearly all informed people now accept as a matter of course the positions that informed people twenty years ago ridiculed our pathetically uninformed group for holding. In 1929 I was much better informed than ten years earlier. But I was coming to believe that the way to true democracy and brotherhood and peace was that of dictatorship and hate and repression and violence. Presently I was brought up hard against the realization that by that very pragmatic test that I had chosen the method did not produce the desired results and that furthermore I was undergoing an inner deterioration and was reduced to judging events and making decisions by purely *ad hoc*, opportunistic standards.

This is Where You Belong

I am, however, setting aside all these valid and I think important answers to the question directed at us, because while I was meditating upon them there flashed into my mind the recollection of three events and the fact that they were significantly related. First, I remembered those mornings with Harold Rotzel in the house on Appleton Street in Boston that I have already mentioned, and the little Christian pacifist comradeship to which I belonged just at the close of the war, and the Society of Friends that had welcomed me into its membership and ministry in those days—and how I had the sense of having found the true church, felt with mingled awe and gladness that I "had come unto Mount Zion, and unto the city of the Living God . . .

to the general assembly and church of the first-born who are enrolled in heaven," and how in that fellowship fear melted away and strength and endurance were supplied according to need, though the need was sometimes immeasurable.[2]

Next I remembered that during my years of absorption in the secular revolutionary movement it had been the doctrine of "The Party"—the nature, structure, and functions of the revolutionary party—which had enlisted my deepest study and concern. I recalled those moments when the sense of "belonging" to a comradeship that had burned away self-centeredness in devotion to the task of making heaven real on earth by building "the workers' world," brought again joy and strength. I recalled also that what came to hurt the most and what really forced me to try to think things through again from the beginning was to find pettiness and duplicity and self-indulgence and ruthlessness and a lack of human sensitiveness and of moral standards in "The Party" itself.

Last, I recalled the circumstances and the form of my "re-conversion." It was in Paris in the beginning of August 1936. I had begun in very tentative fashion to re-examine my beliefs and to consider what I should do on my return to the United States some weeks later. However, at the time I was sightseeing with no conscious purpose except to see sights. One who is seeing the sights of Paris for the first time must see some of the churches. Casually one afternoon I walked into one of them. It was being repaired. There was a certain impression of solidity about it, but it had too many statues of saints for my taste. I sat down on a little bench near the front and looked at the cross. Without the slightest premonition of what was going to happen, I was saying to myself: "This is where you belong," and "belong" again in spirit to the church of Christ I did from that moment on. I felt as if the hand of God had drawn me up out of those "titanic glooms of chasmèd fears," of which Francis Thompson sings, and had catapulted me back into the church.[3]

The True International

Even as these events were passing before me, I was saying to myself: "You see how it is. What you have all along been seeking is what the Marxist calls 'The Party' and what the religious person calls the 'true church' and that is indeed the crucial question of our day: what is the instrument by which the

2. Hebrews 12:22–23.

3. Francis Thompson, "The Hound of Heaven," *Poems* (London: E. Mathews & J. Lane, 1893), 48.

revolution is to be achieved, the kingdom of God established? We cannot go on as we are. The great deliverance must come. But how? Where is The Party? Where is the true church?" I could not rest without an answer.

Lenin, it is interesting to note, was really concerned about two things: the nature and structure of a revolutionary party and how the party might acquire state power. The great split of the Russian social democratic movement into Bolshevik and Menshevik wings was not over a great philosophical or economic issue but over the question of a highly centralized party such as Lenin was determined to have versus a decentralized, "democratic" party such as the Mensheviks wanted. It is a patent fact that in the fascist or Nazi, as in the Bolshevik, scheme the idea and the fact of The Party are all-important. Are we not all in Christian circles rediscovering the "church"?

Let us return for a moment to Lenin. It is astonishing how many of the marks of the true church are included in his doctrine of The Party. The Party must be revolutionary. The existing order is corrupt; it is also unable any longer to function; it is doomed. The Party must therefore aim to overthrow it, not to come to an understanding with it. The Party stands over against "the world" therefore. It is despised, it is weak, it is in a hopeless minority, it is outrageously persecuted—until the day of revolution dawns. Then when the more imposing and less intransigent parties stand paralyzed before a world falling to pieces, The Party will fill the breach.

The Party is the instrument of God—of destiny at any rate, of those "historical forces which make the triumph of socialism inevitable." A force that makes for the reign of righteousness and brotherhood, to which individuals must surrender themselves utterly, and that cannot fail—that comes close to being a definition of, let us say, a Calvinist God. The Party accordingly cannot really fail. "Fear not, little flock."[4] It has the deposit of the truth. It cannot do wrong, since at a given moment nothing can be nearer right than the instrument of historic destiny.

There can on these terms be only one true party. Individual members, if they be true members who have no will but The Party's will, will find ineffable joy in its service. Without The Party, the proletariat is lost. Of itself, through its own experience, without being led and for its good manipulated by The Party, it will not rise to revolutionary heights and be able to save itself. "The basic error," Lenin wrote, "is the idea that political consciousness can be developed in the workers from within. . . . Political consciousness can only be impressed on the workers from outside," and through The Party, of the elite, the elect, through the "ecclesia."[5]

4. Luke 12:32.

5. See Vladimir Ill'ich Lenin, *What is to be Done?: Burning Questions of Our*

The Party, Lenin contended, must be international, universal, in scope and in essence. Violently he contended against the leaders of the Second International who thought in terms of a British, Dutch, German, Russian party affiliated to the International. There could be only one International party with British, Dutch, and so forth sections, but sections without autonomy. "One, holy catholic Church." When finally The Party triumphs, history as we know it comes to an end, or rather history begins for the first time. Humanity will pass, in Engels's great phrase, "from the kingdom of necessity into the kingdom of freedom."[6]

Problems with Lenin's Party

It was a magnificent attempt to sketch and to create the true church for which people long, and because of its daring and its partial truth and because of the apostasy of Christ's church, not least in Russia itself, it was given to Lenin's church to have power for a season, and to win many devout adherents, and to be the midwife for the "historical forces" in one of the great hours in human history—and Lenin has become an icon.[7]

Why is Lenin's party failing, its members in the United States today, for example, being engaged in recruiting for the United States army, and why can we not accept it as the true church? Of the many things that need to be said in answer to that question, I must confine myself to mentioning two. For one thing, Lenin rightly discerned that if you are to exercise control over the flux of the historical present, you must believe that you have a position outside and above it; and that if you are to have the strength and the courage to break down the pillars of this temple and in three days to build another in which the goal of all history will be achieved, then you must be in league with destiny itself.[8] But this, as I have already suggested, is to speak of God, the true God, the Almighty. Then, as Lenin did, you have to wage relentless war against all those you regard as false gods, which for Lenin meant above all against Christ. But then, also, the question is obviously raised: Is your God truly God? And just as in the case of the human being the question

---

Movement, ed. Alexander Trachtenberg, trans. J. Fineburg (New York: International Publishers, 1929), 76; Vladimir Ill'ich Lenin, *What is to be Done?: Burning Questions of Our Movement*, trans. S.V. and Patricia Utechin (Oxford: Clarendon, 1963), 101. It appears Muste used a different translation than either of the translations cited.

6. Friedrich Engels, *Socialism: Utopian and Scientific*, trans. Edward Aveling (Chicago: Charles H. Kerr, 1907), 82. This quotation differs from the original.

7. See Revelation 13:5–8.

8. See John 2:19.

as to whether someone is "really" human has to do with their character, so the ultimate question about your God has to do with your God's character.

This leads to a second and closely related question. If you have The Party, which is international, universal, the depository of the truth, the sole instrument for the redemption of humankind, without which there is no salvation, that can brook no rivals since to do so would be to deny its divine commission and to turn humankind over to destruction—and this party is composed of human beings albeit "the elect"—how can you prevent such a party from becoming the instrument of unspeakable pride and tyranny and hence tearing itself to pieces? Obviously you cannot, and your advice to the inner circle of your party, "Don't make the mistake the leaders of the French Revolution made and get to killing each other off," will go unheeded if you begin as Lenin did by assuming that the character of its members, save in the one respect of self-effacement for The Party, is not of first-rate importance and that the party may employ any means in order to achieve its end.

The True Church

The positive phase of the answer to this most crucial question about the International Party or the Universal Church is stated in the classic chapter on Karl Marx in J. Middleton Murry's recent *Heroes of Thought*:

> To keep alive within any human society the sense of the reality of Good and Evil as absolutes, independent of the convention of the society, or the ordinance of the secular state, is the function of a Church. . . . Therefore the institution of the Church is precious, but precious only in so far as it asserts and justifies in act the claim to possess an authority superior to that of the secular state, because derived from its knowledge of the absolute Good, which is God. . . . Further, it is self-evident that there is but one safeguard against the abuse of this authority of the Church, namely, that the absolute Good in obedience to which its authority consists should forbid persecution, and command nonresistance to evil. This the God of the invisible Christian Church does command.[9]

The only true God is not the God of impersonal historical or economic forces that "automatically," apart from the human agents and regardless of the quality of the human agents, redeem society. To think this is to try "to abolish the problem of human society, which is the problem of human

9. J. Middleton Murry, *Heroes of Thought* (New York: Julian Messner, 1938), 341–42.

nature."[10] The true God is the God of love who can and does redeem people. This God is revealed in Jesus Christ. The true church is the "ecclesia" of those redeemed by infinite love. It must seek to redeem the world and must assert that it is the channel of the grace of God without which there is no salvation, and that to it are entrusted "the keys of the Kingdom of Heaven."[11] But it can rightfully do this only in the degree that it exercises no violence except that of a love which will not be gainsaid and which is ever ready to die for sinners, and if it is in itself a true community of love.

What has been said reminds us, of course, why it is that the church has so largely failed and why multitudes have turned in their passionate hunger for a truly redeeming church to The Party of Lenin, or Stalin, or Hitler, or Mussolini. Too often when it has dared to claim divine authority the church has sought to exercise power by worldly means. Often it has not dared claim to be an instrument of historical forces, much less of the Everlasting God, the Creator of the ends of the earth.[12] Instead of challenging its members and subjecting them to a mighty and joyous discipline, it has tried to be a sanctified Rotary Club or League of Women Voters for them. It has not laid claim, as its Lord authorized it, to being the True Scarlet International of those who "have washed their robes and made them white in the blood of the Lamb" and among whom is neither Aryan, Negro, Slav, Japanese, Malay, since all are one in Christ.[13] Instead all of its branches including those called "Catholic" have been in effect mainly national, state-worshiping or picayune provincial sects.

One God, One Church

How do I explain the return to such a church and a sense of coming back to my eternal home in thus returning? Let two remarks suffice. In the first place, at the moment the visible church is by way of becoming a more faithful replica of the invisible. It is a magnificent portent that the figures in our world today that symbolize challenge to the state, the final refusal to make a bargain with totalitarianism, are not, as would probably have been the case a few years ago, secular radicals, but religious, Christian, church figures such as Martin Niemöller and some of the Roman Catholic bishops of Germany. And it is many centuries since the sense that the church is in essence universal, ecumenical, and must in fact become so, the conviction that the

10. Ibid., 341.

11. Matthew 16:19.

12. See Isaiah 40:28.

13. Revelation 7:14, see Galatians 3:28.

church must redeem and rule the world in Christ's name, has been so strong as it is today.

But more important than this, there is no greater presumption than that one should undertake to build one's own church, and since community, communion, is of the essence of life, no more heinous sin than that of schism. There is one God and one Lord Jesus Christ. There is despite all its divisions and disfigurements and sins but one church, one Christian movement. In it one must, one does, humbly and joyfully take one's place. What branches may yet be lopped off from the church, what changes in outward form may come, what stern prophetic denunciations the Lord of the church may call upon us to utter, God shall reveal. It is palpable error to think that getting out of the church of Christ and joining one of the internationals that aims to replace it will bring salvation to us or to the world.

10

Fragment of Autobiography (1939)

As in two of the previous pieces, here Muste describes the encounter with God that led him to reject Marxist-Leninism and return to the church. In this selection he focuses primarily on the inner, spiritual process that led to his reconversion and speaks honestly about his faith and personal experiences of God. In the process, he shares some of the core foundations of his theology.

Early in the summer of 1936 friends of nearly all shades of views, from fairly conservative to extreme "left," provided me with funds to make a two months' trip to Europe. The main purpose was to enable, in a sense perhaps to compel me to loaf for a while after several years of intense and uninterrupted activity, which had included direct participation in many serious and dramatic industrial conflicts, such as the Marion, North Carolina strike in 1929 in which six men were wantonly killed, shot in the back, by strike deputies; coal miners' strikes in West Virginia in 1930 and 1931; and later some of the movements that led up to the formation of the C. I. O.[1] and the organization of hundreds of thousands of workers in hitherto non-union industries, such as the Auto-Lite strike in Toledo in 1934, the General

1. The Congress of Industrial Organizations was a federation of unions.

Motors strike of 1935, and the Goodyear Rubber strike in the spring of 1936 where the wave of sit-down or stay-in strikes had its origin.

These years had also been years of intense political activity and controversy. For some time I had been one of the leaders in the Trotskyist movement in this country. I held a thoroughgoing Marxist-Leninist position and accepted the metaphysics of that movement. I rejected Christianity utterly, believed religion was nothing but "opiate of the people," the church simply a bulwark of an iniquitous status quo.[2]

Though in conformity with the wishes of my friends, I planned conscientiously to loaf and see sights in Europe, except for a one week's visit with Trotsky, I was saying to myself that when I got surfeited with rest and simply had to do something, it would be an article exposing the anti-revolutionary position of such left-wing religionists as Reinhold Niebuhr, and pointing out that it was precisely such people who were most dangerous to the revolutionary cause: the workers would not pay any attention to the Machens and Fosdicks anyway, but they might listen to the Niebuhrs who, not hardened in dialectical materialism, would nevertheless also betray them when the revolutionary crisis came.[3]

When I sailed out of New York harbor on a June day I had not the faintest idea that I should return with my basic outlook and convictions changed and that my first act on returning in August would be to sever my connections with the Trotskyist movement.

When I returned from that journey, I was again a Christian believer looking to the love of God revealed in Jesus Christ as the one fountain-head of salvation and life. I had again become convinced that there will be no revolution, no new world in which righteousness dwelleth, unless people are revolutionized. "The kingdom of God is at hand"—the great change, the new day—so what? Organize, agitate, fight! No, first of all, "Repent."[4] There are not a few in the left-wing, by the way, who are beginning to see that. To see that the ultimate question has to do with the nature of humanity, whether people are essentially children of God capable of making moral decisions and therefore of living in a free society or whether they are essentially animals, in which case every society, every state, every economic order, no matter how it may be camouflaged temporarily, will be a wolf-pack with the strongest and most brutal of the wolves as the dictator, and

2. See Karl Marx, "Contribution to the Critique of Hegel's Philosophy of Law," in *Karl Marx, Frederick Engels: Collected Works* (New York: International Publishers, 1975), 3:175.

3. John Gresham Machen was a conservative Presbyterian theologian fiercely opposed to liberalism. Harry Emerson Fosdick was a prominent liberal minister.

4. Matthew 3:2, 4:17; Mark 1:15.

business and politics will always be "the game of who gets what when," and the distant as well as the immediate future will be with the dictators since in that case they are building on fact, on what is real in the structure of humanity, and not on illusion.

I was convinced before that summer was over that the labor and revolutionary movement had in so many places suffered defeat, and in others had come to an impasse, largely because of ethical and spiritual shortcomings. "There shall be no classless state—no abundant life—no peace, until each of us shall have said, 'Lord, is it I!'"[5] I was convinced that if you resorted to violence, dictatorship, terrorism, chicanery, if you elevated ruthlessness, temporarily you told yourself of course, into a major virtue to gain your goal—not of course because you wanted to but because it was "the only realistic thing to do"—you would get the violence, dictatorship, terrorism and chicanery that you practiced, not the fair goal about which you dreamed and orated. The movement that began with the contention that "anything goes" in dealing with the class-enemy would presently find each of its myriad factions believing that "anything goes" in dealing with every other faction and would end in the enforced unity and futility of a fascist concentration camp. I became again a Christian pacifist as I had been during the last war.

It is not my purpose in this paper to amplify the statement of these views or to present the theoretical and practical considerations that in my opinion give them validity. That is of course important. To some extent I have tried to do this elsewhere. What I wish to attempt here is to recall for myself and to picture for the reader the inner, psychological process that led to the change that I have sketched.

There are times when it seems impossible or indelicate or even blasphemous to speak or write of certain personal experiences. Obviously, too, the way in which a person arrives at views or convictions does not in and by itself prove their truth, at least not for others. These convictions must submit to the test of reason and of practical experience. How often also when one has tried to speak in the simplest and most honest way of that which lies deepest and is most precious, one wonders whether a human being can ever approximate to self-knowledge and still more to simple and truthful utterance about that which nearly concerns oneself. "The heart is deceitful above all things."[6] On the other hand, there are moments when one is moved or forced to testify. And is it not an apt saying of Arnold Lunn's that "it is difficult to understand why reticence should be a virtue in religion and

5. Josephine W. Johnson, "Year's End," in *Year's End* (New York: Simon and Schuster, 1937), 77. Muste altered punctuation, omitted material, and altered the word order of this quotation.

6. Jeremiah 17:9.

self-expression an essential of art. No sense of reticence restrains the poet or the artist . . . from his attempt to translate into words, form or color the beauty which he had experienced. Why should self-expression be a virtue in the artist and self-suppression a virtue in the apologist?"[7] As Mr. Lunn goes on to suggest, not all reticence is commendable; there is also a "reticence of doubt."[8] He quotes Father Bede Frost in a passage that many perhaps need to take to heart: "If the average Christian of today is reticent about his religion it is not because it is so deep and intimately dear a thing to him, but because it is so shallow and so cheap. . . . Touch one of these 'reticent' people upon a matter in which he is interested—politics, sport, business—and how easily he passes from impersonal discussion to personal reminiscence and personal experience."[9]

God is a Seeking God

Toward the end of July in 1936 we were in Paris. We were devoting ourselves to sight-seeing. When you go sight-seeing in Europe you go to churches even if you believe that it would be better if there were no churches for anyone to visit. So one afternoon I walked into the church of St. Sulpice, having been attracted to that particular edifice partly by this general sight-seeing interest, partly because I had a vague recollection that some of the famous French preachers had in the past occupied its pulpit. I am not ordinarily greatly attracted by Roman Catholic churches, often quite distinctly repelled by the profusion of cheap-looking images. St. Sulpice seemed very much cluttered with statues; besides repair work was going on and there was a good deal of scaffolding about, especially in the vicinity of the altar. Yet somehow almost from the moment I had set foot in the sanctuary, a deep and what seemed a singing peace (though I did not think I heard any physical sounds) came over me. I do not wish to give the impression that this peace took the place of a felt turbulence. I had all along acted pretty conscientiously according to my lights and was not aware of any inner conflict. For the rest I had a sense of comfortable though not exuberant physical well-being on that afternoon. Yet the sudden new sensation was one of a deepened, a fathomless peace,

7. Arnold Lunn, *Within that City* (New York: Sheed and Ward, 1936), 160. This quotation differs insignificantly from the original.

8. Ibid., 161.

9. Bede Frost, *The Art of Mental Prayer*, rev. ed. (London: Philip Allan, 1932), 42; quoted in Lunn, *Within that City*, 161. Everything after "business" is Muste's paraphrase of Lunn; it is not original to Frost, who concluded the sentence with "and note the difference."

and of the spirit hearing what I suppose people are trying to describe or point to when they use the, to me, stuffy and banal phrase, "the music of the spheres," but to what the Bible refers in words worthy of experience when it speaks of the time "when the morning stars sang together."[10]

Then I seated myself on a simple bench and looked toward the altar and the cross. Something inside me seemed to say: "This is where you belong, in the church not outside it." I was immediately certain that when I returned to the United States in a couple of weeks, I should sever my connection with the Trotskyist movement and rejoin the church. Perhaps I should add that at the time I did not think about re-entering the ministry. When I reflected on that some days later, I felt indifferent about it. Two or three weeks later I began to hope that I might have an opportunity to enter the ministry again; but I doubted whether any church would have me and felt that if this proved to be the case, it would be what I deserved. Perhaps this is also the point at which to run ahead of my story a little and to mention an incident in which it may be the hand of God is to be seen. One of the people whom I wanted to tell about my return to the Christian movement at the earliest possible moment was Ted Chaffee, the director of the Labor Temple, who had remained a dear friend through all the years, though we differed about religion and the church. However, during the first week or two after my return, I was fully occupied in trying to formulate and write down my new position and the reasons for it, and in talking with my Trotskyist associates who were of course profoundly shocked. So it was toward the end of September that I wrote Ted a note telling him briefly of what had happened, saying that I wanted to have a talk with him and asking him to lend me his copy of *Younger Churchmen Look at the Church*.[11] The next afternoon I picked up an afternoon paper in Grand Central station before taking a train to see friends at Williamstown. It was about time Ted might have been reading my letter had he been at home and alive. As I opened the paper after getting seated in the train, the first thing that struck my eye was the headline about his sudden death in Minneapolis, as he was beginning an address the burden of which was that our age is not shut in to a choice of "fascism or communism."

One of the things I thought about after that experience in the church of St. Sulpice was Francis Thompson's poem, "The Hound of Heaven." I had first come upon it about 1916. I was introduced to it, as to other great literature, by a group which included Willard Sperry, J. Edgar Park, Ambrose W. Vernon, and others with whom it was my privilege to be associated in

10. Job 38:7.

11. Ralph H. Read, *The Younger Churchmen Look at the Church* (New York: Macmillan, 1935).

the years leading up to America's entry into the World War.[12] It had made a great impression on me because it depicted an element in spiritual experience with which, as I shall indicate presently, I was familiar. Snatches of lines from "The Hound of Heaven" came back to me as from day to day I pondered on the meaning of my most recent experience. As soon as possible I obtained a copy and read the poem again "with exceeding great joy."

> I fled Him down the arches of the years;
> I fled Him down the labyrinthine ways
> Of my own mind.[13]

Truly, I now realized, it was in a labyrinth that my mind had been wandering, as with the clue of Marxist-Leninist thought I had sought to understand what was happening in the world and had striven for the goal of a just and brotherly world-order—a labyrinth in which the next step is always so clear, so inevitable, so promising, but the goal is no nearer.

I went on to those vivid lines about being "shot, precipitated, adown Titanic glooms of chasméd fears."[14] I had indeed been aware of no fears as I had participated in recent years in many of the most bitter American strike struggles and only a week or two before in a secret meeting of Trotskyists from many parts of the world. Yet as I now reflected again upon the terrorism which was proceeding under Stalin in Russia and reflected further that, in spite of its criticism of the Stalin regime, Trotskyism with its belief in terrorism and dictatorship would inevitably have ended in doing much the same things if it had come to power and what a tragic outlook for humankind all this meant, Thompson's arresting figure came back to me: Would not humankind and I be "shot, precipitated, adown Titanic glooms of chasméd fears," with horrible destruction at the end of that flight, unless some Hand came out of the dark and snatched us to safety before the crash?

12. The three men mentioned were all, like Muste, pastors in the greater Boston area. William Sperry was pastor of Central Church of Boston. In 1922 he became the Dean of the Theological School at Harvard University. J. Edgar Park was pastor of Second Church, West Newton, Massachusetts. In 1926 he became the president of Wheaton College in Norton, Massachusetts. Ambrose W. Vernon was pastor of Harvard Church, Brookline, Massachusetts. In 1919 he took a professorship at Carleton College. Leilah Danielson lists other members of the group in *American Gandhi: A. J. Muste and the History of Radicalism in the Twentieth Century* (Philadelphia: University of Pennsylvania Press, 2014), 51.

13. Francis Thompson, "The Hound of Heaven," *Poems* (London: E. Mathews & J. Lane, 1893), 48.

14. Ibid.

Once more that Hand had been laid upon me—"shade of His hand, outstretched caressingly."[15] Three other times in my life I had had transforming experiences that ever after I was compelled to regard as experiences of contact with God and with one exception they had come just as did this experience in Paris—without conscious preparation or seeking on my part. I did not go or try to go to God. He came.

The first time was on an Easter Sunday afternoon when I was thirteen and had not the remotest notion that there was such a thing as experience of God that could come to people in Michigan in the twentieth century, or at any rate could come to me. I was walking in the pleasant spring sunshine near the little house in which we lived. Suddenly the world took on a new brightness and beauty; the words, "Christ is risen indeed," spoke themselves in me; and from that day God was real to me.

A second experience occurred two or three years after I had entered the ministry. I had gone through the experience of adjusting my religious views, or at least the formulation of them, to new insights, scientific and otherwise. The process had been somewhat painful and difficult, but in my own thinking about it, it had been completed in satisfactory fashion. I was not thinking about the matter anymore, and was in a contented and happy mood. I was walking late one morning down the corridor of a hotel where we were staying for a few days. Suddenly came again that experience of a great light flooding in upon the world making things stand forth "in sunny outline brave and clear" and of God being truly present and all-sufficient.[16] With it came the feeling that I had not the same gospel as ever to preach but a much greater gospel, in the sense that my understanding of it was enriched and my personal hold on God firmer.

The other experience of this kind came in another way. It was in the late spring of 1917 when the United States had entered the war. So far as my intellectual processes were concerned I had, after intense concentration, continued to be firmly convinced of the soundness of my Christian pacifist position both on Scriptural and on practical grounds. But it was a desperate crisis. Other people whose honesty and fidelity to the Master I could not doubt were abandoning that position. Isolation is a dreadful thing. To feel the ties that have bound you to an enlightened and affectionate congregation snapping one after another. I prayed as I never, I think, have prayed before or since for assurance, for strength, for a sign if it might be of God's presence. The sign came one afternoon in the same kind of experience of

15. Ibid., 54.

16. Richard Chenevix Trench, "Lord, What a Change Within Us One Short Hour," in *Poems: Collected and Arranged Anew* (London: Macmillan, 1865), 139.

illumination and "Real Presence" as in the other cases. The burden of fear and anxiety was rolled away.

As I have already said, in and by themselves such experiences have little or no evidential value for others. But to the one who has them they are simply fact. Having seen one cannot not see. Accordingly, to me God seems above all to be a seeking God. It is we who run away, not we who seek and pursue him. But his love will not let us go. To a certain point, therefore, and in conformity at that point with my Calvinistic upbringing, I have always sympathized with theologies that emphasize the divine transcendence and initiative and human nothingness. Even the doctrine of election, in so far as it strives, as I suppose it does, to express the initiative of God in all things and especially in our salvation, has real validity. I can well believe at any rate that it grew out of the experience of certain of God's people and their honest attempts to interpret that experience.

Looking the Other Way

The question naturally arises: If you had experiences such as you describe in which you believed in the reality of God and his presence, then how could you desert Christianity, leave the church and so on? The answer to that question is in one sense a long one. It would certainly include a reference to the extent which the church fails people, as it is so well put in the findings of Madras, by "its lack of social guidance," its failure honestly to carry out the implications of its own gospel in various spheres of social life.[17] It would include a discussion also of the extent to which the movement of social revolt takes on religious forms, is even in its imperfect way a true expression of religion. For example, the noblest participants in the revolutionary movement are inspired by the faith expressed in the Marxian phrase that "historic forces make the triumph of socialism inevitable." But a force which makes for a world of righteousness and brotherhood, to which individuals must surrender themselves utterly, and which is invincible—that is a pretty fair definition, I believe, of God and of a Calvinist God! For our present purposes, however, and from our present approach dealing with the inner workings of the soul, the answer to the question I have raised may be simple and short. Josiah Royce has a great sentence upon which I happened only a few months ago which supplies the first part of this answer; Aldous Huxley

17. Muste is referring to the Madras Conference of 1938, also known as the Tambaram Conference. See *The World Mission of the Church: Findings and Recommendations of the International Missionary Council, Tambaram, Madras, India, December 12th to 29th, 1938* (London: International Missionary Council, 1939).

who quotes Royce has the second part. Royce's sentence is this: "Finite beings . . . are always . . . such as they are in virtue of an *inattention* which at present blinds them to their actual relations to God and to one another."[18] Huxley's contribution to our answer is in a paragraph from his *Ends and Means*, which explains how, often, this "inattention" comes about.

> I had motives for not wanting the world to have a meaning; consequently assumed that it had none, and was able without any difficulty to find satisfying reasons for this assumption. Most ignorance is vincible ignorance. We don't know because we don't want to know. It is our will that decides how and upon what subjects we shall use our intelligence. Those who detect no meaning in the world generally do so because, for one reason or another, it suits their books that the world should be meaningless.[19]

The fact of the matter is that whenever I did think of those experiences that had meant so much to me, I was never in my Marxist-Leninist days able to bring myself to believe or say: "You were mistaken, you had a dream, God is not real and you have never felt his Real Presence." I could never bring myself to say that, any more than I could bring myself to say that I had not seen a certain sunset in the Berkshires, or lived through an evening on a little lake in Michigan when the fireflies formed a ring of golden fire a foot high around it, or that I had not read and been transfigured by the understanding of Keats' "Ode to a Grecian Urn."[20] For to say that one has not seen what one has seen, experienced what one has experienced, is to say farewell to sanity. Since I could not look at my former experiences and say with the fool "There is no God," what did I do when I no longer wanted to live under the dominion of such experiences? I simply stopped looking at them!

Human beings have an almost infinite capacity for looking the other way, for evading the issue, for not reckoning with the whole, even of such experience as they have had, for this thing which Royce so aptly calls "inattention," the effect of which is that they are "blind to their actual relationships to God and to one another." Partly this is the effect of our weakness—the effort of really looking at anything, even a flower or a face, of being objective, getting out of ourselves into the Other even to that extent, is exceedingly

18. Josiah Royce, *The World and the Individual: Gifford Lectures Delivered Before the University of Aberdeen*, vol. 2, *Nature, Man, and the Moral Order* (New York: Macmillan, 1901), 307. Emphasis Royce's. Ellipses have been added where Muste omits clauses.

19. Aldous Huxley, *Ends and Means: An Inquiry into the Nature of Ideals and into the Methods Employed for Their Realization* (New York: Harper & Brothers, 1937), 312.

20. John Keats, "Ode to a Grecian Urn," in *The Complete Poetical Works and Letters of John Keats*, ed. Horace E. Scudder (Boston: Houghton Mifflin, 1899), 135.

painful, though the results are infinitely rewarding. But far more than the most sophisticated persons, at any rate, would admit, our "inattention" is, as Huxley points out, whose humble confession surely brings him near to the kingdom of heaven, deliberate. We see what we want to see. We turn our backs upon what it does "not suit our books" to see—and then we tell ourselves that we are very realistic and informed and sophisticated and quite superior to the poor peasantry who bow their knees to God and want to be humble followers of the gentle Jesus.

The satanic element, the true principle of evil in the universe, according to orthodox tradition, is pride, self-will, self-sufficiency. That is a profound truth and there is none that our age needs more desperately to learn.

A Child-Like Faith

As I look back now on the change that took place in me nearly three years ago, I think I can see two things that had happened that summer and of which I was as yet but dimly if at all aware, which served as preparation for the utterly unexpected and unsought experience that overtook me in the Church of St. Sulpice. For one thing, my mind had been resting. The ear of the spirit was not deafened as is the case with us most of the time by the clamor of the demands, the speech-making by ourselves and others, the activities of life. If God did speak, there was under those circumstances a chance that he might be heard. One hour a day spent in such "silence" would mean daily, joyous, cataclysmic transformation for any of us. That is, alas, why we do not practice it. The demands God makes upon us are so much more exacting than our own, or our friends' or the potentates' of this earth. But surely the reader has often experienced the light and power that silently roll in upon us in those rare moments when our souls are quiet.

The other thing that had happened was that I had become less cocksure of my philosophy, how much less sure I was totally unaware of until after I began the intellectual process of reflection on my inner experience and the attempt to revaluate my Marxist-Leninist views. But I can recall clearly how I had been sensing that the revolutionary movement in Europe had come to an impasse, how the idealism and *élan* seemed to have largely gone out of it, how factionalism and lack of confidence on the part of the membership in the leadership and in each other had been eating at its vitals. I recall also how the speeding up of the armament industry, the maneuvers of bombing planes in the skies, the marching soldiers everywhere had made me feel that the world was again in a prelude-to-war period. I must have been much more ready than I had realized to come out of my coma of "inattention" and to pose the question: "If you turned out to be essentially right in your reading of the situation and of your duty in 1914–18, despite the fact that you were unbelievably ignorant and unsophisticated, because you believed in the way of the cross, may it be that you are dead wrong now in spite of your learning and sophistication because you no longer believe in that way?"

In any case, I am persuaded that whenever there is a breach made, no matter how small, in the citadel of human pride and self-will and self-sufficiency, a work of grace may take place, the bread of life may be broken and the wine of God's love poured out for our revival and sustenance.

The last subterfuge of pride and self-will in people of the intellectual and sophisticated type is expressed in the nostalgic plaint: "I want to believe, as I did in my youth or as my parents did; but alas, for me with my experience, my analytical, critical mind, I cannot." How that attitude is essentially, though the one who has it may not be aware of it, an expression of pride and self-glorification has been brilliantly suggested by William Hard, one of our leading reporters and political analysts who some years ago was converted to the Christian faith, in a poem entitled "St. Thomas."

> Kindle, O God, that Inner Light in me
> That lighteth every man—but ah! not me. . . .
>
> Give it to me, O God, to be a saint
> Who am not and can never be a saint, . . .
>
> O stop! For what, dear God, am I now saying?
> That Thou didst choose me out for such a saying?
>
> That I, this Thomas, was by Thee selected
> Out of men's millions, millions, I, selected
>
> To merit Thy damnation, I, I, I,
> Thy foe, Thy high foe, and Thy marked foe, I!
>
> See! God and I! He notes me! And His Light,
> He says, shall never change my dark to light![21]

That is to say, when one doubts that child-like saving faith can be one's portion, it is only the old business of setting oneself apart from one's fellows, thinking of oneself as a superior sort of being that means thinking of other people as belonging to a humbler, lower order. In fact it means making the preposterous, arrogant assumption that one is the highest form of being that

21. William Hard, "Saint Thomas," *The Atlantic Monthly* 162, no. 4 (October 1938), 483.

exists, for one thinks of God either as unable to convince one's own towering intellect or as a mad, sadistic power which will not listen to one's prayer for salvation and purification and peace. When one thus understands that one has once more been tricked by the arrogance, the self-sufficiency of the dependent being who thinks they can stand alone, independent, then one cries out in self-abasement and child-like faith:

> Oh, Thomas! Kneel thee down! Abate thyself!
> Strike from thy self thy centering pride of self!
>
> Thou art not strange nor high, but only he,
> And he, and he, and he, and he, and he,
>
> Man, any man. So pray thy prayer anew.
> I shall, I do. I pray my prayer anew.[22]

Final Remarks

There are two remarks that must be added to forestall misunderstanding of my position. The experience of being humbled by and before God that I have tried to describe, in no sense implies, as I see it, any such thing as a stultification of the intellect, an anti-scientific or obscurantist attitude, a war of religion against science. It is precisely when the mind no longer considers itself to be the teacher of God, when the mind knows that it is a learner in the universe, that the true and fruitful and endless labors of philosophy and science become possible. Science is a product of Jewish-Christian rather than Greek tradition, partly at least because there is more humility and less "pride of intellect" in the former.

Lastly, the salvation which God in Christ brings I have never been able to think of as "individual," in the sense of "not social." For one thing, in its most intimate, personal form, it is an experience of abasement of the self before God, in which one knows—knows with one's whole being, "existentially"—that they are the murderer, the thief, the ingrate, the lustful one. Thus they become one with their fellows. Perhaps no one has ever expressed the attitude which flowers from such experience more clearly than Gene Debs in his speech before being sentenced to Atlanta during the war: "While there is a lower class, I am in it; while there is a criminal element, I am of it; while there is a soul in prison, I am not free."[23]

22. Ibid.

23. Eugene V. Debs, "Statement to the Court Upon Being Convicted of Violating the Sedition Act," September 18, 1918, http://www.marxists.org/archive/debs/works/1918/

A person in such an experience is always as Moses who once was stirred by the affliction of his people, but who has burned out. God is as the bush that burns and is not consumed—that principle in history, that Being who has willed history and who burns and burns with sorrow and love for his people afflicted in "the house of bondage." And the sign that God has truly come is therefore necessarily that one identifies oneself in a deeper, more intelligent and sacrificial way with God's oppressed people and works for that one true revolution, which is material-spiritual, individual-social, by which those who accept the salvation and the law of God are led out of concrete social bondage into a real, not mythical or "beyond-history," freedom in a "good land and a large, unto a land flowing with milk and honey."[24] Or, in New Testament terminology, that revolution in which those who trust and follow Christ, seek "first the kingdom of God and his righteousness" and also and necessarily since he is the God of the living and not of the dead, have "all these things"—food and drink and raiment gay as Solomon's and the lilies of the field—"added unto them."[25]

court.htm.

24. Exodus 3:8.

25. Matthew 6:33.

Facing Another World War

11

The Knowledge of God (1936)

Muste preached this sermon for Armistice Day 1936.[1] *At the time, he had just started a brief tenure working for the Fellowship of Reconciliation as the chair of its Committee on Industrial Relations. He might have been expected to speak on war or pacifism, but instead he preached an evangelistic sermon, arguing that a world full of the knowledge of God would consequently be a peaceful one. Anyone who has experienced the power of God's love knows that it is powerful enough to remake the world and conform it to the prophet Isaiah's vision of a peace so complete that wolves and lambs will lie down together. He argues that religion holds the only hope for peace and critiques those who are led by a scientific worldview to reject religion, noting that science should lead them to explore, examine, and try out religion rather than dismiss it.*

1. Armistice Day, now called Veterans Day in the United States, is November 11. This selection has never before been published. While the exact date Muste preached the sermon is unknown, it is relatively certain that it was in 1936, despite the fact that Armistice Day was a Wednesday that year. It is not known where Muste preached the sermon.

"The earth shall be full of the knowledge of God, as the waters cover the sea."[2]

Drop one phrase out of that sentence and it reads: "The earth shall be full of knowledge, as the waters cover the sea." Thus abbreviated it has a very modern sound. Truly the earth is filled with knowledge of all kinds. With the telescope, the spectroscope, the microscope and with the even more subtle, intangible instruments of daring mathematical formulas, our astronomers, physicists, and chemists have mastered many of the secrets of the remote corners of the universe and of the constitution of matter itself. Similarly, psychology in its various branches and schools has immensely extended our knowledge of the human organism and its behavior. Almost every day medicine and surgery through some beautiful, intricate, long-continued research bring to birth some new knowledge to alleviate suffering or prolong human life. To say that in the realm of technology the past century has wrought a greater revolution than had occurred in all the previous centuries since the dawn of civilization is to utter a commonplace. No other generation has possessed so much knowledge about the part of the human race itself as we possess. The institutions devoted to learning and research—schools, colleges, laboratories, libraries—are without parallel in history. Nor does it appear that the process of acquiring knowledge with the instruments we already possess and others that scientists seem capable of inventing is in any field nearing exhaustion. Yes, the earth is full of knowledge as the waters cover the sea.

But probably no one would think of our age as one which exemplifies the utterance of the prophet: "The earth shall be full of the knowledge *of God*, as the waters cover the sea." The world is full of knowledge of almost everything except God. The various sciences proceed about their work of observing, measuring, analyzing, noting uniformities or "laws" without making any use of the hypothesis of God, and science and the so-called scientific outlook dominate our world. The findings of science may indeed under suitable conditions contribute to the knowledge of God but until recently a mechanistic philosophy mistakenly regarded as scientific was widely prevalent. This philosophy saw the world as a machine. Physical and chemical processes were alone real and potent. Humanity was described as "a highly temporary chemical episode on a most petty planet" or "tiny lumps of impure carbon and water."[3] God was ruled out of the universe. Religion was a discarded relic of the dark ages of humanity's prescientific

2. Isaiah 11:9b. The original manuscript reads "earth" instead of "sea."

3. Harry Elmer Barnes, *Living in the Twentieth Century: A Consideration of How We Got This Way* (Indianapolis: Bobbs-Merrill, 1928), 38; Bertrand Russell, *Sceptical Essays* (New York: W. W. Norton, 1928), 31.

past. In Russia we have the government of a great nation basing itself upon a philosophy that denies God and seeks to root out religion as "the opiate of the people."[4] In Germany we have a regime in some respects very different from the Russian, but it also is seeking to destroy the churches and is carrying on a militant struggle against any conception of religion that a Christian might recognize. It is the first time in 1,500 years that this has been true of great nations in Europe or America. And no one can question that the tendency to confine life to secular interests, to discount if not altogether to banish religious concerns, is powerful throughout the Western world.

We shall do well to remind each other, also, that we can hardly characterize the churches today most accurately and [naturally][5] by saying: "The churches are full of the knowledge of God as the waters cover the sea." They are full of activity, of good works, of ethical idealism possibly, of concern for a better economic and social order perhaps. But not often full of a clear, vital, joyous knowledge and experience of God. Someone remarked recently that nine out of ten sermons nowadays begin with the statement by the preacher: "We are commanded to love God and to love our neighbor as ourself. Setting aside the first commandment for the present, let us meditate for a few moments on the second."

Science

Now there are certain observations to be made about this age of ours which tends to discount or decry the knowledge and experience of God. In the first place, scientists generally are much more modest about the claims they make for their method and their findings than was the case a few years ago. Most of them will hold that within their field scientific results have validity and usefulness and represent aspects of reality; but that the same is true within their respective fields of the insights of the poet and the religious seer or of humble human beings who experience love for each other. They grant validity to the findings of botanists and their descriptions of trees and flowers—but also to the insight of Bliss Carman who wrote and the lovers of beauty who are stirred by the lines:

> The scarlet of the maples can shake me like a cry
> Of bugles going by.

4. Karl Marx, "Contribution to the Critique of Hegel's Philosophy of Law," in *Karl Marx, Frederick Engels: Collected Works* (New York: International Publishers, 1975), 3:175.

5. This sermon has been transcribed from Muste's handwritten notes. Where interpretation of his handwriting is uncertain, the most likely possibility appears in brackets.

And my lonely spirit thrills
To see the frosty asters like smoke upon the hills.[6]

They recognize the significance of biological research, but they recognize also that a man and woman who have for many years loyally loved each other and struggled together through the experiences of married life know something about each other and about the meaning of life that they did not learn from a diligent study of biology and that will never be contained in any textbook of biology or physiology or sex hygiene or even psychoanalysis.

More than that, many of the greatest scientists assert that within their own fields they constantly bump into mysteries that leave them baffled or else lead straight to the thought of a religious hypothesis or explanation. Says Sir James Jeans: "The universe begins to look more like a great thought than like a great machine."[7] Dr. Alexis Carrel in that thought-provoking—and sometimes also perverse—book, *Man, the Unknown*, has stated after years of research in which he is universally recognized as a genius that we do not know the relations between our muscles and our mental and spiritual activities. "We do not know the relations between consciousness and nervous processes, between the mental and the cerebral. . . . We understand still less how unpredictable phenomena spring from the brain, how thought is born."[8] He calls attention to the astonishing fact "that human thought, which has transformed the surface of the earth, destroyed and built nations, discovered new universes in the immensity of the sidereal spaces, is elaborated without demanding a measurable amount of energy. The mightiest effort of our intellect has incomparably less effect on metabolism than the contraction of the biceps when this muscle lifts a weight of a few grams."[9] His scientific studies lead him to the conclusion: "It is impossible not to count mysticism among fundamental human activities. . . . By the exercise of the normal activities of his consciousness man may endeavor to reach an invisible reality both immanent in and transcending the material world. Thus he throws himself into the most audacious venture that one can dare."[10]

But we can go still further. Not only do many of the most eminent scientists grant validity to religion and the religious method in its own field. Not only do they proclaim that scientific investigation constantly

6. Bliss Carman, "A Vagabond Song," *More Songs from Vagabondia* (Boston: Copeland and Day, 1896), 39.

7. James Jeans, *The Mysterious Universe* (Cambridge: Cambridge University Press, 1930), 137.

8. Alexis Carrel, *Man, the Unknown* (New York: Harper & Brothers, 1935), 97.

9. Ibid., 81–82.

10. Ibid., 134n, 136.

leads them into the presence of mysteries and to the threshold of spiritual assumptions or explanations. They confess also that the scientific method transplanted by some out of its own proper field and made into a philosophy, a worldview, a "religion," arrogating to itself the right to dominate over people and over their lives, driving religion and religious experience out of the modern world in so far as it was able—that this so-called scientific outlook has brought the modern world to the brink of the abyss. For science deals with the abstract, with uniformities, with what can be measured and weighed and counted. To science everything is an *object* to be regarded from the outside, to be laid upon some literal or metaphorical dissecting table and taken apart. And since the mind likes to get things down to simple formulas and we live in a civilization dominated by the machine, the sciences present everything under the analogy of a machine. But when you have added together the various abstract aspects of humanity presented by physics, chemistry, physiology, psychology, economics, everything that the sciences tell you *about* humanity, you do not yet have a single flesh and blood, thinking, [illegible], loving, laughing, crying human being. People are not essentially objects that are observed; they are that which observes; they live from within. Let two people live together for twelve hours and simply, coldly, dispassionately observe each other, study each other, as objects under a microscope and have no other thought or attitude toward each other except that of the dispassionate observer—and if they could really do it, at the end of the twelve hours they would be stark mad, wandering in an utterly unreal world. And when science so-called makes the universe a machine that grinds majestically on, and history a machine into which historical forces are somehow fed and events come out like sausages at the other end, and society a stage on which class-antagonisms mechanically clash, and people themselves a machine or cogs in the machine—then we know many things about the universe and history and society and ourselves but we must either be profoundly disinterested and inexpressibly bored with it all or if we still retain any drive for life we must go mad with fear in the presence of this monster.

Science is the creation of the mind and will of humanity, devised to make life richer, freer, better. Made into an idol, a god, it devours its creator. And since humanity is the creator of the conception of life that destroys us, we may say quite literally that in the realm of the spirit humanity commits suicide.

And behold how, in this age that is full of many kinds of knowledge but in large measure empty of the knowledge of God, humanity's suicide in the realm of the spirit, our slaying of our own souls, has its counterpart in the physical world and on the stage of history.

Humanity has become capable of building enginery to make life varied, interesting, and secure. But we build the vast enginery of destruction—technically beautiful guns, subtle gases, mysterious germs—so that the race may commit collective suicide. A few days ago the papers reported that an old man in Paris had been only just prevented from committing suicide. When he was revived, it was learned that he had heard the sirens sound in the [streets] and concluded that war had been declared and the first air raid was on. Rather than face that experience he sought to end his life. I am convinced by my observations in Europe this summer that there will be literally hundreds, very likely thousands who will do just that if another large-scale war breaks out. But what will the entire populations in countries that go to war—under modern conditions with modern weapons—be doing except committing collective suicide?

In this age so full of knowledge and so largely empty of the knowledge of God, we have the means of turning out material goods in quantities undreamed of by our forefathers. But in the midst of abundance people suffer want and having produced much goods the producers find themselves unemployed. And under these conditions class antagonisms become more widespread and bitter until it too bears the fruit of wholesale collective suicide as in Spain today.

In the realm of the individual life we find multitudes who have had and have access to every material and cultural advantage, people of great ability and charm, who yet have lost all real interest in living, are the prey of nervous and mental afflictions, turning to the cultists, the faddists, the psychoanalysts for relief. C. G. Jung, the great psychoanalyst, has written recently: "During the past thirty years people from all civilized countries of the earth have consulted me. . . . Among all over thirty-five there has not been one whose problem in the last resort was not that of finding a religious outlook on life. Every one of them fell ill because he had lost that which the living religions of every age have given to their followers and none of them has really been healed who did not regain his religious outlook. . . . Man is never helped in his suffering by what he thinks of himself, but only by revelations of a wisdom greater than his own."[11]

11. C. G. Jung, *Modern Man in Search of a Soul* (New York: Harcourt, Brace, 1933), 264, 278. This quotation differs from the original. Most changes are minor and serve to shorten the quotation.

The Knowledge of God

In one realm of modern life after another we are forced back upon the question: Is it possible for us to gain that knowledge of God of which the prophet said the earth should one day be full? Not knowledge *about* God, not knowledge concerning doctrines of God. But that knowledge, that experience of the final ground of our being in which the sincerely religious of all lands and ages have found rest and redemption and power.

All those who have had this living and transfiguring knowledge of God, whether they have been numbered among the great saints and prophets or among the humble children of the Father, testify that this knowledge comes to people, is given to them, by revelation. It is not something that you have to reason your way into by long and terrible mental effort. This wisdom is also "revealed unto babes."[12] God, they tell us, was here all the time. The eternal Love pressed all about us like the air we breath. The Hound of Heaven, says Francis Thompson in his great poem, pursued me "down the nights and down the days. . . . down the labyrinthine ways of my own mind."[13] We had eyes, but we did not see.[14] And then suddenly one day our eyes were opened. We saw and felt the God who had been there always, from whom flows life and the meaning of our life. To quote another of Thompson's poems,

> Does the fish soar to find the ocean,
> The eagle plunge to find the air—
> That we ask of the stars in motion
> If they have rumour of thee there?
>
> But (when so sad thou canst not sadder)
> Cry;—and upon thy so sore loss
> Shall shine the traffic of Jacob's ladder
> Pitched betwixt Heaven and Charing Cross.
>
> Yea, in the night, my Soul, my daughter,
> Cry,—clinging Heaven by the hems;
> And lo, Christ walking on the water
> Not of Gennesareth, but Thames![15]

12. Luke 10:21.

13. Francis Thompson, "The Hound of Heaven," *Poems* (London: E. Mathews & J. Lane, 1893), 48.

14. See Mark 8:18.

15. Francis Thompson, "The Kingdom of God," in *Complete Poetical Works* (New York: Boni and Liveright, 1913), 357. These stanzas have been selected by the editor. Muste did not include the material he planned to quote, only a note to himself to

It cannot well be otherwise. If God is, if God is love, then he cannot be far from any of us. God must always be trying to make us see, to break through to us, to get the attention of our world.

It follows, therefore, that if you do not see and know God, it is probably because in some way, for some reason, you refuse to see him. The first thing for you to do at any rate is to ask yourself whether for some reason you are closing your eyes and turning away your face from the vision of God. For many in our day pride in one of its many guises stands in the way. Here is a great, brilliant, learned person. But in the religious experience you have to become as a little child. The knowledge of God is not a knowledge that you build up by painful research, it is not a knowledge that you hold and possess. It is a knowledge that possesses you. You have to lean back into its arms, so to speak, to let it hold you, possess you, make you over again. I have friends in the radical world who will not really try to get the religious point of view because it would mean a revolution in their ideas and a new idea is painful to them as it is to so-called conservatives. Friends might scoff at them. I know delightful, bright young people, many serious, some wise-cracking, who breathe in from the air of these times the idea that religion is something out of date, or childish, or essentially reactionary. And a certain kind of pride holds them back from an effort to understand it. To all such we have a right to say at least this: you will hardly contend that religion is the dominant influence in our age and you will admit that this age is today in a rather tragic plight. You will grant also that there has been in human history something that we call religious experience. Very well, then, if you are really scientific, open-minded, you should at least be willing to sit down in scientific humility before the fact of religious experience, before the solution that religion proposes, and try to understand them. If you do not, then certainly you have no right to call yourself scientific; then *you* are the dogmatist, the sentimentalist, the victim of superstition or fake pride.

With many others it is some form of selfishness that causes them to refuse to see the vision of God. They know only too well that if God comes into life, something else will have to go out. "For, though I knew His love Who followed / Yet was I sore adread / Lest, having Him, I must have naught beside."[16] The everlasting love will come into our hearts and put an end to weakness, to fear, to the strife that rends our being. But it lays upon us with a power that cannot be denied the awful commandment to love God with all our being and to love our neighbor, our fellow human being, as ourself. The

"Quote F. Thompson: The Kingdom of God." Muste's copy of this work is extant (it is in the collection of Van Wylen Library at Hope College, his alma mater), but he did not mark up this poem.

16. Thompson, "The Hound of Heaven," 48–49.

Everlasting Love has been known to nail his own Son on a cross. And here are men and women in this church today, and men and women like them outside, who are saying to themselves that they cannot understand religion, they do not know what the preacher is driveling about, when the truth of the matter is that they know only too well and because of that are trying to run away from God. Men and women in business, in the professions, in politics, in church activity, in their personal relationships, who are running away from the experience of God and making themselves miserable and frequently not a little [ridiculous] because they are leading crooked, or hypocritical, or brutal, or self indulgent, or prejudiced, or merely superficial and indifferent lives—and how well they know, how well they know, that the love of God that saves the soul is to all this a consuming fire.

Two Suggestions

But if there are are those among you who do thirst for God, who are eager for a living contact with that love which is the center, the most real thing in the universe, and which can fill our lives with peace and power, or those who have once seen the vision splendid perhaps, but for whom it has become dim and who long to dwell again in its glory, to you we can make two suggestions, assured that if they are faithfully followed out the ultimate [reward] will not fail to come to you.

First, you have to take time to practice the art of contemplation, of prayer. The religious experience, the experience of the presence of God, is in many ways like the aesthetic. How if you want to see a landscape, or a sunset, or a great picture, or if you want to hear—deeply and truly—a great oratorio or symphony, then you have to quiet your spirit, you have to relax, to compose yourself. And you have to look or listen intently. You have to open the pores of your being, as it were, and let the vision or the music sink into you, penetrate into every fiber of your being, possess you. Then, as many of you have experienced, comes the moment when you *really see* the landscape or the picture, really *hear* the music. The vision and the sound have been transfigured into something you could not imagine before, because *you* were transfigured, your eyes were opened, your ears unstopped. And it was as if you had entered into a different world—at once more glorious and more real than the world of our conventional days.

Even so, if you will take time—in the solitude, in the services of the church—to gaze steadfastly not upon this picture or that but upon the vast picture of life, of reality itself; time to listen not to any partial music but to the music of the whole, to no earthly sound but to the voices of the Spirit, a moment will come—doubt it not, my friend—when again you will be carried out of yourself and you will see reality—the final truth of things—as never before. And what you will see in that hour will be a cross and a man upon it who walked the way of love to the end. And you will also see "the Lord seated upon a throne, high and lifted up," and the heavenly hosts veiling their faces before him.[17] And you will see that the man on the cross and the eternal God are the same. For love is the final truth, the ultimate reality, the kingdom, the power, and the glory in this universe.

Secondly, if you desire the presence of God, its light, its help, its comfort, then even in moments when the light is dim and the angel voices are stilled, you can *act* as if God were. You can make an assumption for the time being as the scientist does, and see if it works. You can try living as if Jesus were right, as if you were a child of his kind of God. Who will say amidst the tragedy of modern life that having tried so many other knowledges it might not pay to try this way in our individual and in our corporate life?

Armistice Sunday

Finally, this is Armistice Sunday and it may be that someone wonders why we are not having an Armistice Sunday sermon, some special message on the tragic question of war and peace about which we are asked to think by our various church councils on this day. The answer is, my friends, that you have been hearing an Armistice Day sermon—in a sense the only message that can mean much on such a day.

The passage in Isaiah of which our text is a part paints a picture of a certain kind of world. In that world, says the great prophetic voice, "the wolf shall lie down with the lamb, and the leopard shall lie down with the kid, and the calf and the young lion and the yearling together, and a little child shall lead them. . . . They shall not hurt nor destroy in all my holy mountain, saith the Lord."[18] A peace among people so profound and real that the whole creation is transfigured by it. Why, how, shall this thing come to pass? "Because the earth shall be full of the knowledge of God as the waters cover the sea."

Do you see? The passage from a world in which it almost seems that we do nothing but hurt or destroy and in which the very earth is wounded and [butchered] by humankind to a world in which people no longer hurt and destroy and the whole creation is delivered from the bondage of corruption—this is not effected by any machinery as such, it will not come to

17. Isaiah 6:1.

18. Isaiah 11:6, 9.

a world devoted to secularism, to nationalism, full of knowledge and empty of the knowledge of God. War between nations is but the last, inevitable expression of the self-destruction that people visit upon ourselves when we turn our backs upon the God of love revealed in Christ. Whatever we may think of this type of machinery or that, the basic truth is that the core of any effective movement for peace must be composed of those who by the grace of God and out of a deep religious experience have renounced the very spirit and method of war and accepted the way of love—in their [own] souls first and thus necessarily in all the spheres of life. Those who know the overcoming power of prayer and humility and sacrifice. Those who are not led astray by the pipings of the war-makers in any realm because for them a trumpet sounds from the hid battlements of eternity and when they look up they are able to say: "His name I know and what his trumpet saith."[19]

"They shall not hurt nor destroy in all my holy mountain, for the earth shall be full of the knowledge of God as the waters cover the sea. And it shall come to pass in that day, that the root of Jesse"—the man on the cross—"that standeth for an ensign of the people, unto him shall the nations seek; and his resting place shall be glorious."[20] Too good to believe? Yes, and so is the experience of the vision of God, of God being born, in a single human soul, too good to believe—until it happens. And it does happen. The person who has experienced that love smashing to bits, dissolving into nothingness, their pride, their bitterness, their prejudice and hate and fear, cannot even entertain the idea that there is any power in heaven or on earth that can prevail against it. Whither there be knowledge, it shall be done away—all our sciences—for we know in part. But love never faileth.[21] "The earth shall be filled with the knowledge of God as the waters cover the sea."

19. Thompson, "The Hound of Heaven," 53.

20. Isaiah 11:9–10.

21. See 1 Corinthians 13:8–9.

12

The Church's Responsibility for Peace (1937)

Given in June 1937, the month after he started as the director of the Presbyterian Labor Temple in New York City, this speech at the General Synod of the Reformed Church in America is one of Muste's most moving calls for Christians to embrace the gospel of peace and reject war. The denomination later published it as a pamphlet.[1]

It is in a spirit of humility and gratitude that I accept this opportunity to address this Assembly of the church of my fathers and of my own early years. It is fitting that I should begin with a word of confession. For a number of years I definitely renounced the Christian position and adopted the Marxist-Leninist. Although during those years I acted conscientiously according to the best insight I had, it is nevertheless true that in a real sense I

1. Although the Labor Temple was not an RCA church, Muste was raised in the RCA, attended its schools through seminary, and pastored his first church in the denomination. He left it in 1914 amid proceedings against him due to his unwillingness to accept a literalist interpretation of Scripture and his rejection of certain points of Calvinist doctrine.

was an "enemy of the cross of Christ" and that in so far as they were influenced by me I led people at important points astray.

Though I have repented, I do not cease to grieve over the harm I may have done during those years, nor to pray daily that it may be given me so to live that I may in some measure make up for that harm. It is in this spirit that I hope I may be used today of that God whose power to transmit his grace through most unlikely channels is not shortened.

The introductory sentences of the Pronouncement Concerning World Peace adopted by the General Synod of 1932 are accepted as the basis on which the Reformed Church approaches the problem of war. These sentences read as follows:

> The Church of Jesus Christ is faced again with the responsibility of proclaiming anew her faith in the Gospel of Peace. As long as the existence of, or preparation for, war continues, so long must the Christian Church give of its life and power to teaching the ways of peace and to supporting those agencies which strive to bring peace to the world.
>
> The present world situation reveals the one-ness of the human family, the inter-dependence of all nations, and the need of applying Christian love and goodwill to interracial and international as well as individual relations. War in our generation has demonstrated its futility as a means of solving international conflicts and its destructiveness of moral and spiritual values for which Christ stands. The hour has struck for the ending of our reliance upon it. We therefore affirm our unflagging opposition to the war system. We purpose as Christian citizens living in a democracy to exert our influence among our fellow citizens and upon our government toward the realization of a warless world. To this end we declare our allegiance to the principles and resolutions adopted at the general Synods of 1930 and 1931; we renew our obligation to educate the conscience of the Church until preparation for war in any form becomes impossible.[2]

Three things are stated or directly implied in this pronouncement. First, the standard by which as Christians we are to judge, in this matter of war as in all other issues that confront us, is the teaching and Spirit of our Lord Jesus Christ—nothing else and nothing less. In every realm we must strive to make "the moral and spiritual values for which Christ stands" regnant.

2. Reformed Church in America, "Report of the Permanent Committee on International Justice and Goodwill," *Acts and Proceedings of the One Hundred and Twenty-sixth Regular Session of the General Synod of the Reformed Church in America*, vol. 30 (New York: Board of Publication and Bible School Work, 1932), 134–35.

This position is in accord with the essence of the Christian religion. It is in accord also with the special genius of Protestantism, especially in its Reformed expression. No one would have been more surprised than John Calvin to learn that there might be some sphere of life in which Christians might act by some other standard than that of Christ!

Second, the Statement of 1932 says that war cannot be reconciled with the Christian position. It is "destructive of the moral and spiritual values for which Christ stands." The statement affirms "unflagging opposition to the war system." Synod pledged itself "to educate the conscience of the Church until preparation for war in any form becomes impossible." On this matter I shall have more to say presently.

Third, it is implied in the Pronouncement from which we have quoted that the church has a distinctive task in the struggle to put an end to war. The church is not a political party. It is not itself a government, a state. But to the church has been entrusted, so to speak, the keeping of the conscience of humankind. It has the revelation of the will of God, of the moral and spiritual standards by which people must govern themselves, the ideals which must be their goal.

The church is, however, more than that: it is the channel through which in a special manner and degree the grace of God flows. It is a power-house. Not only does it place the ideal before people but the dynamic by which people may, through grace, achieve the impossible.

And it follows from the very nature of the church and its message that in carrying out its mission its method is not that of force, of compulsion, but of education—teaching, preaching, persuasion—most of all, that of example, of contagion. Thus do the churches and Christians exert their influence on their fellow citizens and on governments.

In this connection it is interesting to note that there is a growing realization, often in most unexpected quarters, that a truly effective movement against war and for peace must have a spiritual basis and a spiritual dynamic. Aldous Huxley, until recently one of the most sophisticated, cynical and irreligious of novelists, now openly proclaims this conviction.[3] Even Bertrand Russell in his latest book, "Which Way to Peace," states: "The movement in favor of war-resistance is not to be viewed primarily as political, but rather as a matter of personal conviction, like religion."[4]

The core of any effective movement against war must be composed of those who by the grace of God and out of a deep religious experience

3. Aldous Huxley, *What are You Going to Do about It?: The Case for Constructive Peace* (London: Chatto & Windus, 1936), 30–34.

4. Bertrand Russell, *Which Way to Peace?* (London: Micael Joseph, 1936), 220. Muste Americanized Russell's British spelling and altered the punctuation.

have banished the whole concept and spirit of war out of their own hearts, and therefore are able to help banish violence out of all relations of life; those who really believe in the overcoming power of prayer and humility and sacrifice; and who are not led astray by the pipings of the war-makers in any sphere because for them "a trumpet sounds from the hid battlements of eternity" and when they look up they are able to say: "His name I know and what his trumpet saith."[5]

If this is true, if the world must look chiefly to the church to limit or to rid it of the curse of war, then a terribly solemn responsibility as well as a glorious opportunity confronts the church today. Then indeed the "education of the conscience of the church" becomes our first and deepest concern. If its light be hidden under a bushel, how shall people see? If the salt have lost its savor, wherewith shall it be salted?[6]

We must seek for a deeper, surer understanding of the mind of Christ and we must come, I think, to see that there can be no reconciliation of war and that mind. We have to take the position: "We are through with war, all through with all war," because it is of the very essence of the Christian view of life that we should do so.

To say this is not to impugn the motives of those who in the past may have participated in war, or who may do so today or in the future. Unquestionably people have gone to war believing that they were doing it in obedience to the will of Christ. It would be ironical and tragic if those who believe that we must renounce all war in conformity with the ethic of love were to pass angry, censorious, and bitter judgment upon those members of the Christian fellowship who honestly hold another conviction and who are willing to pay the price of fidelity to that conviction.

But it is our business to open our minds to receive all the light God has to give us and to live up to such light as we have, not counting the cost. Parents with the best intention in the world have exposed their children to contagious diseases; if we were to do the same, we should be our children's murderers. Good Christian people have in the past held slaves. That does not mean that we can hold slaves and claim to be Christians; nor did it mean that upon some of our fathers God did not lay the command to witness and work against chattel slavery as un-Christian even though their contemporaries did not share that insight.

5. Francis Thompson, "The Hound of Heaven," *Poems* (London: E. Mathews & J. Lane, 1893), 53.

6. See Matthew 5:13–16.

Objections

Perhaps it will be well at this point to deal with two other points about which many Christians when confronted with the challenge to renounce war are honestly troubled. In the first place, there are those who think they find a justification for participation in war in certain Pauline utterances counseling obedience to the state, to "the powers that be which are ordained of God" and which do not "bear the sword in vain."[7]

Assuming that this passage must be read as a part of the total Christian teaching, in its context in the New Testament, and not as representing in isolation the full Christian position, we may be sure that the basic meaning of this passage in Romans 13 is that earthly governments have a place in the divine providence and that normally the Christian obeys the laws and is a good citizen. This is an attitude which the church in all ages has accepted. Beyond this the reference to "the sword" may be taken to justify such use of force by the state as meets these three conditions: it is required strictly in order to maintain the public peace, i.e. police force; it does not involve denial of the basic Christian motivation of love; and it is positive, constructive, reforming, and redeeming in its effects.

It cannot mean that the state has a right to our obedience when as has often enough happened its commands are plainly contrary to the law of Christ, e.g. forbid the practice of the Christian religion itself. The reference to "the sword" cannot be taken to justify any and every use of force by the state, for in that case it would justify that use of it which was presently to send Paul himself to a martyr's death. We have only to remember, furthermore, that when Paul wrote and for more than a century thereafter, service in Caesar's army was regarded as impossible for a Christian, to realize how surprised Paul would have been if his readers had taken this text to be a justification for participation in war. The ground given by all the early Church Fathers for refusing participation in carnal warfare was not only that service in Caesar's army meant idolatrous worship of his image, but a straight-out Christian pacifism. Tertullian's saying: "The Lord in disarming Peter ungirded every soldier" is highly typical.[8]

Do those who deduce a justification of Christian participation in war from this passage take note of the fact that it is immediately preceded by the counsel: "If thine enemy hunger, feed him . . . Be not overcome of evil but overcome evil with good"—and is followed by the command: "Owe no man

7. Romans 13:1, 4.

8. Tertullian, *On Idolatry*, chapter 19.

anything but to love one another; for he that loveth another hath fulfilled the law"?[9]

In the second place, there are those who argue that the world is subject to sin, that until the kingdom of God is finally established war as well as certain other evils will continue to exist, and who draw from this assumption the conclusion that Christians may participate in war. Time does not permit us to discuss the intricate theological problem raised by the premise of this argument, nor do I think it necessary for our present purpose. For it suffices to point out, for one thing, that we may believe that certain grave evils may remain until the end of the world and yet not be shut up to the assumption that certain specific evils may and must be removed, such as dueling and chattel slavery in the Western world or the burning of widows in India. Also, the same argument for the fear that war may continue may be made with regard to the liquor traffic or the traffic in women. Does that justify Christians in participating in such evils, or excuse them from witnessing against them? No more, even if it be true that war will continue until the "end of the age" is the Christian thereby justified in participating in it or excused from witnessing against it.

The Christian Position

Let us fix our gaze for a moment then upon the essential Christian message and from that viewpoint try to determine what the Christian conscience must say about war. Definitions of what constitutes the essential Christian message have of course varied. It seems to me, however, that if we read the New Testament honestly, we do find there a certain interpretation to which at any rate the saints and the church have come back repeatedly. When we do not preach and practice this interpretation, it is rather because we shrink from its implications, than because there is any doubt as to what Jesus and the New Testament were trying to say. What then is this conception of the essence of Christianity?

First, the Christian revelation has something to say about the nature of the universe in which we live. Jesus put it in the simple human terms which he constantly used and said that God is Father, God is love. Now if that is anything but a soothing form of words, it must mean that the mightiest thing in the universe, that which is ultimately real, is love. It must follow that any human association—family, state, church—is stable, is able to function, precisely in the degree that some element of love, of fellowship, of cooperation in action, enters into it; and any human association is unstable in the

9. Romans 12:20–21, 13:8.

degree that this element is lacking. There has to be "honor" even among thieves, something that transcends ulterior considerations, some element of simple human confidence and fellowship. And the societies of "thieves" are so notoriously short-lived and precarious because there is so little of love in them.

Christianity, in the next place, has something to say about the nature of humanity. Again Jesus put it in simple human terms. We are the children of this God of love. Therefore, personality for the Christian religion is sacred. The human individual "for whom Christ died" is of infinite worth. Violate personality in yourself or your fellow, and you strike at the heart of God himself. No lines of nationality or race or class wipe out this basic fact. All are before God under sin, and all are the objects of his free grace.

All are members of one family. The relationship is so close that it is difficult to find human terms to express it. "Love thy neighbor as thyself."[10] The neighbor is, as it were, the "other self," so that I can no more think of wanting to humiliate them, or put them in the wrong, or dominate over or injure or destroy them than I could want to do these things to myself. I cannot wrong my neighbor without wronging myself.

God Had to Suffer

But we do not seem to be living in this kind of world where love reigns and we are members one of another. There is opposition, sin, evil. What to do about that? The New Testament answer is clear, is it not? God faced this problem. And his answer is: "God so loved the world—this sinful world, us while we were yet sinners—that he gave his only begotten Son."[11] It is of the very essence of the divine nature that God did not meet evil with evil, but with good. God has no power and no wisdom in dealing with us save the power and wisdom of a father in dealing with his children. God did the only thing he could do in face of sin, he kept on loving.

If you continue to love in the face of evil and rejection, then you suffer. We may put it another way and say that since God would not condone the sin and would not hate the sinner, or seek to overcome it by evil, God had to suffer. That is why the cross is the central truth and mystery, the crowning symbol of the Christian faith.

It is when the meaning of all this dawns upon the soul that it is utterly prostrated by the vision of its unworthiness and sin: "Against Thee, Thee only have I sinned"—against such utter love as this I have fallen short and

10. Matthew 22:39, Mark 12:31.

11. John 3:16, altered.

risen in defiance.[12] And in that same instant the soul is exalted to heaven by the sense of forgiveness, by the assurance that if in the end it is with such love as this we have to reckon, then it is literally possible that we should die to our old selves and that it should no longer be we that live, but Christ who lives in us.[13]

But surely no one will in some genuine measure thus understand that it is the cross that alone overcomes sin and evil in ourselves and is the means by which God redeems us, without realizing that we too can overcome evil in our fellows and in society only by the same grace of love and the same method of the cross.

Plainly Jesus faced this whole problem in the temptations at the beginning of his public ministry.[14] Here was Israel conquered by Rome, looking for the Messiah who was to put himself at the head of the Messianic army and so deliver them. Jesus rejected that way as Satan's way. He saw the symbol of his own mission and method in the Suffering Servant of Jehovah. He would not seek to overcome evil with evil, an impossibility in a world ruled by love, by his Father in heaven. He set his face toward Jerusalem on the way of suffering love.

This it is that was a "stumbling block" to the Jews. Caesar they could understand and his aims and ways; also Barabbas the violent revolutionist and his aims and ways. But not this kind of Messiah who seeks to overcome by love and voluntary suffering. "Let him now come down from the cross, and we will believe in him."[15] Whenever in any of the relationships of life, we trust in the way of strife, of domination, of violence, we once again mock and spit upon Jesus and join the Jews of old in saying: "Let him come down from the cross—use another way—and we will understand and believe in him."

But does the method of the cross really "work"? Does it represent a divine power for overcoming evil? Let me remind you of the verdict of history in the case of Jesus himself. You recall Paul's exultant and perhaps somewhat defiant cry in First Corinthians: "We preach Christ crucified, to the Jews a stumbling-block and to the Greeks foolishness, but to them that are called, both Jews and Greeks, Christ the power of God and the wisdom of God."[16]

What the Jews saw in that age was the might and majesty of the Roman Empire and that seemed to them to represent power, reality, victory,

12. Psalm 51:4.

13. See Galatians 2:19–20.

14. See Matthew 4:1–11, Luke 4:1–13.

15. Matthew 27:42, Mark 15:32.

16. 1 Corinthians 1:23–24.

that would stand. And on the other hand they saw a dead man on a cross, completely discredited at the early age of thirty-three, rejected by the rulers of his people because he was constantly exposing the hypocrisy underlying their position and rejected by the common people also because he would not put himself as a conquering warrior at their head—and this was to the Jews a stumbling block. What the Greeks saw was the imposing culture of that Roman civilization, much of it coming down out of their own tradition, and this to the Greeks was wisdom. And on the other hand, they too saw a dead man on a cross, a very interesting personality in some respects, but he probably did not know Plato and Aristotle well and besides he was one of those "prophets without a sword" about whom Machiavelli was later to write that they always fail and this to the Greeks was foolishness.[17] And what the Jews and the Greeks and the Romans heard were the disputations in the great academies of this period and the clanking of the coins on all the busy exchanges of that world, and the laughter in the palaces, and the steady tramp of the Roman soldiers on all the roads of that world—and that to them was reality, that would last, that was power. And, for the most part, they did not hear Jesus at all, for was he not dead? Nor his followers, for they were just a discredited sect of fanatics.

Now what Paul and the early Christians saw was nothing like that at all. For them all that mighty civilization already lay in ruin: "There shall not be left here one stone upon another that shall not be torn down. Fallen, fallen, is Babylon the great."[18] It was built on false foundations and would not stand. On the other hand, they saw their crucified Lord "seated on the right hand of power on high."[19] And they did not hear the disputations, the clanking coins, the laughter, the tramping soldiery: all this for them was already silenced. What they heard was the angelic hosts and the ages to come shouting; "Crown him with many crowns, the Lamb upon his throne."[20] "The Lamb that is in the midst of the throne" is the symbol of the meekness, the gentleness, the seeming weakness in the presence of evil, the suffering love, which is at the heart of all real power and the secret of every final victory in this universe.[21] It could not be otherwise since it is the creation and the kingdom of the God who is love.

My friends, how wrong the Jews and the Greeks and the Romans proved to be, and how right Paul was. When in the midst of the perplexities

17. This does not appear to be a direct quotation.
18. Matthew 24:2, Mark 13:2, Luke 21:6, Revelation 14:8, 18:2.
19. Matthew 26:64, Mark 14:62.
20. Matthew Bridges, "Crown Him With Many Crowns," 1851.
21. Revelation 7:17.

of our own day, I am tempted to think that we may have to trust in the method of the sword, that we cannot really be sure of the way of the cross, I reflect what would have become of Jesus, how little anyone after these two thousand years would care whether he had ever existed, if he had chosen the way of Caesar or of Barabbas!

A Matter of Life and Death

Let us come much closer home for one more illustration. Twenty years or so ago the so-called Christian nations fought in a great war. So far as the masses of people in our own country are concerned, there is no doubt that they hoped thereby to extend democracy, to make the world safe for democracy, to put an end to war itself. It has been estimated that that war cost, directly and indirectly, thirty million human lives and four hundred billion dollars worth of wealth. No one seriously argues today that after that terrific expenditure we gained any of the objects we set out to achieve in the last war. Must we not face the fact that once again God has given us a demonstration on a colossal scale of the eternal validity of Christ's command: "Put up thy sword into its place, for they that take the sword—for whatever cause—shall perish by the sword."[22] God's universe is so made that the way of the cross alone is the way of victory.

I am convinced that it is quite literally a matter of life and death for the church today that it should recognize and bear witness to this truth. There is a sense, of course, in which the church is eternal: "the gates of hell shall not prevail against it," even though it may have to find refuge again in the catacombs.[23] But a church or churches, as the Book of Revelation reminds us, may have their candlesticks removed.[24] So the organized church, as we know it, must, I am convinced, renounce war and thus become qualified to lead the world in its abolition, or that church itself is doomed.

Consider for a moment. Those who deal in statistics tell us that another general war will cost at least five times as much as the last one—one hundred and fifty million lives, more than the entire population of the United States, that would be, and as much wealth as the United States in boom times could produce in twenty-five years or England in a hundred years. Does anyone suppose that any of the institutions of our Western world can survive such a holocaust! Or again, in every country that goes into the war, some form of fascism will be established immediately. It is impossible to

22. See Matthew 26:52.

23. Matthew 16:18.

24. Revelation 2:5.

wage modern warfare save through the most extreme regimentation of all life—of business, labor, agriculture, the schools, the church, the home. As is being made clear in certain European countries, this means the destruction of the church or its survival as a mere vassal of the totalitarian state, a church of anti-Christ.

The decision is squarely up to the church. None of the Western nations can go to war unless the church consents and gives a substantial measure of cooperation. If civilization goes to pieces under the impact of another war, it will not be because God willed it, but because we willed it.

If, on the other hand, the church today dares to believe in the way of the cross, dares to obey the command to put up the sword, to renounce all further participation in war—that will cost something and the church will be persecuted by Caesar and his agents in our day as was the church in the early Christian centuries. But the cost will not be nearly as great as the cost of a general war is certain to be; and into that persecuted church the masses desperately seeking for a way out of war will flock as the masses flocked into the persecuted church of the early centuries. If the church is given grace to provide such leadership, we shall know a joy and peace "beyond all human ingenuity." People shall sing again and know what they mean when they sing:

> In the cross of Christ I glory,
> Towering o'er the wrecks of time.[25]

And of us and of our age it shall be said: "These are they that have come out of the great tribulation and have washed their robes and made them white in the blood of the Lamb. They shall hunger no more, neither thirst any more. . . . The Lamb that is in the midst of the Throne shall be their shepherd and shall guide them unto fountains of the waters of life; and God shall wipe away every tear from their eyes."[26]

25. John Bowring, "In the Cross of Christ I Glory," 1825.

26. Revelation 7:14, 16–17.

13

The Church's Witness to Her Faith (1938)

Muste gave this sermon-speech to a Reformed Church in America conference on evangelism. He argues that Christians need a faith in God and in Jesus that overcomes the world. To put this faith into practice, the church must do five things: 1) be the church and not anything else, 2) be able to meet the world intelligently, 3) not defend or condone what is evil in economic or political life but instead raise a prophetic voice, 4) lead the world to the renunciation of war, and 5) be ecumenical, a body in which there are no national, racial, or class divisions.

Many Scripture passages would constitute an appropriate text for these remarks. The one that has come to my mind repeatedly in preparing them is 1 John 5:4, "Whatsoever is begotten of God overcometh the world. And this is the victory that hath overcome the world: our faith."

The faith of John and of the early Christians did overcome the world. It enabled them in their individual lives to fight down its temptation and to rise above its cares and its hostility. They were thrown to the lions—literally and figuratively. But theirs was the perfect love that casteth out fear.[1]

The faith enabled them—enabled the early church—to "overcome the world" also in the larger social sense. Nothing seemed more likely by ordinary standards than that this vast, rich, materialistic, tyrannical, "totalitarian" if we want a modern word, Roman Caesarism would swallow up the church; that future ages would know nothing of Jesus, not to mention Paul or John or Stephen. Nothing seemed more unlikely than that this great civilization would go down into the dust, while ages to come would shout, as the early Christians heard the angelic hosts singing: "Crown him with many crowns, the Lamb upon his throne."[2] Nothing more unlikely than that 1,500 years after Rome was destroyed in this year of grace 1938 more people than ever before would sing: "Jesus, the very thought of Thee, with sweetness fills my breast."[3] But so it was. The faith did overcome the world, but in the sense of making the individual who embraced it immune from its temptations and lifting them above its turmoil into peace; and in the sense that history validated the Christian faith as the way of life and progress for humankind as against the other philosophies of that age. Today we need—each in our individual lives and the church in its corporate life—a faith that overcomes the world. On the surface it looks very much as though "the world" were overcoming the church today. True, Christianity in our time is not being challenged as it once was by its historic rivals such as Buddhism or Islam. But today on the very soil of Christendom great rival faiths—pseudo-religions—are challenging the faith. We think of fascism and communism, and the persecution to which the church is being subjected at their hands in such countries as Germany and Russia. Dictatorship and brutality stalk the earth and the future seems to be with them. Nor do we need to look beyond the borders of our own country. We know something about materialism and worldliness here also. A ministerial friend of mine tells how recently four of the most prominent businessmen and civic leaders of Los Angeles were spending their Sunday morning playing golf. During their game they talked about the danger of communism and how it would shut up all the churches if it came to this country! Well, communism has not yet closed any churches in the United States and is not likely to for a long time to come, if ever, but many who consider themselves highly respectable and patriotic people have already done all they could to empty if not to close the churches!

1. See 1 John 4:18.
2. Matthew Bridges, "Crown Him With Many Crowns," 1851.
3. Bernard of Clairvaux, "Jesus, the Very Thought of Thee," trans. Edward Caswall.

Does the surface appearance tell all? Or is there still "the faith that overcomes the world"? I am convinced that there is. I have experienced something of the power of God's love in my own life. And there is no one who has experienced that miracle of grace by which their own self-will is broken and their soul redeemed who can believe that there is any limit to what the divine power and grace can accomplish: the faith can and will overcome the world!

I want to try to state quite simply, without any attempt at being exhaustive or profound, what is the essential content of that faith to which the church must bear witness if it is to overcome the world.

Faith in God

First, overcoming faith may be said to be *faith in God*. Humanity stands, as did that poet who wrote the first chapter of Genesis—and an inspired poet he certainly was—in the presence of the awful mystery of this universe in which we are placed. The earth is "without form and void." Darkness broods upon the face of the cosmic deep. What does it mean? Must we not all be crushed sooner or later by this machine of power? Then there dawns that ray of light by which we are enabled in part to understand, to endure, to live amid this awful mystery: "In the beginning—God!" And though "the earth was without form and void" and "darkness brooded on the face of the deep," the Spirit of God moved up on the face of those waters and God said: "Let there be light"—and there was light.[4] God!

Here we touch upon that doctrine of the transcendence of God, the centrality of God, the sovereignty of God, the God who is "utterly other," the God of the inscrutable will and the resistless power, which is one of the fundamental elements in every sound Christian theology.

This is the God whom Moses met in the desert and when he asked God's name received only the answer: "I Am." This is the God whom the writer of Psalm 8 apprehended and cried out: "When I consider thy heavens, the work of thy fingers . . . what is man that thou art mindful of him, or the son of man that thou visitest him?"[5] This is that God who descended upon Job and his friends out of the whirlwind, after Job had made demands to understand his providence and said: "Gird up now thy loins like a man, for I will demand of thee, and declare thou unto me: Where wast thou when I laid the foundations of the earth . . . when the morning stars sang together and all the sons of God shouted for joy?" And when that whirlwind had at

4. Genesis 1:1–3.

5. Psalm 8:3–4.

last ceased to speak, Job said: "I had heard of thee by the hearing of the ear, but now mine eye seeth thee: wherefore I abhor myself and repent in dust and ashes."[6]

The inscrutable and transcendent God is the God of Paul, of Augustine, of Calvin, and of our fathers of the Reformed churches, the God to whom certain modern theologians such as Karl Barth are again calling attention. And it is well that we should be confronted with such a God. A faith that is to be capable of overwhelming the world must be able to proclaim such a God.

In a sense this is a hard and austere doctrine, and "the natural person" finds it difficult to accept.[7] Before such a God a person becomes as nothing. One cannot in the remotest sense be the center of one's universe. The deepest truth about humanity if one stands indeed over against such a God, is that one is an utterly dependent being. The basic sin is then pride, self-will. The virtue that most becomes humanity is humility. We are beings capable of falling on our knees, and that is where we belong.

In the presence of such a doctrine of God, of the divine transcendence, any pretension that we can fully understand the universe goes. Any pretension of being able to work out our own salvation, of being able to guide the course of the world, of being able in our own strength to build a just and brotherly world, must vanish. And also, if the ultimate reality is such a God, then we are forever forbidden to find our lives entirely in this present world of space and time: to live for God means to live for the world that is beyond. As we have said, this is hard and austere doctrine. It goes against the grain of modern humanity. Yet people without such a God, unable to look up to anything beyond themselves, presently despise themselves and all things, and find it impossible to go on.

Furthermore, as the fathers well understood, this doctrine of the transcendent God is also a supremely comforting doctrine. For a God who was simple enough for us to understand, we could not respect. A God whose moral attitude was that of an indulgent uncle could not satisfy our conscience. A God whose purposes we could thwart would leave us impotent and terrified in the presence of evil in the world.

It is precisely "the everlasting God, the creator of the ends of the earth," whose understanding is beyond our searching, of whom we can be sure that he "faints not neither is weary," and that in the hour of human extremity when "even the youths shall faint and be weary" he will "give strength to

6. Job 38:3–4, 7; 42:5–6.

7. See 1 Corinthians 2:14.

the weak." We can be sure that they who wait for him "shall mount up with wings as eagles, run and not be weary, walk and not faint."[8]

This God and his universe that we can never fully comprehend can engage the unceasing labors of human philosophy and science.

Furthermore, if this God be the Lord, if we all are under the divine sovereignty, then as Dr. Abraham Kuyper so clearly pointed out in the at present too little read Stone Lectures, there is an end forever to any notion that one person can be lord over another. Then, since we are made in God's image, the possibility that people should live together not as lords and slaves but in a free fellowship exists. The foundations of democracy are then, so to speak, securely laid in the very constitution of the universe, in the very nature of God.

To quote Dr. Kuyper on this point, people

> stand as equals before God and consequently equal as man to man. Hence we cannot recognize any distinctions among men save such as are imposed by God in that he gave one authority over the other or enriched one with more talents than another, in order that he should serve the man with less and so serve God. Hence Calvinism condemns not merely all open slavery and systems of caste, but also all covert slavery of woman and the poor; it is opposed to all hierarchy among men; it tolerates no aristocracy. . . . Thus Calvinism was bound to find its utterance in the democratic interpretation of life, to proclaim the liberty of nations, and not to rest until politically and socially every man, simply because he is a man, should be recognized, respected and dealt with as a creature created after the Divine likeness.[9]

Faith in Jesus Christ

Thus we are brought naturally to the second aspect of the content of a world-conquering faith upon which I wish to comment. We have said that such faith may be described as *faith in God*. It may be described in its other chief aspect as *faith in Jesus Christ*.

You will recall the opening line of our Bible to which we have already referred: "In the beginning—God." Mystery, majesty! Do you recall the last

8. Isaiah 40:28–31.

9. Abraham Kuyper, *Lectures on Calvinism: Six Lectures Delivered at Princeton University Under Auspices of the L. P. Stone Foundation* (Grand Rapids: Eerdmans, 1931), 27. This quotation differs insignificantly from the original.

verse in the canon of Scripture, the one with which Revelation 22 ends? It reads: "The grace of the Lord Jesus be with the saints."[10] How simple, how gentle, how intimate, how "human" this is in contrast to the opening verses of Genesis. And in that contrast we have a symbol of one of those paradoxes by means of which alone our human minds can in some measure grasp the truth. For we cannot see the whole truth in one glance or experience; we must look first at this aspect, then at quite a different aspect and try somehow to grasp and hold them in our minds together. So it is that any doctrine which says God is not "utterly transcendent," indefinitely removed above us, fails to do justice to the depths of the Christian revelation; and just as surely any doctrine which says that God in Christ is not infinitely near to us—"closer than breathing, nearer than hands and feet"—fails to do justice to the depths of the Christian revelation.[11]

Now we are touching upon those doctrines of the immanence of God, of the incarnation (the Word became flesh, dwelt among us at a certain point in this our human history), of the redemption of the individual and society, of the doing of the will of God "on earth as in heaven," which are also an essential part of any sound Christian theology.[12]

Let us think of the significance of this aspect of the faith for the individual. In effect it says to us: "If you want to think of what is at the very heart of God, of the mystery and power which are the universe, then after all you must not think primarily of might, or wisdom, or law but of love. God is like Jesus. He is Father." You recall that verse in the account of the Nativity: "There is born to you this day in the city of David, a Savior who is Christ, the Lord, and this shall be the sign unto you—the proof that the Lord, God, has come—ye shall find—a Babe!"[13]

You see, my friends, how near God is. It is this love as gentle as a baby that watches over us. There is nothing we need fear.

> I know not where His islands lift
> Their fronded palms in air;
> I only know I cannot drift
> Beyond his love and care.[14]

10. Revelation 22:21.

11. Alfred Lord Tennyson, "The Higher Pantheism," in *Select Poems of Alfred Tennyson* ed. Archibald MacMechan (Boston: D.C. Heath, 1907), 168. Muste uses a common paraphrase of this line rather than the exact wording.

12. See John 1:14, Matthew 6:10.

13. Luke 2:11–12, altered.

14. John Greenleaf Whittier, "The Eternal Goodness," in *English Poetry III: From Tennyson to Whitman*, ed. Charles W. Eliot, Harvard Classics, (New York: P. F. Collier & Son, 1910), 1416.

But that is not all, nor even the most important thing. The basic problem for us is, after all, the problem of sin, though people shrink from admitting it. So long as we remain human, do not sink to the level of the animal, we have to try to obey "the Law"; we must seek to be decent, honest, pure. But we are not. And presently it dawns on us that in our own strength we cannot be. In that hour, when we no longer pretend, when we see ourselves as we are, and the cry is wrung from us as from the author of Psalm 73: "I was as a beast before thee"—what then?[15] In that hour what does God do?

In that hour, if we have truly read the Scriptures, if the Christian outlook is ours, we see graven on the very heart of the eternal and transcendent God himself a cross! While we were yet sinners God loved us! In the face of our sin and rejection of him, he does the only thing—being the God revealed in Jesus—that he can do: he keeps on loving. And if you love in the face of evil and rejection, then you suffer. Hence the cross is after all the inmost mystery and the most distinctive symbol of the "faith that overcomes the world." Before that cross we fall down in shame and self-abasement. By the power of that cross, we rise into newness of life, for if it is indeed such love as this with which we have in the end to reckon, then our sins cannot thwart its victory, then it is possible for even such as we that it should no longer be we who live but Christ who lives in us.[16]

This gospel of the cross for every sinful and troubled soul is the faith that overcomes the world. This gospel the church must be able to preach to humanity. When it can no longer do so, it would better stop preaching altogether.

There remains a very important word to be said in closing. There are always those who tend to present us with this half or that half of the gospel, instead of the whole. The faith of the early church that overran the Roman world was this faith of which we have just spoken that saved individual sinners, lifted them above the world so that although in it they were not of it. But it was also and equally a faith which set over against the kingdoms of this world the kingdom of our God and of his Christ. It pronounced doom upon the economic and political systems, "the wickedness in high places," and proclaimed a new world-order was coming that would be built according to the specifications of Jesus.[17] Christianity not only makes new and holy people, it brings to earth the Holy City, the new Jerusalem—a new Washington, London, Paris, a new America, a new Orient and a new Occident. The command of God runs through all the spheres of life and society!

15. Psalm 73:22.

16. See Galatians 2:20.

17. Ephesians 6:12.

This point has also been impressively stated by Abraham Kuyper in the Stone Lectures from which we have already quoted and now venture to quote another notable passage:

> Calvinism did not stop at a church-order, but expanded in a *life-system*, and did not exhaust its energy in a dogmatical construction, but created a *life-* and *world-view*, and such a one as was, and still is, able to fit itself into the needs of every stage of human development in every department of life. It raised our Christian religion to its highest spiritual splendor; it created a church order, which became the preformation of state confederation; it proved to be the guardian angel of science; it emancipated art; it propagated a political scheme, which gave birth to constitutional government, both in Europe and America; it fostered agriculture and industry, commerce and navigation; it put a thorough Christian stamp upon home-life and family-ties; it promoted through its high moral standard purity in our social circles; and to this manifold effect it placed beneath Church and State, beneath society and home-circle, a fundamental philosophic conception, strictly derived from its dominating principle, and therefore all its own.
>
> This of itself excludes every idea of imitative repristination, and what the descendants of the old Dutch Calvinists as well as of the Pilgrim Fathers have to do is not to copy the past, as if Calvinism were a petrefact, but to go back to the living root of the Calvinist plant, to clean and water it, and so to cause it to bud and to blossom once more, now fully in accordance with our actual life in these modern times, and with the demands of the times to come.[18]

If now we attempt to put in concrete form what should be the strategy in this day and age of a church possessing the old conquering Christian, Calvinistic faith, we might very briefly sum it up under the following headings.

1. *"The church must be the church."* It is not and must not seek to be a reform society, a political party, reactionary or revolutionary, a trade union or anything of the sort. We must recover inwardness. Our ministers and our people must have the experience of God in their own lives, or we shall be helpless to communicate it to anyone else. And it is above all the living experience of God in Christ that our age needs.
2. *The church has to be able to meet the world on intelligent grounds.* It must be willing to undergo the tremendous labor of thought, of

18. Kuyper, *Lectures on Calvinism*, 171. This quotation differs insignificantly from the original.

theology, which is involved in putting its ancient eternal gospel into the language and thought-forms of our day, as Paul and John and the Church Fathers who followed them translated the gospel first planted on Jewish soil into the language and thought-forms of the Graeco-Roman world; and as Dr. Kuyper would have us not be slavish copyists of the past but to cause the Calvinist plant to bud and blossom again from the living root. A church that ministers to the heart but not the head is as far from doing justice to the riches of the gospel as one that ministers to the head and not to the heart.

3. *The church must not defend or condone what is evil and un-Christian in our economic and political life.* It must, as the church in all its great ages has done, lift up its prophetic voice against such evils and demand that the will of God prevail in all spheres of life. If the church becomes a mere bulwark of the status quo, if it bows its knee to human wealth, authority or prestige, as the church in Russia did, its candlestick will be removed. We may and indeed should grieve when a church is thus brought low, but Christians first of all will bow their heads at such a spectacle and confess that "the judgments of the Lord are true and righteous altogether."[19]

4. If the church is to overcome the world today, *it must lead the world in the renunciation of war.* Whatever may have been the case in the past, war today can accomplish no good and it cannot be waged without the violation of every principle of morality. As the Oxford Conference put it, war "is sin, being a denial of the nature of God as love, of the redemptive way of the Cross, and of the community of the Holy Spirit," and consequently "the Church will become a creative, regenerative, and reconciling instrument for the healing of the nations only as it renounces war absolutely."[20] We may remind ourselves that the early Christians also refused to bear arms in Caesar's battalions. It was one of the most significant points at which they refused "to be conformed unto the world."[21]

5. *The church must itself be "ecumenical," universal, in character if it is to overcome the world.* The early church conquered that formidable

19. Psalm 19:9. Abraham Lincoln famously quoted this verse in his second inaugural address.

20. J. H. Oldham, *The Oxford Conference (Official Report)* (Chicago: Willett, Clark & Company, 1937), 163. This quotation differs insignificantly from the original, which begins with the assertion that "Some believe that war, especially in its modern form, is always sin."

21. Romans 12:2.

Roman civilization not least because in an age of racial and other hatreds the church within itself was from the outset a unity transcending race, nation, color, and all other lines: "In Christ Jesus there is neither Jew nor Greek. . . . Christ is all and in all."[22] Even so in this age of ours when rampant nationalism, crude racialism, bitter class wars, threaten to rend the fabric of humanity in pieces, the church will be able to heal and to overcome the world only if in its own fellowship there is the unity of the Spirit, if there is neither white nor black nor yellow; neither American nor French nor Japanese—but Christ is all and in all. Let the church in this sense be the church, a fellowship that does not recognize bounds of nation, race or class, united not by human inspiration but by the love of God. Let such a church in all lands, in peace and in war, lift hands of prayer to "the One God, the Father, from whom all comes and for whom we exist, and to the One Lord, Jesus Christ"—and we shall once again see the fulfillment of that ancient word: "Whatsoever is begotten of God overcometh the world. And this is the victory that hath overcome the world: our faith."[23]

22. Galatians 3:28, Colossians 3:11.

23. 1 Corinthians 8:6, 1 John 5:4.

14

The Way of the Cross (1938)

Well aware of the impending Second World War, in this article Muste makes a forceful biblical and theological call to pacifism. He argues that the cross indicates that suffering love is the supreme redemptive power. Christians must either reject Christ—the suffering servant and the lamb—or renounce war and seek to hinder nations' ability to wage it by refusing to participate.

Someone has used the phrase, "the cross as maker and yardstick of history." That suggests, for one thing, that it is on "the plane of history"—not in a "beyond history," but in this history of people, classes, nations in which exploitation occurs and wars break out—that the cross, the way of the cross, is a force and an applicable standard of judgment. The phrase suggests also that it is on the great scale of history, in the affairs of races, classes, and nations, and not merely or chiefly in intimate relations between individuals, that the cross is determining force and conquering ideal and pronouncer of judgment—that it is history which validates the cross.

Such ideas are, however, constantly challenged and the pacifist's espousal of them deprecated and scorned, both inside and outside the church. The world has many maxims in which it conveys its wisdom in the matter to its children: "Business is business"; the dictum of the English statesman, "You can't handle the Irish question on the lines of the Sermon on the Mount"; and the older "God is on the side of the big battalions."

Is It an Impossible Ideal?

What is more important and serious for us is that in theological and religious circles also the implications of that phrase I have quoted are challenged. The problem of politics and economics, we are told, is that of justice, not love. "In the field of collective behavior the force of egoistic passion is so strong" that nothing more than the provisional and precarious harmony of a balance of power can be achieved.[1] Emil Brunner in a familiar passage warns that "the projection of ideal [political] programs is not only useless but harmful. . . . The prophetic demand, which does not concern itself with the possible and impossible, has, of course, its own relevance as proclamation of the unconditioned law. But it has this significance only if it is presented not as a specific program but as a general demand, i.e., if it does not involve immediate political realization."[2]

But it seems to me that in the Jewish-Christian revelation the cross is the crucial event in history, our human history; that the concept of the cross, of suffering love as supreme redemptive power, was a social concept, which was revealed to people who faced overwhelming and bitter historico-political and economic dilemmas as a way of meeting precisely such dilemmas; that it is impossible to build up a scriptural-prophetic theology that does not demand the practice of love in all the relationships of life and promise the reign of God on earth.

The concept of God himself as one who suffers with peoples at a definite historical moment when they groan under quite concrete social oppression and who takes measures to redeem them from this bondage and to set up a kingdom based not on power but on ethical foundations, on a love (covenant) relationship between people and God and among people—this is already prefigured and in part expressed at the very beginning of Jewish religious history. The record is found in the book of Exodus that gets its name from a historic "walk-out" led by Moses.

1. Reinhold Niebuhr, *Interpretation of Christian Ethics* (New York: Harper & Brothers, 1935), 140.

2. Emil Brunner, *The Divine Imperative*, trans. Olive Wyon (Philadelphia: Westminster, 1937), 230. Muste follows Reinhold Niebuhr's translation of the German, not the published English version. See Niebuhr, *Interpretation of Christian Ethics*, 155–56.

But the idea becomes much clearer in later prophets. Israel began with a largely tribal conception of God. God is power. He is patron of your tribe and his law runs in its territory, not beyond. If you have might in relation to other tribes, it means your god is puissant. He is really your "blood" (Jewish or German), your might as tribe or nation, personified and idealized. If you are licked in battle, your god has been licked.

Why Israel Survived

What ordinarily happened then was that your tribe was absorbed, if not annihilated, and you accepted the victorious god. But that did not happen to Israel, hemmed in and presently crushed like some Belgium or Czechoslovakia between the empires of Egypt and Mesopotamia. Israel survived its destruction as a nation. How? Why?

The only answer history gives is that in that crisis Israel through the prophets received and in a slight degree accepted a revelation of God, a deeper insight into the character of God, or ultimate reality. This revelation was proclaimed by the prophets to a nation caught in that definite historical situation, not, as Brunner would have it, as "unconditioned law," a merely "general demand," but for "immediate political realization."

The revelation came to this: God is not power, domination. This is not the finally real. The thing that counts is not a state which has power, economic, political and military, as against other states. Righteousness, and again as in Exodus, "social righteousness," counts. But righteousness is not geographical in character. It reigns if at all, everywhere—also in Egypt and Babylon of your captivity.

The prophets took a further step. Put it this way: If as a nation you suffer defeat and this does not prove that God is weak and therefore to be cast off, you still face the question, Is your suffering, the suffering of the righteous, of the chosen people, then a proof that God is unjust? If you believe that your suffering is basically unjustified, two things will happen. First, you will throw the blame on the other nation that "causes" your suffering. Second, you will presently give up trying to live righteously, for what is the use of following a God who inflicts boils precisely on Job? (The "inscrutability" of the ways of providence is a partial but not a final and complete answer to this problem.)

Not Hate but Repentance Needed

The answer of the great prophets was in substance: Righteousness is still righteousness. So far from being unjust God loves and suffers for the unjust. Now if that is your approach you must first of all measure yourself against that righteousness and love. From that you reach the insight that you suffer, not because of the hellishness of these Egyptians or Babylonians, this sadistic dictator or that; you suffer because you have sinned, have exploited the poor, have tried to become a predatory military power yourself. Therefore you must repent, change yourself. [There is no point in hating; you cannot very well hate the enemy.][3]

When you achieve this height of humility, you are, so to speak, taking sin on your own shoulders, your own heart. First of all your own sin, which you do not now try to project on the other so that you may hate and slay them. But also, by rising to this higher moral position—of self-accusation, nonvengeance—[your attitude toward the "enemy" undergoes a revolutionary change. It has become impossible for you to hate them with the unpeaceable hatred of the self-righteous. Like yourself, though with more excuse because they have not learned the law as you have, they are caught in the grip of sin. Thus as it were][4] you take on your soul the burden of the enemy's sin too, you suffer for them, you want them too to become the subject of Jehovah's law. You, Israel, become "the suffering servant of Jehovah," a redeeming agency, because you become like the One who loves sinful humanity and has a cross graven on his heart.[5] "Pray for the peace of Babylon your great enemy!" cries King Zedekiah in Franz Werfel's novel *Hearken Unto the Voice*. "Shall a man pray for the peace of his slayer who sets the sword to his breast?" Jeremiah replies, "I realize what I have done." Zedekiah cries, "And you do not shudder with horror at—at—the impossible?" Jeremiah bows his head: "The Lord demands of them and of us."[6]

3. Muste crossed out this line in his copy of the published article, which he apparently marked up for republication. It can be found at the Swarthmore College Peace Collection, A. J. Muste Papers, box 9 (microfilm reel 89.4).

4. Muste's copy of the published article contains this addition in Muste's hand. I have added the phrase "grip of sin" where Muste's actual phrase is illegible.

5. Isaiah 53.

6. Franz Werfel, *Hearken Unto the Voice*, trans. Moray Firth (New York: Viking, 1938), 598–99.

Jesus as "Suffering Servant"

Space permits only a brief reference to Jesus' wrestling with the same problem as confronted the prophets of the great age. Anyone who thinks of Jesus as a secular revolutionist, socialist, or communist, is mistaken. But it is quite as mistaken to think of Jesus as a Barthian who could make distinctions as to the spheres of life in which the law of love is fully operative. He too finds his nation ground under the heel of the dictator. He knows himself called to be God's instrument to redeem his people, "to proclaim liberty to the captives."[7] But how to do it? Surely he must achieve influence, power? He must take "the kingdoms of the world and the glory of them"?[8] Then he will be able to use his place and power to establish God's reign. But he rejects that course. His decision was a religious one. The idea was satanic, i.e., contrary to his concept of God. The God whose Son he knew himself to be was the prophets' God of righteousness and love, not a heavenly potentate, a celestial general. So his servant could not be an earthly Caesar. He must be "the suffering servant of Jehovah."

He must summon his people as Jeremiah had done—and clearly the decision is once again a political arising out of a religious decision—to repent of their own sins, to renounce the aim to be a state having power against other states and to become a "church" based upon the worship of God. The end for such a Messiah, his sword and throne, must be the cross. That was what most of his contemporaries could not understand. He had thrown himself away: "Let him now come down from the cross and we will believe in him."[9]

The Prophet in a Time of Crisis

So the prophetic revelation comes each time in a profound political, social, cultural, spiritual crisis marked by the emergence of brute power and its deification. Each time the prophet urges the nation to take the course of repentance, nonviolence, love of the enemy—to take suffering on itself, not to inflict or desire to inflict it. Each time the prophet proclaims God, the Spirit, as mightier than the dictator. "The Egyptians are men and not gods, and their horses are flesh and not spirit."[10] How are you going to meet this horseflesh except with more and better horseflesh, this Nebuchadnezzar, Caesar,

7. Isaiah 61:1, Luke 4:18.
8. Matthew 4:8.
9. Matthew 27:32.
10. Isaiah 31:3.

Herod, except with a bigger and better dictator? No, says the prophet, spirit, spirit of God, righteousness, love is mightier. And in each case the prophet of realism and doom proclaims also the undying hope: the kingdom of God is at hand.

What is the verdict of history upon this religious-political strategy? The Jews did survive—not the Amorites and Hittites, nor yet the Egyptian or Babylonian empires—and survived because the remnant at least responded to the prophetic revelation and centered Israel's life in an idea, in God, not in power. And has not Israel, precisely through "the Law and the prophets," been a savior of humankind?

As for Jesus, whom has history vindicated—the Jews and Greeks and Romans who saw the Roman Empire and civilization as real and victorious and the cross as a stumbling-block and foolishness? Or Paul and the early Christians for whom Rome's schools and palaces and banks and tramping legions were already gone and dead, who exultantly preached Christ crucified and saw and heard none but "the Lamb that is in the midst of the throne"[11]—not bull or lion or dragon or ass, but the Lamb, symbol of gentleness, of seeming helplessness in the presence of evil, of sacrificial love, which is at the heart of all real power and the secret of every final victory in this universe? Thenceforth and until this moment history has been stamped with the seal "Anno Domini."[12]

The Only Way Out

And what of us and our world at this moment? We need not labor the point that we are again in a world crisis marked by worship of the beast, of brute power.

The prophets, including Jesus, have always given one answer to the problem as to what is an adequate political strategy for religion, how the religion of redemption can "come alive" in such a world crisis as ours. Today their message is again that the church must renounce war, the way of violence and domination, and that the nation must renounce war. There is no other adequate religious, Christian answer. There is no other adequate political answer. If Christian forces actually withdraw support from the war machine so that the nation cannot effectively make war, it is impossible for an exploiting capitalism or imperialism to survive. By the same token, if a

11. This is an image from the book of Revelation. Muste may be thinking specifically of Revelation 5:6 or 7:17.

12. The Latin, used for dates (as in 1938 AD), means "In the year of the Lord" or "In the year of our Lord."

great imperialist power such as the United States cannot wage or threaten war, it must consent to basic changes in the international economic setup, and this is the one way out of the international crisis.

Reluctantly, as it were by the back door, we find people sometimes admitting that the way of the cross must be taken and that it can gain the victory, can "overcome the world." Professor Sidney Hook, in a review of Aldous Huxley's *Ends and Means*, speaks of Huxley as belonging to a "perpetual out-élite who have taken to heart Lord Acton's dictum, 'Power always corrupts and absolute power corrupts absolutely,' and must perforce remain outside the arena of active politics."[13] There we have the often heard note of admiration for the person of the Spirit, followed immediately by the shrug of the shoulder that says they "aren't practical." But Professor Hook, being an honest man with a penetrating intellect, cannot after all leave the matter here. He goes on to say in effect that the people who stand without compromise for truth and love are after all the only "practical" people, the universe being what it ultimately is: "Since there are degrees of corruption, the possibility exists that their work may bear fruit even in politics. The only alternative to their view that political means must not be dissociated from the ideal of the good life in the good society is the conception of politics as the game of 'who gets what when' and of social philosophy as a set of rationalizations to conceal the fact."[14]

The Idealists Are Practical

If we put that into somewhat less abstract terms, does it not mean simply that we have got to believe in the political philosophy and methods of the prophets or find ourselves forced to adopt the philosophy and methods of Machiavelli? That people are children of God and that therefore evil may be overcome by good or else we are reduced to regarding them as animals—in which case every human society is in essence a wolf-pack over which the strongest and most brutal of the wolves will be the dictator, and not only the near but the distant future is given over to the ruthless Caesars and their big battalions?

The hour of judgment has again struck for humankind. We stand at such a crisis in history as was the age of the great Jewish prophets and the early Christian era. In those earlier crises, only a remnant rose to the faith

13. Sidney Hook, review of *Ends and Means* by Aldous Huxley, *The Nation* 145, no. 24 (December 11, 1937), 656, 658. This quotation differs insignificantly from the original.

14. Ibid., 658. This quotation differs insignificantly from the original.

that people and nations must make the political decision to renounce might and embrace the way of suffering love, discerned the law of the Spirit that they who lose their life shall find it. Being a remnant they were persecuted from all sides, but no one doubts now that their blood nourished the seeds of a new and ampler age.

There will be a remnant in our day's crisis, regarded by all as fools of Christ, or perhaps of the Antichrist, but members of that church against which the gates of hell do not prevail. But today there must be more than that remnant. A nation or the nations must make the religious-political decision to be Israels indeed, to renounce war and the whole spirit of war. Otherwise the very vastness and delicacy of the mechanisms people have devised, the very complexity and richness of our civilization, the truly monumental intellectual progress made by modern humanity and the sensitiveness of its nervous organism, will but serve to make the coming dark ages more brutal and more ghastly. "O Jerusalem, Jerusalem, if thou hadst known, in this thy day, the things which belong unto thy peace!"[15]

15. Luke 19:42. The original article has "place" instead of "peace."

15

Admonitions for War Time (1940)

In this radio sermon, broadcast nationally in March 1940, Muste gives advice to Christians facing another world war. At the time, he was in the process of leaving his pastorate to become the head of the Fellowship of Reconciliation.

We live in such a day as the Bible speaks of—a day of wars and rumors of war, when nation rises against nation and kingdom against kingdom; a day when "the beast that cometh up out of the abyss" seems to possess people's souls and to rule over human destiny; a day when even the youths shall faint and be weary and the young people shall utterly fall.[1] What does God's word have to say to us? What does our faith teach us in such an hour? Let me try to state some of the admonitions I think it brings us.

1. *Make up your mind whether you believe in God.* The fact that we go to church, that we say prayers, that we sing hymns that mention God, all this does not prove that we believe in him. It is clear that the destiny of humankind, the fate of the universe, is not in our hands. Vast forces utterly beyond our control are at work and they seem to be sweeping people to destruction.

1. Revelation 11:7, Isaiah 40:30.

In the last analysis either blind chance rules, or a cosmic demon, or God the Father of our Lord Jesus Christ. Make up your mind which it is. Until one can say, "I believe in God," or contrariwise say definitely and finally that there is no God, nothing is settled.

2. *Do not try to put yourself in God's place.* God commands you to worship him with all your mind. That means that you must seek out the truth and you must act intelligently. If you will do that and trust God's guidance, you will know from moment to moment what to do. But your mind remains limited and human. There will be many things in this complex and troubled world you will not be able to understand. You must not demand to know all the answers. "The significance of religion," Kagawa the Japanese saint has wisely said, "is not that it explains things that already exist, but that it creates things that did not exist."[2] If you will ask God, you will receive the light you need to create in this world justice and truth and beauty that do not yet exist.

God places great responsibilities upon you. You must discharge them faithfully. Others will suffer as well as yourself if you fail. But you do not have to carry the whole world on your shoulders. You will be able to carry your own load better if you leave something to God to carry. You really do not have to worry that God is asleep. "The everlasting God, the Lord, the Creator of the ends of the earth, fainteth not neither is weary."[3]

3. *Practice the presence of God.* Nothing has ever been more conclusively proved than that men and women who take time to be alone and in the silence, to meditate, to pray, find light and grace and power from a divine and inexhaustible source flowing into them and flowing out in healing and blessing upon their fellows. How else shall the great open sores of the world be healed? How else shall these hungry, stricken multitudes of refugees that wander like lost sheep across the face of the earth be brought into the fold of peace and a decent life again? How else shall war be stopped? But if this is true, is it not time that anyone who will not spend at least an hour every day in prayer and silence so that the power of God may flow into and through them should stop pretending to be a Christian? Stop pretending that they care for the world's suffering? Jesus, once again on his way to crucifixion in this Lenten season, finds us sleeping, drugged with love of comfort, with insensitiveness, with sloth, and he exclaims: "What, could ye not watch with me one hour?"[4]

2. Toyohiko Kagawa, *Meditations on the Holy Spirit* (Nashville: Cokesbury, 1939), 79.

3. Isaiah 40:28.

4. Matthew 26:40.

4. *Practice works of mercy.* Feed the hungry, clothe the naked, heal the sick, visit the forlorn ones and the prisoners.[5] We must all do it directly for those who are near by. We must share to the limit of our means and ability in supporting the organizations that minister to the victims of war and persecution throughout the world. "When the Son of Man shall come in his glory and all the angels with him and before him shall be gathered all the nations and he shall separate them, one from another as the shepherd separateth the sheep from the goats. . . . and shall say to them on his left hand, 'depart from me, ye cursed, for inasmuch as ye ministered not unto one of the least of these my brethren, ye ministered not unto me'"—in the hour when that test is applied and that judgment pronounced, where shall we, where will complacent America be?[6]

5. *Keep the conscience sensitive and alert.* Never condone evil, injustice, oppression. The conscience is the eye of our spirit. In some people that eye is astigmatic, they see everything blurred. Many of us have blind spots in that eye: we see evil and terror when it is practiced by people or groups or nations whom we do not like; but we cannot see the same evils in ourselves and our friends.

6. *"First take the beam out of your own eye."*[7] Repent of your own sin. True, all people and nations have sinned. We should like to see them admit it and stop their evil practices. If they would only do so, we are quite certain that we should gladly follow such a noble example. Alas, my friends, God made each of us the keeper of our own conscience, not of our brother's. Nowhere has any blessing been pronounced on those who will be just and forgiving and honest and kind, when it no longer costs anything because "everybody's doing it." There are no Beatitudes for the morally lazy, cowardly, slackers. If we in America do not believe in racism, for example, we can tackle the huge job of removing from our own eyes such beams as Jim Crowism, lynching, anti-Semitism—which is not unknown in our "best circles"—and the Oriental Exclusion Act. Do you think nothing would happen in Russia, Poland, Germany, Italy, Japan, if we did some of these things? Did them *first*—which is Christ's way, "who while we will still sinners died for us."[8]

7. *Love your enemies and pray for them.* Nowhere is it written that this command is abrogated or suspended in war-time—when there really are

5. See Matthew 25:34–40.

6. Matthew 25:31–32, 41. Muste invents the last portion of this quotation by rewording verse 40 in the negative. This is likely an unintentional mistake made when quoting from memory; it adheres closely to the meaning of the passage.

7. Matthew 7:5, Luke 6:42.

8. Romans 5:8.

enemies! Bitterness and hate toward nations or individuals may not enter into our judgments on the issues involved in war.

8. *Keep the mind's eye clear and the judgment cool.* "Ye shall know the truth, and the truth shall make you free."[9] Nothing else can. Let the channels of discussion, therefore, be kept open in our land, whether in war or peace. Let us jealously guard the liberties of speech, press, assemblage, and worship. In debate, let us try to understand the other person's position and why they hold it. Let us seek the victory of the truth, not of our own clever minds or glib tongues. Let us learn to analyze propaganda from whatever source. Let us strive to become members of the blessed company of those in whom mental brilliance is not a cloak for an arrogant and cruel spirit, nor gentleness a synonym for a fuzzy mind—the company of those who "speak the truth in love."[10]

9. *Remember that as God is the source of all comfort and light, so is God the sole lord of conscience.* Each Christian must therefore assume responsibility before God and their fellows for their own personal decision as to whether loyalty to Christ forbids or permits or requires participation in war. Having made their decision, let them stand by it and take the consequences.

> Our fathers, chained in prisons dark,
> Were still in heart and conscience free;
> And blest would be their children's fate
> If they, like them, should die for Thee![11]

Let the State cherish the brave and independent conscience. And since equally sincere and devout Christians differ on this matter of participation in war, each must respect fully the conscience of the other, maintain Christian fellowship and the unity of the church despite these differences, and pray that the Holy Spirit may further enlighten the mind of the church and of its members.

10. Finally, remember God's purpose for humankind and the certainty of ultimate triumph. "All these things shall come to pass," said Jesus, "wars, upheavals, catastrophe, but the end is not yet. People may refuse to accept my way of love and crucify me. But they will not have defeated my Father God, and they will not have seen the last of me. After three days I will rise again. Of this world which seeks to build another kingdom than mine, there shall not be left one stone upon another that shall not be torn down. But the fellowship of those who accept me as Lord is built upon a rock. The

9. John 8:32.

10. Ephesians 4:15.

11. Frederick W. Faber, "Faith of Our Fathers," 1849.

gates of hell shall not prevail against it. They shall yet see the holy city, new Jerusalem, coming down out of heaven from God. And the dwelling place of God shall be with humanity, and they shall be his peoples and God himself shall be with them and be their God; and he shall wipe away every tear from their eyes."[12]

12. See Matthew 16:18, 24:2, 6; Mark 8:31, 13:2; Luke 21:6; Revelation 21:2–4.

16

Unity in Crisis (1941)

In this sermon from the eve of the United States' entry into World War Two, Muste explores how pacifist and non-pacifist Christians can remain in fellowship during wartime. He argues that Christians who disagree should never see each other as enemies, but instead cultivate an attitude of searching for truth together. The church must maintain its prophetic role of calling for repentance and condemning the self-righteousness of both individuals and nations. Its role is to be salt, light, and yeast.

Every day and nearly every hour of every day brings news that means that we are being drawn more completely into war. The hope that the church, which is certainly more sensitive on the issues of war than twenty-five years ago, might lead the nation into some dynamic peace action that might call a halt to the ever spreading conflict, must probably be given up for the present.

We are aware of the fact that Christian people thus far have not been in agreement, either on the general question of participation (can the church ever participate in war) or on the narrower political question as to whether it is justified in participating in this war.

The question I want to raise this morning is: Granted that in the church we have both pacifists and non-pacifists, what is a program on the basis of which we may have Christian unity in the crisis?

Since whatever unity we may achieve will be fraudulent and not Christian unless it be a unity with Christ as well as with each other, our program must be one that expresses his spirit.

Jesus was apprehensive not that his followers would become wicked but that they would become insipid—salt that has lost its savor—that there would no longer be anything distinctive about them. He frequently used the images of salt, light, and leaven to describe them. Each suggests that the church and the Christian people must not get out of the world, but must be deeply immersed in its life—like salt in meat, light in darkness, yeast in a loaf.

The figures suggest too that often the church and Christian people may be a minority, a small minority in an intractable or hostile environment—a bit of salt in meat threatened with putrefaction, a light at the end of a dark road, a little yeast in a lump of dough.

Above all, these figures suggest the Master's requirement of distinctiveness—we should not become identified with the environment in which we are embedded but continually. . . .

[*One page is missing here from the original manuscript.*[1]]

. . . . but that our apprehension of truth is imperfect.

From one point of view, one of the greatest mysteries and bitterest tragedies is that in such discussions parent and child, pastor and congregation, may find themselves on opposite sides of the question. But it is hardly possible to achieve intellectual and spiritual fortitude unless one is willing to take the stand for what one thinks is right, like Luther, even if all the rest of the world may be on the other side. Furthermore, fellowship is much cheaper and more superficial if it is only with people who think exactly alike.

One of the implications of what I have been trying to say is that when discussion is in the Christian spirit, one should never think of the other person as an enemy whom we must batter down or they will batter us down—whom we must put in the wrong or they will put us in the wrong—we must remember that we are still engaged in a common search for Christ's truth. Therefore we are anxious to understand the person who sees the question differently and to see the validity of what they say—for there will be validity—and to appropriate any light they have to give. Above all, we must remember that they hold the view they do because of what is good in them.

1. Only one manuscript copy of this sermon exists. It has never before been published. An archivist's note informs us that the page was already missing in 1978.

It is their fidelity to truth as they see it. We may then hope that they will receive the light that we have to give.

Whenever we are not in this mood we must examine ourselves, examine what it really means when we must be so sure of ourselves—to see if it does not really mean that we are not quite sure. In theological seminary when I was there a story that was frequently told was that of a minister who wrote out the manuscripts of his sermons and then went over them to mark them for emphasis. Once there was one paragraph he read carefully, then read it a second time, then knit his brows and read it slowly a third time, then wrote in the margin, "Not so clear. Holler like the devil."

If we can maintain an attitude in the church of searching together for the truth, it is sure to be a considerable contrast to the tendency to repress free expression of opinion which will grow—and will be rendering a great service.

Maintenance of an attitude of Christian criticism also means that the church must keep alive discussion of war aims and such questions as whether time has not come to call a halt to the strife. It must be observed that it will not be easy to avoid what will seem like obstruction of war efforts and reduction of the will-to-victory, if we do not permit the question of stopping the war to be pushed aside. But the alternative is much more dangerous, both for religion and for the church. It means to offer no opposition to the terrible forces that threaten to draw one people after another into a dance of death that does not end until the entire Western civilization goes into eclipse. It means fighting for victory, not knowing what you are fighting for, with the possibility of waking up to find that you fought for something utterly different from what you supposed. In any case it will be difficult enough to avoid an atmosphere of national exultation and a post-war moral let-down, under the best of circumstances. It will be utterly impossible to avoid these unless problems of post-war reconstruction are held constantly before the people.

Returning to the attributes of Christian criticism, Christians must keep asking themselves whether war retains any legitimacy at all, whether Christians must not withdraw from it, whatever the consequences may seem to be. In the words of Bishop Oldham, a non-pacifist, "The Christian can approve of war only if there remains a distinction between war and murder. Indiscriminate bombing of civilians is murder. If that were done, one would have to choose between ceasing to be Christian and becoming a pacifist."[2]

2. George Ashton Oldham was an Episcopal bishop in Albany, New York from 1929 to 1950. The source of this quotation is unknown.

A further point for Christian consideration is whether one can pray for military victory. Can Christians ask for themselves what they would not ask for others? All are children of God. In any case, Christian prayers must always be "Not my will but Thine be done."[3]

Closely related to this is the responsibility of the Christian church to witness against smugness and self-righteousness, in self or nation. The prophetic message is always penitence and repentance: "take out the beam in thine own eye."[4] The most terrible evil of today is that no nation is praying like the publican, "God, be merciful to me, a sinner" but all are praying like the Pharisee, "I thank Thee, Lord, that I am not like these others, these Nazi swine, these fascist dogs, these Japanese devils," or, if the person belongs to one of those nations, "these effete Britons, or Americans."[5]

Obviously the church cannot condone or help instill hatred. Christians must pray for their enemies.

Also, Christians must not perpetrate a lie by ostentatiously raising funds and making garments to relieve suffering, when it is their purpose to relieve suffering only on one side while refusing to relieve it on the other side. In that case participation in the war effort is primary, relief of suffering is incidental. If people want to do that, if they are convinced that it is God's will for them, then they must do it, but they should be aware of what they are doing. (Morally it is the same thing as being in the Army.) If their primary purpose is to relieve suffering, it should be done as the American Friends' Service Committee is doing, by relieving suffering wherever it is found.[6] There is much to be said for the view that this is really the Christian approach, for we have the example of God "Who maketh the sun to rise on the evil and the good and sendeth rain on the just and on the unjust."[7]

Certainly if the essential Christian spirit is to prevail in the church, we must maintain full fellowship. One of the most hopeful signs of the times is the full fellowship that is being maintained in Great Britain, between pacifists and non-pacifists as well as between all classes and all parties. If we are to implement that attitude it will mean, for example, that no church has the right to go on the assumption that it is the normal thing for its young men to go to war. No minister has the right to act on that assumption. It must compel each volunteer or selectee to make his own conscientious decision.

3. Luke 22:42.

4. Matthew 7:5, Luke 6:45.

5. Luke 18:13, see Luke 18:11.

6. The AFSC, a Quaker organization, was highly respected for its relief work and steadfast neutrality. It received the Nobel Peace Prize in 1947 with the British Friends Service Council on behalf of all Quakers for their work during and after the war.

7. Matthew 5:45.

If the soldier does that in the spirit that "I can do no other," the church may bless him equally with the conscientious objector. The church must also be ready to counsel and aid conscientious objectors. If recognition services for soldiers are to be held, they should be held likewise for conscientious objectors. It might be well to have special communion services in which drafted men and conscientious objectors would take communion together, would together agree to obey no law but Christ, never to do anything that will prevent their taking communion with any fellow Christians.

It might well be that such support of war and of the nation at war would hardly seem sufficient to the government that desires totalitarian loyalty in totalitarian war. But it is not the business of the Christian to be conformed to the world and to become a tool of any earthly state. It is ever the church's business to play a distinctive role—not to be conformed to the world but to confront the world with Christ and compel it to conform to his truth and demands, though it have no weapons save the foolishness of preaching, the patient practice of love, humility, prayer, and willingness to die for its law.

The church cannot, in any event, identify the fate of the kingdom of God with that of any earthly government. It may be that we are witnessing the end of the French, British, and American Empires. Empires have passed before. There is something harrowing about the passing of an empire, but it is not true that it means the end of civilization or religion. What reason is there to suppose that France, Britain, or America have developed imperialisms with the attribute of immortality—of which it can never be said: "Far called our Navy . . ."[8] If this happens—and I, of course, trust that it will not happen—it would not be true that it would be the end of civilization and religion. It would mean that once again human structures not built on the foundation of Christ have collapsed—but the end is not yet. Rather it is the beginning of a new opportunity to help build a city which hath foundations whose Builder and Maker is God.[9] This, too, the church and Christians may and must proclaim to all rulers and all peoples of the earth.

8. This appears to be a reference to Rudyard Kipling's 1897 poem "Recessional," which warned of the transience of Britain's empire. The line in the poem reads: "Far-called, our navies melt away."

9. See Hebrews 11:10.

17

Unable and Unwilling to Conform[1] (1942)

In this article addressed to the members of the Fellowship of Reconciliation, Muste discusses his refusal to register for the draft.[2] *He did so as a protest, despite the fact that as an ordained minister registering would allow him to claim exemption from military service. Muste's explanation of his choice is a good example of how his Christianity informed his political activism.*

This message to the members and friends of the Fellowship is being written just before I forward to the Attorney General, the highest officer of the Judicial Department of our Government, a letter informing him that on grounds of conscience I am unable and unwilling to conform to the President's order of March 19, 1942, directing men in my age-group to submit, on April 27, to registration under the Selective Service Act.

1. This piece was originally published under the title "April 27—A Message to the Fellowship."

2. Muste had reluctantly left the Presbyterian Labor Temple in 1940 to become the executive secretary of the US branch of the FOR. He held the position until 1953, when age limits forced him to retire.

The question as to the point at which Christian pacifists draw the line in dissociating themselves from the war effort and from the machinery of conscription is not the most important one with which we are confronted. Inevitably there will be differences of opinion on that matter. God does not call upon us all to bear exactly the same witness in exactly the same way. But it is, in the first place, important that we draw the line somewhere and that we draw it where God wants us to. There are, as I see it, two or three considerations that guide us in knowing God's will in such a matter. We must remain sensitive to the evils of war and conscription and we must compromise as little as possible with them, drawing the line where we take our stand at what is for us the earliest possible moment. Wherever that may be and however firm our attitude, we shall still be entangled in the war-effort and shall continue to share in its guilt. A deep humility will become us. But the fact that we cannot extricate ourselves from involvement in war does not mean that it becomes a matter of indifference as to how far we become involved and how clear and vigorous our witness against the evil is. Otherwise, the whole pacifist position becomes untenable.

Love—for God and for all our fellows involved with us in this situation, including the officials of our government and our fellow citizens and fellow Christians who are conscientiously led to engage in war—must be the sole ground for the stand we take and for the way in which we take and express it. That means, also, that we must grow into the position we take, not force ourselves back into a position that does not go far enough, nor forward into a position that may seem "advanced" or "uncompromising."

The other basic concern for all in the Fellowship is that, as we have done in the past, we maintain among ourselves "the unity of the spirit in the bond of love." That we should draw the line at the same point is not fundamental. It is fundamental that we should give heart and hand to each other, however varied our form of witnessing; that each should help the other in making their witness as effective as possible; that no one should be thought a more "orthodox" or "noble" or "sensible" pacifist than the other. The presence or lack of these things indicates whether or not we are indeed a fellowship of the Spirit. If we are that, "all things shall work together for good"; if we are not such a fellowship, it is idle to suppose that in an age like ours it makes much difference what becomes of us.[3]

Having said this, I am eager that the readers of *Fellowship* should understand, as far as it is possible for one human being to enter into the spirit of another, why I am unable to register.

3. Romans 8:28.

1. Registration constitutes, I feel, an integral and important part of the national war effort. The President's proclamation that summons me to register on April 27 states that such registrations are "required to insure victory, final and complete, over the enemies of the United States." As a pacifist I do not wish to sabotage or obstruct others in performing what they regard as their patriotic and Christian duty, but I cannot assist the war effort and I am not free to silence my witness against war. By helping this particular step in the prosecution of the war to proceed smoothly, I should perhaps be making about the most substantial positive contribution that as a minister of the gospel, too old for military or even for physically exacting civilian service, I could make. The very fact that the government attaches so much importance to registration seems to me to indicate that it is not "just a census" but is regarded by those who are charged with the prosecution of war as a valuable gesture of conformity. I feel that I cannot make that contribution to war which, as the Oxford Ecumenical Conference said, involves "compulsory enmity, diabolical outrage against human personality, and a wanton distortion of truth" and is "a defiance of the righteousness of God as revealed in Jesus Christ and Him crucified."[4]

Part of War System

2. Registration is an integral part of a system of conscription for war. To conscript human beings for such a purpose seems to me a crime and a fundamental denial of the democratic faith. If war is truly the only way in which Americans can now defend their homes and loved ones, their civilization and religion, and yet they can be induced to act for these ends only under compulsion by the state, this seems to me to constitute a denial that they are capable of acting as free and responsible human beings. It assumes that the state has to force them to act for their own good and for social ends. The only other explanation for the fact that in no nation can the masses be induced to engage in war except by all sorts of physical and psychological pressures, including conscription, would seem to be that the deep-seated conviction in the normal human being today that war is evil or futile or both is sound and based on truth. But in that case conscription for war is even more definitely a denial of democracy and an outrage against the human spirit. It now seems certain that, barring an experience of national repentance leading to a reversal of our course, conscription in some form, whatever the military outcome of the war, is to be a permanent part of American

4. J. H. Oldham, *The Oxford Conference (Official Report)* (Chicago: Willett, Clark & Company, 1937), 162. This quotation differs insignificantly from the original.

life. In the present historic context that can only mean, in my opinion, that it is a great step toward the establishment of a regime of totalitarianism, wholesale regimentation, in our own land. I believe that I can best serve my country by refusing to give any countenance or consent to this evil.

3. Former Chief Justice Hughes, in an opinion from the bench of the Supreme Court, declared: "In the forum of conscience duty to a moral power higher than the State has always been maintained. . . . The essence of religion is belief in a relation to God involving duties superior to those arising from any human relation."[5]

The Christian church, and any free church, rejects the absolute sovereignty of the state, either over the church or over the conscience of the individual. "God is the sole Lord of conscience." Here is the crux of Christianity's rejection of all totalitarianisms, Nazi, fascist, communist, or any other; for when the state claims absolute sovereignty it degrades the human being, who is a child of God, into the pawn of a human institution. But in relation to conscription for war the American State refuses to recognize freedom of conscience and religion in principle and, instead, embodies in its law and practice the principle of state absolutism.

Thus, citizenship is denied to Christian men and women and persons capable of and actually rendering outstanding service to society, because they will not and cannot swear to "defend the Constitution" by force of arms. The Supreme Court justifies barring from the public schools little children who refuse to salute the flag and so disobey their parents to whom this act seems a direct defiance of the Word of God. And the Selective Service and Training Act under which I am now called to register asserts in effect that, although the State is willing as a matter of expediency to excuse conscientious objectors from service in the armed forces, it nevertheless insists upon its right to compel every man, if it chooses, to do some kind of conscript work as a part of the war effort.

This matter was called to the attention of Congress, but it refused to make provision, as the British Act does, that the man who is adjudged by a suitable tribunal to be sincere in his opposition to any conscript service or in his conviction that the work in which he is engaged is a God-given calling that he may not leave, should be left free in the work that he has chosen or may choose. I cannot by registration put myself in the position of paying lip service or seeming to give inner consent to totalitarian principle and thus countenancing the very thing against which this nation is presumably contending in this war.

5. *United States v. Douglas Clyde Macintosh* 283 US 605, 635 (1931). The punctuation of this quotation differs from that of the original.

The Priesthood of the Believer

4. Two additional considerations strengthen my conviction that I must take a stand at the point of registration. I am an ordained Presbyterian minister. Presumably, if I register, I shall become automatically exempt from conscript service. But I believe that a denial of the doctrine of the priesthood of all believers, and an acceptance of the idea of a priestly class, are involved in the provision that sets ministers and theological students apart from their fellows and gives them automatic exemption. (Incidentally, I believe this is probably a violation of the Constitutional principle of religious liberty.) The idea that a person's work may be a vocation, a God-given task, is a truly religious idea; but that may apply as well to a physician, an artist, or a Brother Lawrence in his kitchen as to an ordained minister.[6] And for religious vocation in this true sense, the conscription act, as I have pointed out, makes no provision.

Apart from ministerial standing, there are considerations of age, etc., that render it most unlikely that I should be called to render any compulsory service, even of a civilian character. If, therefore, I register, I shall at that point make obeisance to the law and to the evil and undemocratic principle that it embodies, and I shall fail to make an effective protest against it. And for the rest I shall be shielded by exemptions provided by this very law, some of them, in my opinion, vicious in character, while younger men who share my views and who have acted upon them are in prison and millions of American boys who perhaps, for the most part, do not share these views are also called upon to sacrifice for the things they cherish.

Some of these conscientious objectors in prison are boys who were willing and even eager to render alternative service of national importance under the Selective Service Act, but the tribunals found them "not sincere" or, though finding them sincere, insisted that they must take non-combatant service in the armed forces. They had no choice, therefore, unless indeed they were insincere, but to refuse induction into the Army, which led to conviction for violation of the law and a prison sentence. To date all efforts to persuade the Selective Service Administration to establish a more satisfactory plan for reviewing such cases have failed. In these circumstances, though I am engaged in work to which I have been called by God and which I pray God may permit me to continue, my conscience was not free to register on April 27.

6. Brother Lawrence, a lay member of a Carmelite monastery in Paris in the 1600s, was assigned to work in the monastery kitchen. Reportedly, it was while working in that kitchen that he developed the spirituality described in his classic *The Practice of the Presence of God*.

Daily the voices of devoted and intelligent leaders of thought and action in this county proclaim that we must find more effective ways to demonstrate to the masses of people everywhere—including the colored peoples of Asia, Africa, South America, and our own land—that we are offering, as an alternative to Hitlerism, not a mere return to the *status quo ante* but a genuine, creative and thrilling advance in the concepts and practices of democracy. It is generally recognized that it would be perilous to postpone such a demonstration until the war is over. One way to prove our will and our ability to make democracy work and triumph would be, at the very time when dictatorships degrade the individual into a pawn of the state, to give more explicit and unqualified recognition to the dignity of the individual. At the very time when the State seeks elsewhere to make itself absolute, we could set limits here to the demands that the State makes, so that people may be free to give an absolute allegiance to the community of humankind and to God who is its Father. At the very time when rigid conformity and regimentation seek to bind the human spirit in iron fetters, we should make room here for that non-conformity and creativity in personal and social life that have been the glory of American history and without which human progress must end.

As we face the unknown future together as members of our far-flung Fellowship of Reconciliation, there is still, I think, no more certain and helpful guide than that which has been found these many years in the closing paragraph of our Statement of Purpose:

> It is intended that members shall work out these purposes in their own ways. . . . The movement depends not upon a large number of nominal adherents, but upon those who, accepting the principles fully for themselves, will give time individually and in groups to thinking out what is implied, and will set themselves seriously to apply their conclusions. Such an endeavor inevitably brings a consciousness of insufficiency; but strength and wisdom, far beyond the limits of our present experience, are available to all who open their lives to the leading of the Spirit of God.

Civil Rights, Cold War, and the Church

18

What the Bible Teaches About Freedom (1943)

Writing to both African Americans and whites, Muste explores the narrative history of the people of Israel in the Hebrew Scriptures as an archetype of an oppressed people. He warns against the age-old tendency of oppressed people to essentially exchange roles with their oppressors and argues that equal fellowship regardless of race should be the goal. As a result, violence is not a helpful method for combating discrimination like that codified in Jim Crow laws. Of course, inaction is even worse. The NAACP and the March on Washington Movement both distributed this pamphlet, the substance of which Muste had previously given in numerous sermons.[1]

More than three thousand years ago there was a group of people who were being persecuted as a minority. Through most of their history,

1. Jo Ann Robinson, *Abraham Went Out: A Biography of A. J. Muste* (Philadelphia: Temple University Press, 1981), 110. The exact origins of Muste's desire to combat racism and racial inequality are not known. It was clearly present as early as his involvement with the labor movement. Later, he supported efforts by conscientious objectors

before and since, they have been a persecuted minority. They still are. They are the Jews.

Long ago these people made a tremendous discovery about what true religion and true religious leadership are. You can find the story in your Bible.

They made this discovery during a time of great trouble, while they were exiled from their own land. But there were persons and events in their past that helped them in thinking the thing through, and in telling about what religion is they tied the story up with this past.

Moses: "Let My People Go!"

They tied it up with Moses and an earlier experience of exile and deliverance in which he played a big part.[2]

Moses lived in a period of dictatorship. His people were slaves. The bosses made them work under a speed-up system, and committed horrible atrocities, such as trying to kill all the boy-babies born to the Jews.

Moses himself was saved from such a death only because his mother hid him in a reed basket in the Nile River. There he was found by the daughter of the Pharaoh, which is what they called their dictator in Egypt. (Notice how much *Pharaoh* sounds like *Führer*!) The princess took Moses to the royal palace and had him brought up as her own son.

When Moses was a young man he became curious about the Hebrew slaves, and one day went to the brickyards where some of them were working. The first thing he saw was an Egyptian boss hitting a Hebrew laborer. Moses was a powerful young man. He lost his temper. He hit the boss—and killed him! He buried the body hastily in the sand, and went back to the palace.

But a fire had been kindled in Moses' heart, a fire of concern about his people and their suffering. The next day he went back to the hot brickyards. Then he learned two things that those who try to help their fellows often discover.

He found, first, that slaves often spend as much time and energy fighting each other as they do fighting their common oppressors, and second,

---

to end prison segregation during the Second World War and helped make civil rights a major focus of the Fellowship of Reconciliation. He mentored a number of prominent leaders of the civil rights movement, including Bayard Rustin, who later claimed that when he was an advisor to Martin Luther King Jr., he never made a difficult decision without talking about it with Muste first (see Robinson, *Abraham Went Out*, 118).

2. The story of Moses is told in the book of Exodus.

that slaves do not always welcome their deliverers. They get accustomed to being slaves. They cling to the ills they have, as Shakespeare pointed out, rather than fly to others that they know not of![3] Even after they have been freed, if freedom brings hardship, they may want to go back "to the fleshpots of Egypt."[4]

This time Moses found two Hebrews fighting each other. When he rebuked them, they turned on him and said, "Who made you our boss? Do you mean to kill us as you did that Egyptian yesterday?"[5]

Moses feared that in order to turn suspicion away from themselves they would tell the Egyptians that he killed the boss. He concluded that it might not be healthy to stay around those parts, so he ran away.

On his flight he met a young woman and her sisters who were having a hard time getting water for their flocks. Moses still felt in a fighting mood. He drove away some shepherds who were bothering the women. Later he fell in love with one of the women, and presently they were married. Then—so the Bible goes on to tell—his father-in-law gave him a job and he settled down to a nice comfortable life, raising a family and feeding the flocks of his father-in-law Jethro.

God Is All Burned Up About Something

Only, after a while, God came into the picture. What was the sign that God had come? It was a bush that burned and burned and did not stop burning. Moses had had a fire kindled in his heart once, but it went out, or at least died down. God is the being whose heart does not stop burning, in whom the flame does not die down.

What was God all burned up about? The voice that came out of the bush said, "I have seen the affliction of my people that are in Egypt and have heard their cry by reason of their oppressors."[6] It was the physical, economic, and spiritual suffering, the injustice, the degradation to which actual people were subjected here on earth, that caused God concern.

And the proof that God had entered into Moses, and that Moses had really been "converted," was that he had to go back and identify himself with his enslaved people—"organize them into Brickmakers' Union Number

3. William Shakespeare, *Hamlet*, 3.1.81–82.

4. Exodus 16:3. In this passage, the Israelites lament the lack of food in the desert ("fleshpots" refers to pots of meat). In the story, God responds by miraculously feeding them with manna.

5. Exodus 2:14.

6. Exodus 3:7.

One"—and lead them out of hunger and slavery into freedom and into "a good land, and a large, a land flowing with milk and honey."[7]

At the head of the Ten Commandments stand these great words: "I am the Lord thy God which have brought thee out of the land of Egypt, *out of the slave-house*. Thou shalt have no other God before me"—before this God who is in the hearts of his prophets as the eternal flame that will not let them rest where there is injustice and inequality until these have been done away with and people set about building God's house instead of the slave-house.[8]

To be religious, the Hebrews discovered, is to get out of Egypt into Canaan; to refuse to be slaves or contented draft-horses; to build brotherhood in freedom—because that is what people, the children of God, were created to do!

And religious leaders are those who identify themselves with the oppressed, so that people may carry out this, their true mission in the world.

Injustice and Tyranny Don't Work

The world and human beings are so made that you can't organize life securely on injustice and oppression. All kinds of things happen to "ball things up." The top dogs always get to fighting each other about the spoils. Besides, people really can work efficiently only in freedom, and if oppression is pushed beyond a certain point, people either stop producing anything to speak of, or, because they don't find living and having children worthwhile, they may even just die off (as happened to the slave population in the Roman Empire)—or else they revolt.

So, in a way, the oppressed always go free. And, very often, the minority gets its chance to become a majority.

What happens then, when the tables are turned? What usually happened was simply that the tables *were* turned. The "minority," the oppressed, promptly proved that they were humans, too, made in the same mold as the oppressors, and started to behave very much as their former exploiters had done.

That happened in the history of Israel, too. There came a time in Canaan, the Land of Promise, when the Hebrews decided to be like other peoples, who had kingdoms and empires. They began to organize armies to fight, plunder, and rape. At first, of course, this was just in "self-defense," to make themselves "secure." But it wasn't very long before they became frankly imperialistic. *The kingdom was not completely established until the*

7. Exodus 3:8.

8. Exodus 20:2–3.

time of David. His son, Solomon, was already an arch-imperialist. Nothing could satisfy his appetite, as illustrated by his thousand wives and concubines, symbols chiefly of his *political* alliances and ambitions.

But exploitation and imperialism do not work for the former underdogs, either. Under Solomon's son—it worked that fast—the Hebrew kingdom already was split in two! Before a great while one of the parts was destroyed. The other led the existence of an ancient Belgium or Czechoslovakia—one of the little countries on whose soil big countries like to do their fighting. Presently this Hebrew kingdom also was shattered and the people driven into exile.

Still later the wheel turned again, and under the patronage of a benevolent monarch named Cyrus a little band of Hebrew exiles went back to the dear homeland. One of those who went back was a priest named Ezra.[9]

When Ezra first thought of making the long journey through territory infested by robbers and hostile armies he decided to ask the king for an armed escort. But then—much like Gandhi—"he proclaimed a fast!" For he said, "I was ashamed to ask of the king a band of soldiers and horsemen to help us against the enemy in the way because we had often told the king, 'the hand of our God is upon all that seek him for good.'"[10] Ezra was not like the clergyman who, after Britain passed through a crisis, wrote, "We must give fervent thanks to Almighty God for delivering us and now we must be careful not to be caught in such a defenseless position again."[11]

The Bitter Fruits of Power

These events in the life of the Hebrew people were taking place at a time of turmoil in the history of the ancient world. Presently Alexander the Great appeared and conquered Palestine. Under some of his successors the Hebrews had to endure horrible persecution again. Of course, there were Fifth Columnists among the Jews, and these helped the infamous Antiochus Epiphanes get control over their people. There were others who refused to toady to the conqueror, and met his attacks with non-resistance and non-cooperation, and died as martyrs. But there were still others who said this was not enough. You must fight fire with fire, give the conquerors some of their own medicine. So there was a heroic revolt led by the Maccabees, and the Hebrews were an independent nation again.

9. The story of Ezra is told in Ezra 7–10.

10. Ezra 8:21–22.

11. The source of this quotation is unknown.

This time they said that although they must have a king, the people would elect him. They would be democratic about it. But alas, the old business of the oppressed behaving like oppressors as soon as they got into power occurred again. The first king in the new line, Simon, was murdered by his son-in-law, who nevertheless did not succeed in becoming king. So Simon's son, John Hyrcanus, succeeded him and promptly set out on a career of conquest that included forcing the Jewish religion on conquered peoples!

Members of the Jewish ruling class quarreled among themselves, and presently made the mistake of inviting Pompey, a Roman general waging war in those parts, to arbitrate their dispute. Pompey brought their land under the control of the Romans.

By the time Jesus was born, Judea was ruled by Herod, a puppet of the Roman Caesar. As his first act of kingly power, Herod put to death all the old aristocracy. He introduced a spy system like Hitler's Gestapo or Stalin's Ogpu. Herod assassinated Mariamne, his own wife, her mother, and three sons.

Not many decades after Jesus died, Jerusalem was razed to the ground, Palestine devastated, and the Jews scattered in an exile from their country, which was to last for eighteen centuries. This was after a war against the Romans in which Jews fought each other about as bitterly as they fought the foreign dictator. As one Jewish scholar has recently put it: "Amidst a terrorism comparable only to that which took place later in the French and Russian revolutions, the Jewish state, like a building burning from within and without, collapsed in the flames of war."[12]

The Way of Jesus

It was in such times that Jesus lived. He knew the history of his people that we have sketched; it was a part of him. You cannot understand him unless you see him in the midst of all this.

One thing that was not true of Jesus is that he told his people simply to submit to dictatorship and oppression. No one could have been more un-submissive to human laws, institutions, and dignitaries than he. No one ever learned subservience or false humility from him.

Jesus began his public career with the proclamation: "the kingdom of God is at hand."[13] It was like someone saying today, "the revolution is here; the end of the reign of oppressors, native and foreign; the beginning of the rule of justice and brotherhood."

12. The source of this quotation is unknown.

13. Mark 1:15.

If Jesus had been safe and respectable, the powers of his time would not have put him away as they did. Rulers are almost always somewhat dumb and often very dumb, but not that dumb.

What Jesus objected to was not the great religious act of human beings moving out of Egypt into Canaan, out of bondage and insecurity into freedom, security and peace. What grieved him was that people were forever moving out of bondage—*into bondage*! They escaped from the violence of another to fasten the chains of violence on themselves. This terrible evil circle must be broken.

Jesus said: "It is really very simple. You cannot expect Satan to cast out Satan. You cannot overcome evil with evil. Evil can be overcome only by its opposite, good."[14]

Jesus Shows the Way to Freedom

Now let us see if we can describe in our own language, in terms of our own problems, how Jesus believed people could overcome evil and injustice in such a way as not to fasten new chains of tyranny and injustice on themselves.

1. *The way to overcome your enemy is to love them.*[15] This may sound sentimental or positively crazy to you. You may think that if large numbers of ordinary blacks have to begin by loving the white enemies who oppress them and Jim Crow them, we may as well stop talking about nonviolence as a method for liberating black people. But Jesus is still a mighty force after nineteen centuries. It may not be wise to dismiss him as a fool. Besides, the leaders of most of the great religions have said much the same things about the power of love over brute force that Jesus did. Let us see how much common sense there may be in these teachings.

When we cry out for justice and equality, on what do we base our demand? We say that racial discrimination is contrary to the findings of science and the principles of reason and religion. People—all people—are human beings, members of one family, children of one God. Discrimination denies people their standing as human beings, shuts them out of the family, deprives them of the moral dignity with which God clothed them. So runs the argument for democracy and equality.

14. See Mark 3:23, Romans 12:17, 21.

15. The headings and numbered subheadings are from the Fellowship of Reconciliation's 1943 pamphlet version of this sermon; they were omitted when it was reprinted in Nat Hentoff's *The Essays of A. J. Muste*.

For Jesus, who saw all people thus as sisters and brothers, the worst sin is the denial of brotherhood by drawing lines that shut some in and others out. When people think of Jesus' symbol of wickedness, they do not think of robbers, or prostitutes, or bloody tyrants, or Quislings like the publicans of his time who became tax-gatherers for the foreign dictator. Jesus' symbol of sinfulness was the Pharisee. The Pharisee was a good and respectable person; a devoted churchman and an ardent patriot. But the Pharisee set himself apart from other people; he prided himself on his separateness from them. He prayed: "God, I thank thee that I am not as other men are . . . or even as this publican."[16] But suppose that the publican in his turn had turned around and prayed: "God, I thank thee that I am not as other people are—or even as this Pharisee"? Then he would have been a Pharisee too, shutting people out, putting them in a lower rank.

We cannot have it both ways. Either there is a fundamental kinship among all people—in the old Quaker phrase, there is "that of God" in everyone—or else there is not. If there is not, and we are not all fundamentally the same breed, then there never can be any real understanding among people. They simply think and feel differently. In that case, whenever any real difference develops among them, people can only fight it out and those who prove the strongest, most clever, and most ruthless will always be on top. There will be no point in crying over it or getting up a lot of moral indignation about it. There is no question of morals between a tiger and a cobra, or between two-legged animals that belong to essentially different breeds that have no kinship with each other.

Another thing, if people are not members of one family in God, then the pattern of human society will always be that of domination-subordination. There will always be some top dogs and many underdogs. And then Hitler and all the imperialists and exploiters and exponents of racism are right and the idea of a democratic society is bunk, as they say it is.

But if the oppressed black people and their white friends today accept the biblical, democratic concept of the kinship of all people and reject racism, then we have to be governed in our own actions by this fact of human kinship or we shall only be plotting our own defeat.

That means that we must always remember that our enemy, the exploiter, is not an abstract word—not a nation or race or class, for example. A nation, race or class cannot have pneumonia or chickenpox, cannot be warm or cold, cannot cry or laugh. Only human beings can. And these who injure and degrade us are human beings, very much like ourselves. Our

16. Luke 18:11.

strategy must always be based on that fact. The human in us must try to reach and touch the human in them.

Our object always will be to build up a family relationship, a brotherhood and a democratic society with them; to put an end to separateness and to the top dog-underdog business. When the Japanese took Hong Kong from the British, they put white men in front of the Chinese rickshaws, and then made a point of putting colored folk—Chinese, Hindus, Filipinos—in the seats, telling the white men to "hurry up." People in this country who had never been much shocked when Chinese coolies were used like animals were shocked very much. The Japanese broadcast the news throughout Asia and many colored people chuckled and thought that it served the dirty whites right.

They were both wrong. Nothing really had changed. It is no better and no worse for white people or colored people to be humiliated and exploited. The only worthwhile objective is to have them walk together as sisters and brothers; to destroy the pattern of domination and slavery altogether.

One of the brilliant young black writers recently said it—"The fallacy is that the Negro is a problem both *in vacuo* and *in toto*, where in reality the Negro is only an equation in a problem of many equations, an equally important one of which is the white man. To know and understand and love the Negro is not enough. One must know and understand and love the white man as well. . . . It was in this direction, in the direction of knowledge and understanding and love that I had come a little way."[17] That is J. Saunders Redding in the closing pages of *No Day of Triumph*, which is a terribly realistic and not at all a sentimental book.

The emphasis on problem rather than conflict, on understanding rather than victory, is another technique that flows from Jesus' teaching that we must love our enemies because they are our sisters and brothers. Ordinarily when differences occur, we get all emotional and hysterical about it. We think in terms of God's hosts versus the devil's, the good versus the evil, the people who are "perfectly willing to listen to reason" versus those who "don't understand anything except force"—and our side being, of course, God's host and the good and the rational! The Hebrews of old were always doing that. They blamed the devilish Egyptians and Babylonians. If only they would behave better, or were not on top! The prophets always came back at them and said: You should repent first; that is, change your focus on this thing. You and the Babylonians and Egyptians are all in the same boat, all faced with a problem. Devote your energy to solving it.

17. J. Saunders Redding, *No Day of Triumph* (New York: Harper & Brothers, 1942), 339–40. This quotation differs insignificantly from the original.

The oppressor is always involved in the same perplexing and calamitous situation with the oppressed. How obvious that is in the situation in India today. The whole future of the British in the war and afterward is tied up with what they do in India. How true it is also of whites and blacks in this country today. The black problem is the white problem. The white problem is the black problem. So we can always include the "enemy" in our strategy—the enemy as a human being—and the black person can say to white folks today: "Here we are in this mess. Obviously, it cannot go on this way. We cannot continue to accept this discrimination and degradation, even though submission to it seems to have certain initial advantages, and resistance may bring suffering upon us. But neither can you continue to practice this discrimination that has brought us all to this sorry pass, and the continuance of which can lead only to more woe. Let us then face our common problem together."

Thus to recognize the essential humanity of the enemy and to see, as Gandhi has emphasized, that the changing of the enemy's will and spirit is involved in all real overcoming of evil, is also to recognize that the enemy in the situation is one's "other self." It is, in the practical, social sense, to obey the great command: "Thou shalt love thy neighbor—including the Samaritan, the publican, the enemy—as thyself."[18]

From this flow two other basic approaches in overcoming evil which Jesus taught and practiced.

Openly Refuse

2. *Openly refuse to submit or conform to laws that deny love and brotherhood.* We must be true to ourselves, to our moral dignity, to the spirit of God in whose image we are made. When people have lost all respect for themselves, they are no longer human. That is why we strive so desperately to keep a little self-respect. But people who grovel before another, or before laws and customs that degrade them—as Hitler's laws degrade the Jews and Jim Crow degrades blacks—are wounded in their self-respect. If they continue to grovel, their self-respect, their essential self, will die.

What do people do under these circumstances? Too often they do obey the evil laws and submit to the degrading customs, unless they can sneak out of doing so. But sneaking does not make for self-respect either. So very often, when they think they can succeed in a revolt, and perhaps even put themselves on top and bind oppressive laws on others, they strike back. They demand justice from an evil government or institution and, as Gandhi

18. Leviticus 19:18, Matthew 22:29, Mark 12:31, Luke 10:27.

puts it, they say: "We will hurt you, if you do not give this." When they do not like certain laws, they "break the heads of the lawgivers."[19]

Where they or their own nation or group is the victim, nearly everybody believes that it is a noble thing thus to strike back. Every nation and race reveres as liberators and heroes those who were successful in thus striking back. Of course those who struck back and lost are not remembered or, if remembered, are probably regarded as rash fools. Of course, too, the liberator of one people or group is likely to be regarded as a scoundrel by another. However, probably everybody would agree that those who consider themselves grievously wronged and enslaved and who strike back are morally on a higher plane than those who submit to evil in a cowardly or passive fashion.

Nevertheless, fighting back against laws and customs that degrade people is not a solution. Suppose, as often happens, you are not strong enough to organize and fight back? Must the crucifying of the human spirit go on? Does wrong become right if the wronged are weak?

If black people in this country today were to resort to violence in order to achieve liberation, it would serve chiefly to give fascist forces the excuse to take power openly. Does that mean that blacks must continue to submit to being Jim-Crowed? Do the preachers, black or white, believe that the God of Moses and Jesus desires this?

Furthermore, as we have already shown, fighting back does not change things essentially. At most it may reverse the role of the top dogs and the underdogs. J. Saunders Redding, whom I quoted a moment ago, wrote in the same book about the communist movement: "What I had seen of it did not convince me that it was interested in broadening the basis of human relationships but rather that it aimed only at transposing them, so that those at the top—the rich and the mighty—would come to the mud at the bottom. It seemed not to be interested in leveling barriers of caste and class and race but only in scaling them. Surely this imbruting struggle is not all."[20]

Faced with the wastefulness and futility of violence as a means of righting things in a fundamental way, many say that the oppressed—as for example black people today—should stick to gradual, democratic ways of amending laws and customs. Unquestionably this procedure has its place, and an important one. Efforts of black organizations and their friends along these lines must continue and be strengthened. In dealing with certain

19. M. K. Gandhi, *Indian Home Rule* (Madras: Ganesh, 1922), 82, 88. The punctuation of these quotations differs from that of the original.

20. Redding, *No Day of Triumph*, 113. This quotation differs insignificantly from the original.

conditions ordinary educational, legislative, and judicial processes are all that need to be used.

There are, however, other spiritual and social issues that cannot be met satisfactorily, or at all, in this way. Henry David Thoreau, the great American exponent of nonviolence and civil disobedience, pointed out one of the difficulties in the days of the Fugitive Slave Law. Such a law, he said, "requires you to be the agent of injustice to another." By obeying it while you work to amend it, you become an evildoer and a supporter of evil. The very fact that you are ordinarily a law-abiding and conscientious person actually may make your influence for perpetuating this evil greater. "Those who, while they disapprove of the character and measures of a government, yield to it their allegiance and support are undoubtedly its most conscientious supporters, and so frequently the most serious obstacles to reform."[21]

As there are laws and customs that require one to be "the agent of injustice to another," so there are laws and practices that directly and deeply bind and degrade one's own spirit—the laws, for example, that at various times have forbidden Christians to practice their religion or teach it to their children. Also, the law that makes people agents of injustice to another may serve to destroy the self-respect and the soul of this other if they yield to it.

The laws against the Jews in Germany, for example, if enforced or accepted degrade both Germans and Jews. The same is true of those who practice and those who submit to Jim Crow in the United States. Every time such laws are obeyed the deepest sin is committed, the Spirit of God is denied and trodden underfoot. It will not do to say: "I will obey, submit, but hope and work for change."

What is one to do then? Those spiritual leaders whom we most revere have given one answer: *Refuse to obey or conform to such laws as deny love and brotherhood.* The most sacred law and custom of Jesus' own group was that relating to the Sabbath. Jesus broke it openly, unmistakably, completely. When the three young men in the book of Daniel were told they must worship an idol, they said: "Be it known unto thee, O King, that we will not." When Daniel was forbidden to worship his God as he had been accustomed to, "he went into his house and he kneeled upon his knees three times a day and prayed, as he did aforetime."[22] If the law is of such a nature that it requires you to be the agent of injustice to another, declared Thoreau: "then I say, break the law."[23]

21. Henry David Thoreau, "Civil Disobedience," in *Walden and Civil Disobedience* (New York: Signet Classics, 2012), 284, 282.

22. Daniel 3:18, 6:10.

23. Thoreau, "Civil Disobedience," 284.

Often people are afraid to break such taboos and laws as Jim Crow today. They tell themselves and others that it is dangerous, that it will make trouble and breed anarchy if the law and practice are violated. Gandhi calls the idea that such a law must be kept a "superstition." He is exactly right, for superstition means making something real and sacred out of something that is unreal and unholy.

He adds: "So long as the superstition that men should obey unjust laws exists, so long will their slavery exist. And a passive resister alone"—that is, one who will not cooperate with, who breaks the law nonviolently—"can remove such a superstition."[24] Jesus said essentially the same thing about his people's Sabbath observance: "The Sabbath was made for man, not man for the Sabbath."[25]

It is our timidity and blindness that makes us observe manmade law while we break God's law. We keep up Jim Crow practices, for example, because, whites and blacks alike, we think only of the unpleasant and dangerous results that might follow if we do anything else. We simply do not see the frightful sin we constantly commit by acting upon the Pharisee's principle of excluding and degrading others: "God, I thank thee that I am not as other men are."[26]

If we really did see the truth, in the light of God's law, it would become impossible for us, from that moment on, to observe a single Jim Crow law or practice. We would be impelled to act on Thoreau's challenge: "Let your life be a counter-friction to the machine. . . . Cast your whole vote, not a strip of paper merely, but your whole influence."[27] A minority is powerless when it conforms to the majority; but it is irresistible when it clogs with its whole weight. As with the early Christians, "They only can force me who obey a higher law than I. They force me to become like themselves."[28]

Before such faithfulness to God we might find unbrotherly institutions crumbling much more easily and quickly than we had supposed. For it is not God, not anything in the true nature of life or the universe, that

24. Gandhi, *Indian Home Rule*, 89.

25. Mark 2:27.

26. Luke 18:11.

27. Thoreau, "Civil Disobedience," 284, 286.

28. Ibid., 289. Here I have followed the wording found in Hentoff's *The Essays of A. J. Muste*, except that I removed the unnecessary ellipsis that preceded the quotation in both versions. The original pamphlet version reads: "A minority is powerless when it conforms to the majority; it is not even a minority then; but it is irresistible when it clogs with its whole weight. '. . . They only can force me who obey a higher law than I. They force me to become like themselves.'"

sustains them, but only the fact that we uphold them by our support, active or passive.

Wake Up the Conscience of the Privileged

3. *Do not permit the conscience of the privileged and the powerful to sleep.* If for the oppressed and their friends the conclusion to be drawn from the moral dignity and kinship of all people is the duty of nonconformity with evil laws and practices, the conclusion for those who have privilege and power is that they must not eat the fruits of their position in smugness and peace. It is when we realize that they do have consciences and refuse to permit them to slumber that we deal with the privileged in the one way that recognizes their moral worth and our kinship with them.

Here again we confront a basic problem in social action. Generally, the oppressed take one of two attitudes toward the privileged. Some obsequiously accept injustice and even regard the oppressor as a benefactor. He is "such a nice boss." So the master is morally justified; he tells himself that he is waxing great and rich, not at the expense of his victims but "for their own good." Or else the oppressed pour out their scorn, hate, and thirst for revenge upon the master group. Again the latter continue to feel morally vindicated and secure: "The underdogs are no better than we are; they simply want to put themselves in our place."

Often both of these attitudes are found side by side in the same person. Many a Jew in Jesus' day would bow obsequiously to a Roman dignitary and then spit out of the corner of his mouth at him when he was past. Jesus did not spit out of the corner of his mouth at the conquerors of his people; neither did he do groveling obeisance to them.

Space does not permit consideration of the many instances in the Gospels when Jesus confronted people, especially the privileged and mighty, with the moral realities of their position and the hypocrisy that underlay it. For example, to his hometown people who expected a flattering speech from the hometown boy who had made good, he administered a rebuke to their nationalism and to all group pride: "There were many lepers in Israel in the days of Naaman the Syrian; to none of them was the prophet sent, but to this foreigner." To the virtuous, he said, "This publican is justified before God rather than you"; to the philanthropists: "This poor widow who has contributed a penny has given incalculably more than you all."[29] So must we find ways to keep conscience in those who impose discrimination on black

29. Luke 4:27, Matthew 21:31, Mark 12:43.

people awake and hurt, with the hurt that heals in the end because it makes the oppressors whole and unites them with those they have injured.

We have to understand that when we speak to the conscience of our fellows, we have to come with truth and with principles, not with half-truths and expediency. There is often timidity and evasion in the way blacks and their friends present their case. They want such and such improvements in the condition of black people, but they suggest or permit it to be understood that this does not mean equality in *all* respects. We are going to "do justice" to black people, but things will remain very much as they have been. And we give various reasons why it would be prudent or clever to introduce these reforms. And truly there is a good deal of ground for such arguments. Herbert Agar, editor of the *Louisville Courier-Journal*, writes in *A Time For Greatness*: "We can no longer think in terms of what we are willing to 'do' for the colored peoples of the world. That is not the question. We must force ourselves to understand that the question is whether *we* can join the human race in time, while the white man has still the chance to be treated as an equal in a world where the people of his color are a small minority."[30]

But all this misses the main point. The real question, the only question, is whether or not we believe the great truth that God taught Peter in the vision on the housetop and that caused Peter later to say: "I am a man"—not a Jew or Roman or Greek—"and God hath taught me not to call any man common or unclean."[31] Whether we shall so act that we can say honestly as did the early church: "In Christ Jesus there is neither Jew nor Greek"—white, black, yellow, brown.[32] In Christian teaching and in democratic concepts there is *no moral basis for Jim Crow*, for segregation of any kind, no basis for anything but complete brotherhood. In the face of that all questions of expediency pale into insignificance and all half-measures are mockeries. In face of that, the attitude of the churches and of Christian people, North and South, smells of the same hypocrisy that Jesus was constantly exposing in his contemporaries.

We have to confront these Christians with the stark question—whether, in this matter of Jim Crow, theirs is the program of the one who says, "I am a Christian, therefore," or the program of the person who says, "I am a Christian, but." So long as people can believe that there is some moral justification for Jim Crow it can endure. As soon as the churches quit

30. Herbert Agar, *A Time For Greatness* (Boston: Little & Brown, 1942), 63. Emphasis Muste's.

31. Acts 10:26, 28.

32. Galatians 3:28.

pussy-footing on the issue and people know that Jim Crow has no ethical and Christian justification, its end will be in sight.

Oppose Evil

4. *Oppose evil wherever it shows itself.* Especially oppose evil in yourself. Much of the time people generate no real power in combating an evil because they are not really against the evil at all. In the United States today, for example, we are against racism when practiced by Hitler and the Japanese militarists, but we practice it ourselves against black people. We are against occupation and rule by a foreign power in Belgium, Norway, and so on; but we want it to continue in India. We are against concentration camps, but we put our own citizens of Japanese descent into them. Such things show that we are not really against these evils at all; we are simply against those results that happen to inconvenience ourselves. No wonder this device of casting out Satan by the power of Satan gets us nowhere.

This is why the great teachers of nonviolence always have taught their followers that before they can really fight to overcome evil, they must purify themselves. It is common knowledge that the United Nations have suffered tremendously in this war because in their treatment of black people and in other respects they have not practiced the democracy they preach.[33] They have enabled the Japanese to pose before millions of Asiatics as "liberators" from white domination. No one can estimate how many American and British lads have had to die and will die from our failure to destroy what Gandhi calls "the canker of white supremacy."[34]

Black people also will be strong exactly in the proportion to which they put their own house in order and remove from their own midst the evils they condemn when practiced by whites. Among blacks, as among other exploited groups, there are those who will exploit their own people as ruthlessly as any outsider does. Black leadership is often guilty of selfishness, smugness, and pettiness. Many blacks are as self-seeking and cynical as those who oppress them. Unless they develop a tremendous moral and

33. Muste is referring to the allies who were fighting against Nazi Germany, not to what we now know as the United Nations, which had not yet been founded when this piece was published.

34. Mahatma Gandhi, "The Bombay Interview," *Harijan* 9, no. 19 (May 24, 1942), 168. Gandhi, writing during the Second World War, argues that "Both America and Britain lack the moral basis for engaging in this war, unless they put their own houses in order. . . . They have no right to talk about protecting democracies and protecting civilization and human freedom until the canker of white supremacy is destroyed in its entirety."

spiritual dynamic themselves, blacks will not be delivered from Jim Crow. Will the black churches meet this challenge?

You Can Overcome

5. *You can overcome evil if you care enough.* Care enough to be willing to die in order that the evil may be overcome. This is the law of the seed, Jesus pointed out, which bears no fruit except it fall into the ground and die.[35] This is the way of the cross.

Few expressions are used more often than the saying: "If a man would save his life, he shall lose it; he who loses his life, shall find it."[36] Yet people will not face up to the truth and the inexorability of that law they talk about so often. They want an easy, cheap, painless way out. Let any black reader of these lines, or white friend of black people, sit down some time for five minutes and ask yourself how often you have been willing to die that Jim Crow might be abolished—yes, how often you have been willing to risk a little unpopularity, a day in jail, the loss of a job. White people generally have bad consciences about Jim Crow and want to "do something about it"; but as soon as it appears that this may result in some disturbance, they draw back. They think God will be indulgent; that in this case there will be remission of sins without shedding of blood. But if there is any sense in the Christian symbol of the cross at all, this cannot be.

There will be suffering, there will be a fearful price to be paid for removing Jim Crow. There is always the choice of inflicting suffering upon others or taking it upon ourselves. The Christian way is to refuse to cooperate with evil and to accept the consequence. The consequence is the cross. Only as blacks and whites who are concerned with abolishing the denial of brotherhood as represented by Jim Crow take up the cross of suffering can Jim Crow be done away with. When we are ready for that, God himself will give us victory.

This idea that evil cannot be overcome by inflicting suffering in the effort to stop it, but by accepting suffering unto death rather than acquiescing in the evil, profiting by it, or obeying its command, seems to many sheer "moonshine." If we reflect for a moment, however, we shall see that it is sober realism.

For one thing, as Gandhi has pointed out, unjust laws and practices survive because people obey them and conform to them. This they do out of fear. There are things they dread more than the continuance of the evil.

35. John 12:24.

36. Matthew 16:25, Mark 8:35, Luke 9:24.

So long as there is still something the oppressor can take away that we fear to lose or selfishly cling to, their power over us continues. So long as we are still afraid of death we can be bought off. We are not yet hard enough to overcome evil. That is why so much thought and effort are expended in trying to drug or paralyze the fear of death in the soldier. So also when we become true, i.e., fearless, nonviolent resisters, we have the courage against which evil cannot stand. The degree of suffering we, blacks and whites, can endure for our cause of establishing brotherhood without qualification in race relationships will determine the measure of our success. Gandhi said, "Who is the true warrior—he who keeps death always as a bosom friend, or he who controls the death of others? . . . That nation is great which rests its head upon death as a pillow. Those who defy death are free from all fear."[37]

Back in 1933 when Hitler already had come to power a great statesman whom most people would consider more "practical" than Gandhi stated the same truth. Thomas G. Masaryk, the first president of the Czech Republic, expressed confidence that democracy would prevail. "How can it most speedily be brought about?" he was asked, and answered, "Follow your convictions. Do not merely talk your politics. Live them. Tell the truth and do not steal. Above all, do not be afraid to die."[38]

To put it another way, the capacity to suffer unto death on behalf of our fellows is the real power that makes human life possible, and creates and maintains human society. If it were the regular thing that in a pinch the mother sacrificed her babe in order to save herself, the human family long since would have ceased to exist. Not even animal life, for that matter, can be sustained on that basis of each for him or herself and the devil take the hindmost. Thus it is that whenever love that will suffer unto death is manifested, whenever a true crucifixion takes place, unconquerable power is released into the stream of history. The intuition that says that God has been let loose on the earth when such devotion is manifested is absolutely sound.

This is the true road to liberation. Chiefly, humankind must always depend on its minorities, on the downtrodden, to show the way, since the privileged are too much bound by their vested interests. Gandhi, in India, is practicing nonviolence today on a great scale. If the black churches of this country were to give the lead to their own people and their friends in the use of this basically Christian way of redemption, it would constitute another great step toward the achievement of a revolution greater and more beneficent than all the revolutions of the past.

37. Gandhi, *Indian Home Rule*, 91–92.

38. Edgar Ansel Mower, "Tomáš G. Masaryk," in *Dictators and Democrats*, ed. Lawrence Fernsworth (New York: Robert M. McBride, 1941), 185. Originally from a 1933 interview in the *Chicago Daily News*.

19

The Man on the Cross Against the Atomic Bomb (1947)

In this chapter of Muste's book, Not by Might: Christianity, the Way to Human Decency, *he responds to problems raised by the Second World War and the use of the atomic bomb by the United States. Muste deconstructs the anti-pacifist argument that it is better to use sinful and violent means to defend others against violence and oppression than it is to stand by and do nothing. Instead, he argues that Jesus taught nonviolence—that there are better ways to combat evil than by resorting to evil ourselves. In the previous two chapters he had discussed "The Individual Conscience Against the Atomic Bomb" and "Love Against the Atomic Bomb."*

What, then, is the ultimate risk involved in refusing to resort to violence, to try to cast out Satan by Satan, to do evil that good may come? This brings us to the final consideration that we must face, the profoundest mystery of human life and the moral universe.

In the play *Jakobowski and the Colonel*, Jakobowski, the refugee, says to a Nazi engaged in tormenting certain victims: "There is one advantage the hunted has over the hunter—that he never becomes the hunter."[1] The inference is that the victim has an overpowering, an infinite advantage over their tormentor. The victim is the fortunate one of the two. The victim is blessed. The victim is to be envied.

This is the implication of what we have been saying about the moral order, and conscience, and the nature of humanity and the universe. The moral order either does not exist at all, or it is the supreme good, the ultimate value, for the sake of which people will gladly "count all things but loss."[2] All human beings are creations of spirit and equal before God, or else none is. We are all of us parts of a spiritual unity, bound together so that what happens to any, happens to me, or there is no unity. The maintenance of that unity by love in every moment, to every person, is either the ultimate good or it is sheer illusion.

When a person suffers cold, hunger, thirst, injustice, imprisonment, slavery, humiliation, it is a terrible thing. But it is literally as nothing compared to what has happened to us when we have committed a wrong, when we have treated another human being as a thing instead of a person, when we have injured another or been lacking in love and fellowship toward them, when we have failed even to the extent of withholding a cup of cold water. People can suffer and still be beings of moral dignity and worth. They can suffer, and the moral universe, the fellowship of spirits, still holds together. But when a person violates conscience and inflicts injury on another, then the moral universe is shattered; a soul is shattered. In the spiritual realm an atomic explosion has occurred. It is what moral beings do to themselves, within, that constitutes the incomparable evil. It is this tragedy that has occurred in the spiritual—the most real—realm that leads to the evil and suffering that happen to other people and in the outward order. Therefore, also, evildoers are the ones most to be pitied, most in need of help. Upon them catastrophe has descended. They have banished themselves, though they may not be aware of it and may even glory in their shame, from the circle of life and fellowship, and are lost.

Most people pay at least lip service to this idea that the hunted has the moral advantage—hence the only meaningful advantage—over the hunter, the victim over their tormentor. But it is a difficult idea for people to grasp and hold securely. They need to "repent," change their whole focus on life, in order to see it clearly and hold on to it with the mind and so practice it. Most of the time most of us are bothered a great deal more even about little

1. Franz Viktor Werfel and S. N. Behrman, *Jacobowsky and the Colonel* (New York: Random House, 1944), 136. Muste's recollection of this quotation is not worded the same as the published English version of the script.

2. Philippians 3:7.

annoyances than about our sins, are much more afraid of those that kill the body but cannot kill the soul than we are of "him who is able to destroy both body and soul in hell."[3] That is, of course, why our moral force is usually so weak. We then go on to conclude that moral or spiritual force is inherently weak as against Hitler or the atomic bomb, for example. But perhaps we are all along aware, somewhere deep within us, that this is a rationalization of our unwillingness to face ourselves and our true situation.

It is, nevertheless, eternally and unquestionably true that the hunted has the advantage over the hunter. It is better to suffer than to inflict suffering, to be deceived than to deceive, to be killed than to kill, to have atomic bombs dropped on you than to drop them on others.

This is why the greatest religious teachers and saints have virtually all in one way or another arrived at and preached the doctrine of nonviolence or nonresistance. It is surely remarkable that there is such unanimity among them on this point. Yet a moment's reflection makes it clear that it could not possibly have been otherwise.

If the supreme evil and tragedy is indeed not in the realm of the suffering that is endured by people but in the soul of the person who inflicts suffering on another, is in treating another human being as a thing and not as a person and a sister or brother, then the temptation that must at every cost be avoided is the temptation to meet evil with evil, violence with violence.

This is the most insidious and terrible temptation that besets "good people." They are not inclined to turn into hunters and aggressors. They may even submit willingly and cheerfully to injustice and suffering inflicted upon themselves. But when it is the innocent Jews who are persecuted, the "defenseless" little nations that are attacked, the cause of democracy and human decency that is threatened, must and may people then "stand by and do nothing"? Granted that, if they resort to war or other forms of organized violence in the effort to curb aggressive evil and to save its helpless and innocent victims, they must in turn practice evil and violence, is this not a lesser evil and loss than if no positive effort is made to curb the aggressors? And is not the pacifist who refuses to take up the sword even against Hitler in part responsible for the material and spiritual suffering of Hitler's victims and hence an evildoer in the same way as those who, reluctantly, drop bombs on German cities in order that Nazi domination may be broken?

3. Matthew 10:28.

The Case for Violence

It is proper and necessary to point out that, whether we assess motives or results, in so far as it is possible to calculate the latter, where complicated issues and conflicts on a global scale are under consideration, the case of those who resort to violence is open to serious criticism.

For example, the pacifist is not the only one who at times and at least to outward appearance stands by and does nothing about injustice and suffering. If, that is to say, going to war about them is the only way to do something. In a world where there are always multitudes who are oppressed and mistreated in the most outrageous fashion, people often feel helpless to take any action that seems at all effective. They are after all not omniscient and omnipotent and are not morally responsible for the ordering of the entire world. Those who have no faith at all recognize that much has to be left to chance. Those who believe in the reality of a moral order and in God know that God is the ruler of the universe, that God has indeed given humanity a limited and sufficiently awful responsibility, but that beyond that limit people do well to remember that "the everlasting God, the Lord, the creator of the ends of the earth, fainteth not, neither is weary" and that in the day when "even the youths faint and are weary, and the young men utterly fall, they that wait for the Lord shall renew their strength."[4] When pacifists say that in certain circumstances they are seemingly helpless, can only "stand by and do nothing," they are in principle doing the same thing that their nonpacifist sisters and brothers also do in many instances.

In other words, people choose the occasions when evil is so outrageous that they "must" resort to war to stop it; and the motives and occasions which lead to such decisions require more careful scrutiny than is usually given them. As a young minister in 1916, I was taught a lesson in this connection which has a great influence on my subsequent thinking. The Protestant ministers in the section of a suburban city in Massachusetts where I lived were much disturbed by the "Belgian atrocities" that were then allegedly being perpetrated by the Germans. (I leave out of account here the fact that these allegations were later proved largely baseless and in some instances deliberately manufactured by Allied propaganda.) It was agreed that the community should bear its witness against these outrages. Since some of us were pacifists who were opposed to going to war over them whereas others believed that the United States should enter the conflict, it was also agreed that our protest should be so worded that both groups could unite wholeheartedly in the demonstration. I was sent to the rector of the Roman

4. Isaiah 40:28, 30–31.

Catholic parish in our community to ask him to participate with his people. He and they were Irish. I told him my story, to which he listened politely. Then he said: "Mr. Muste, have you and your colleagues ever heard of the Irish atrocities?" It was about the time of the "Easter Massacre" in Dublin! I told him, of course, that we had. He then said: "Well, they have been going on for several centuries; and as soon as you and your friends have joined us in a few protest meetings against the Irish atrocities, we shall join you in a meeting to protest the Belgian atrocities."

Our excitement about the Belgian atrocities was not as purely and clearly motivated as I had assumed. It was tied up with ancestral and emotional associations and, to a much greater extent than even the pacifists in the group were aware, with the side we were on in the war. The practice, often unconscious, of a double standard of morality that affects both our ethical and our political analysis constitutes in my opinion one of the basic evils of our age. As Americans and Russians, whites and blacks, Orientals and Occidentals, Catholics and Protestants, left-wingers and right-wingers, we constantly condone or justify in ourselves and in those who are on our side what we subject to the severest condemnation when practiced by others. At the moment of writing, it is generally admitted that the Russians are subjecting Germans in territories taken over by Russia and Poland to the most ruthless treatment as they are driven out of their homes. Not only do those who pleaded most vociferously that we must go to war to stop Nazi atrocities not suggest that we go to war against Russia. Many of them become highly excited when the outrages perpetrated by the Russians are so much as mentioned and brand as fascists and war-mongers those who do speak of them.

It is especially noteworthy in this connection that for the most part those who demand that we go to war as a nation for a "cause" or to stop suffering inflicted on unfortunates abroad are not equally stirred about the injustices to blacks or laborers at home and that practically without exception they unequivocally condemn resort to violence on the part of these victims and on behalf of the cause of social or economic emancipation. Here they are sure there is "a better way," and insisting that this better way than violence be found is not condemned as merely standing by and doing nothing. They are sure that resort to violence would be the greater evil in this case. As Randolph Bourne said of certain elements in 1918: "Numbers of intelligent people who had never been stirred by the horrors of capitalistic peace at home were shaken out of their slumber by the horror of wars in Belgium. Never having felt responsibility for labor wars and oppressed masses and excluded races at home, they had a large fund of idle emotional capital to invest in the oppressed nationalities and ravaged villages of Europe."[5] Incidentally, the war expends the "emotional capital" of most participants, and we witness, therefore, after cessation of hostilities, the indifference and self-indulgence that mark such periods, including the one in which we now live. Surely this is another consideration that should lead us to reflect on who they are who "stand by and do nothing" and what it is that produces this attitude in individuals and nations.

Furthermore, it is a sheer illusion that nations go to war when they can no longer stand by and watch injustice or the sufferings of the victims of persecution. That moment when war breaks out is not chosen by those who feel moral indignation. Nations that stand by when democratic Czechoslovakia is raped go to war when reactionary anti-Semitic Poland is attacked; and having contended that this was necessary in order to put a stop to unilateral action in respect to Poland, they ratify and legalize similar unilateral action in Poland and elsewhere in eastern Europe when it is taken by an ally in the war. Moral indignation and the morally indignant are used as tools by those who go to war for amoral or immoral purposes and serve to place a cloak of respectability over the latter. After the war the morally indignant have to stand by for the most part and do nothing while the consequences of the war work themselves out and then they are likely to become pacifists of a sort again!

Resorting to Atrocity

We have dealt in an earlier chapter with the question whether intervention by the method of war and violence is effective in stopping war and violence and achieving the results that its idealistic defenders strive and hope for, and we shall not attempt here to adduce further proof of the self-defeating character of this method. With reference to the specific ethical problem under consideration at the moment, we may make this further observation. What the pacifist does in certain situations in which others resort to violence is often in our opinion more effective than nonpacifists may be willing to admit. We grant, however, that there are times when they may be likened to a person who stands by helpless when their own or their neighbor's house goes up in flames because there is no water or other means of extinguishing the fire to be had. If the neighbors at that juncture discover a lot of gasoline and begin throwing it on the fire, we think a person is rational and behaving as a responsible moral being when they choose to stand by and let the fire burn itself out rather than joining in and adding fuel to the flames.

5. Randolph Bourne, *Untimely Papers* (New York: B. W. Huebsch, 1919), 36.

We have also pointed out previously how the United States, in resorting to war in order to put a stop to Nazi and Japanese militarist atrocities, itself descended to the lowest depths of atrocious conduct and left itself and the rest of the world with no moral or other defenses against the illimitable atrocities of the atomic wars of the future. That is the logic of resort to atrocious means even with the best intentions. Since writing those earlier observations we have come upon a striking confirmation of them from an unusually authoritative source in an article in the February 1946 issue of the *Atlantic Monthly* entitled "One War Is Enough." The author, Edgar L. Jones, saw forty months of war duty, much of it in the front lines, as an ambulance man and later witnessed the fighting in the Pacific as a special correspondent for the *Atlantic Monthly*. He says: "What kind of war do civilians suppose we fought anyway? We shot prisoners in cold blood, wiped out hospitals, strafed life-boats, killed or mistreated enemy civilians, finished off the enemy wounded, tossed the dying man into a hole with the dead, and in the Pacific boiled the flesh off enemy skulls to make table ornaments for sweethearts, or carved their bones into letter openers. We topped off our saturation bombing and burning of enemy civilians by dropping atomic bombs on two nearly defenseless cities, thereby setting an all-time record for instantaneous mass slaughter."[6]

Since war in the future will necessarily be atomic or "super-atomic" war and more diabolical than anything we have yet seen, it might seem that our argument could rest here, since it may well appear inconceivable that any moral justification can be found for such irrational and indiscriminate slaughter. But, alas, this is not the case. Unless we abolish war altogether, those who do not undergo a spiritual revolution will, after a period of protesting that atomic war "simply must not be," find a moral justification, or more accurately excuse, for engaging in it—always, of course, on the right side, "our" side. Those on the other side will be devils incarnate. Furthermore, there are other forms of violence than international war. And we are now at the very heart of the moral issue we started to explore and must grapple with it.

Nonviolence May Fail

When people and nations resort once more to violence in order to overcome or limit violence, all the rationalizations and miscalculations of which we have spoken will enter into their thinking and their decisions. Our

6. Edgar L. Jones, "One War is Enough," *Atlantic Monthly* 177, no. 2 (February 1946), 49. This quotation differs insignificantly from the original.

nonpacifist friends are under moral obligation to take this into account; and this applies particularly to nonpacifist Christians who must disregard or "interpret" so much in the New Testament—so much that is, furthermore, at the very heart of the Gospels and Epistles—when they take up the sword which the Lord told Peter to "put up into its place."[7] But the behavior of our nonpacifist brethren cannot be altogether accounted for as the result of thinking which can be safely dismissed as coming under the head of rationalization and miscalculation. They take up the sword because they feel that they cannot stand by and see the weak and innocent struck down and that, if they were to do so, they would lose their moral integrity and violate the command of their Master as it comes to them. If they have to face the risks that their course involves, pacifists have also to attempt a final reckoning with the possibility that they are accomplices in the suffering, material and spiritual, of the weak and innocent, that they fail to advance the kingdom of God on earth in the only practical and possible way that is open to people in a given situation. In other words, can pacifists guarantee success if individuals and nations try their way?

All the greatest religious teachers and saints, as we have pointed out, are in some form expounders of nonviolence or nonresistance as the methodology of love in both personal and social relationships. They are also—and as we shall see presently, necessarily—expounders of the law of suffering and crucifixion. They are people who confess, and in a sense glory in, weakness and failure.

There is a kind of pacifist who thinks that if only people will meet evildoers, the Hitlers, for example, with kindness and gentleness and a smile, we shall quickly convert them, atrocities will soon stop and all will be well. We do not live in such an idyllic world. Those who go to war take terrible risks, risks that in my opinion cannot be justified on any basis. But those who will not meet violence with violence also take risks. For the good of their souls they must realize this and must not hesitate to admit it to others. It may be that the innocent, or at least the relatively innocent, will perish. Multitudes may be subjected to suffering. But the religious pacifist in the final awful showdown takes their stand on their interpretation of the essential nature of the moral life, their evaluation of what is essentially and supremely evil. The hunted has an incalculable advantage over the hunter. Never, whatever the provocation may be, must one add to the essential evil in the world by hunting, hurting, killing another human being. We cannot, except in a very small degree, control the world and determine the course of history. The amount of suffering on earth is also in only a limited degree subject to our

7. Matthew 26:52.

determination. But there is one thing that is absolutely within the control of each of us, namely, our own moral decisions and acts. I can refuse to add to the hurting and the violence of the world. I can in face of all that comes strive to love, to reconcile, to heal. I can act on the maxim that it would be terrible for the American people to be wiped out by atomic bombs but far, far more terrible for the American people to wipe out another people by atomic bombs—even though America's refusal to do the latter might subject it to the risk of suffering the former.

It seems to me beyond a shadow of a doubt that Jesus faced this dilemma that love and nonviolence may fail, fail utterly and horribly. I cannot but believe that it was his wrestling with that awful problem that wrung the bloody sweat from his brow in Gethsemane and from his lips the cry: "Father, if it be possible, let *this* cup pass from me."[8] What cup? He had been certain that God had called him to liberate his people. He had been certain also of the way he must use, the way of nonviolence and love, love even for the enemy, a way so contrary to the thought and expectation of most of his people. Yet it was God's way: "*Thou* art my son in whom I am well-pleased," not these other Messiahs, nor Caesar.[9] And since it was God's way surely it must succeed. But now it was clear that there would be failure. His people would not heed his call. Rome would go on its way of dictatorship, and of terror for all who would not yield to that dictatorship. Calamity would overtake his people: "There shall not be left here one stone upon another."[10] His disciples would betray and desert him. They would be exposed to danger. He would be killed. The cause would fail. Even now it need not be. There were "ten legions of angels."[11] Even now he could turn the tables on his enemies. But that would mean turning upon his hunters and in the name of the hunted, of righteousness, of God and his kingdom, becoming a hunter. This he could not do without violating his deepest conviction, denying himself, denying the Father who had been revealed to him in the deepest hours of his life since boyhood, the God who did not requite evil for evil, who made his sun to shine on the evil and the good, who would have sons and daughters, not subjects and servants. Whatever might betide, in the face of utter failure and the imminent triumph of the satanic powers, he would not relinquish that conviction, deny this God of love. He would stand by—helpless, despised—and let the blows fall on him and on the cause. He would die

8. Matthew 26:39.

9. Matthew 3:17, 17:5; Mark 1:11, 9:7; Luke 3:22.

10. Matthew 24:2, Mark 13:2, Luke 21:6.

11. Matthew 26:53. Muste misquotes this passage: it is twelve legions, not ten.

and fail. "Father, if it is be possible, let this cup pass from me. Nevertheless, not my will but thine be done."[12]

The Law of Suffering

We suggested a moment ago that the expounders and practitioners of non-violence are "necessarily" also expounders and practitioners of the law of weakness, suffering, and crucifixion. There are at least two basic reasons for this, both of them repeatedly set forth in the New Testament and especially by Jesus himself.

In the first place, in a world of moral beings made to live in a community of those who know that each must find their good in the welfare of the others, but in whose midst disruption has entered, where people have sought to deny the truth of their being by turning to hinder and hurt others, the supreme need is a love that insists the community must not be broken, that insists no one must be permitted to banish themselves from it. Under these circumstances, the love that embraces only the worthy and the lovely is obviously a poor, inadequate thing. It is not worthy of the name of love at all. All the great religious teachers have said that, too, in their various tongues. "If ye love them that love you, do good to your benefactors, what reward have ye? Do not even those you esteem least do that?"[13] The love of God for humanity is always love for the unworthy and undeserving. Forgiveness is primary and essential in it. "While we were yet sinners, Christ died for us."[14]

It is these sinners who have suffered the greatest calamity in causing their brothers and sisters to suffer. If there can be said to be degrees in love at all, it is these who have sinned rather than those who have been sinned against who must be pitied and loved the most. They, in the language of religious symbolism, are in danger of eternal damnation. They must be cleansed, restored to the family of God.

The fact that in a universe governed by moral law sinners suffer the inexorable consequences of ignoring or defying reality does not solve the problem. They may be driven to greater excesses or to despair. Alternatively they may strive by prudential behavior to avoid unpleasant consequences. Since freedom is of the essence of the moral life and the universe is built to permit the exercise of such freedom, people may in considerable measure "get by" with such prudential behavior, by being discreet when the police

12. Matthew 26:39.

13. Matthew 5:46.

14. Romans 5:8.

are watching them. But in none of these ways can a truly human society, a family, a community of love, be built or restored.

The sinner must freely, from within, choose to renounce their sin and must be assured that forgiveness is available, that there is a community of love to which they can be restored. This can happen only if there is exerted a love that cannot be provoked or transformed into indifference or hate by evil, a love great enough to hold on to and draw back the unlovely, those who in no sense merit love.

Since the use of violence is excluded, since evildoers encounter no "resistance" in the conventional sense of the term but are given freedom to choose the evil and to visit its consequences not only upon themselves but upon others, the God of love, the Father in heaven, inevitably appears weak, rather foolish and not altogether fair. See the parable of the Prodigal Son and the Sermon on the Mount.[15] God makes his sun to shine and his rain to fall on the just and the unjust alike.[16] Prudential morality and religion are not the same thing at all.

If God will not make the evildoer to suffer, the evildoer will mock God and make God suffer. If God keeps on loving in the face of rejection and evil and sin, God must suffer. The concept of God as weak and foolish and enduring contempt and suffering, of God as represented not by power but precisely by the renunciation of power, is in one way so difficult to accept, seems indeed so sacrilegious, that people constantly try to find formulations which may enable them to avoid a complete acceptance of it. God himself does not suffer, they try to make out, but he "so loved the world that he gave his only begotten son."[17] But then they have to turn around at once and say that if you want to know God you must know and believe in "Jesus Christ and him crucified. . . . God was in Christ."[18] For Christians certainly there is no escape: God is the Father and his children carve the cross on his heart.

The Nature of Nonviolence

This brings us to the second reason why practitioners of nonviolence are "necessarily" the victims of crucifixion and the exponents of failure. They have to be true to the inner nature of the love and nonviolence to which they have committed themselves, they must follow out its logic to the end,

15. Luke 15:11–32, Matthew 5–7.

16. See Matthew 5:45.

17. John 3:16.

18. 1 Corinthians 2:3, 2 Corinthians 5:19.

even though that spells defeat, even though it nails them, "forsaken of God," to the cross.

Those who, however reluctantly, resort to violence are also bound by the inner nature of the weapon they employ. Material or physical force finds its ultimate expression in the power to kill, to destroy the adversary. If you resort to violence, then you have to be prepared, if it is required for the accomplishment of the end in view, to kill. Otherwise you are bluffing, and your bluff will be called. War, as we have seen, has its own logic. It becomes ever more destructive and indiscriminate. But that does not deter people, except those who renounce war unequivocally, from engaging in it. The next war or its successor will probably bring Western civilization to an end, and with it the American republic. It may quite possibly mean the annihilation of the human race. The American government is, nevertheless, devoting itself wholeheartedly to preparation for this war. There will also be churches to bless it in the name of Christ, if not explicitly, then by way of giving their members to understand that it is right and necessary to engage in atomic war—but "penitently."

If the ultimate expression of violence is killing the opponent, the "aggressor," the ultimate expression of nonviolence or soul force is quite as obviously the willingness and ability to die at the hands and on behalf of the evildoer. Pacifists must be ready to pay that price. If they are not willing to go that far, they are bluffing, and their bluff will be called. Until people are willing to pay for the way of peace something like what they pay for war, they do not truly want peace and they certainly will not get it.

The suffering need not be sought. Indeed it must not be. Martyrdom for the sake of martyrdom is suicide by exhibitionism, not redemptive crucifixion. But we may not seek to evade suffering. It must be voluntarily accepted. The son must trust the Father, though he forsakes and slays him. He must do the Father's will, though that means drinking the cup of defeat and failure. Love must seek no return. Its ultimate vindication, the seal that it is indeed divine love, will be that, no matter what the suffering imposed upon it by evildoers, it will not resort to violence and hate in turn. It must be willing to accept death on behalf of evildoers and in the hour of death love them and pray for their forgiveness. That price may in fact be exacted.

When such love is manifested, then the paradox at the heart of the universe is revealed and the miracle that transforms people and history takes place. Out of weakness comes strength; out of defeat comes victory. Out of death springs life. When love is confronted by evil in its most irrational and inexcusable form—evil that would crucify even Jesus—and triumphs because it will not alter its nature, because it insists on loving still and forgiving, because it asks no boon at all from God, no "well-deserved" victory, then God himself in his inmost being stands revealed. Then God has entered into history and its course has been forever changed. Here is released the power that in the political and social realm is the counterpart of the fission of the atom and the release of atomic energy in its realm. If the Christian religion means anything, it means this. If the experience of humankind has taught anything, it teaches this.

It is not—be it noted once more so that there may be no mistake—that God can be inveigled into making a bargain: love, refrain from violence, pretend to be willing to sacrifice, and peace and comfort and well-being will be yours. Nothing is guaranteed. The element of risk and cost cannot be removed from the life of people or nations. The nation that goes to war has no guarantee of victory. The strong person fully armed guarding their court may suddenly be confronted by one stronger than them who overcomes them and takes from them their whole armor wherein they trusted and divides the spoils. God will not make a bargain with the nonviolent either. Pacifism cannot guarantee a cheap and painless solution. Life is dynamic and unpredictable. We have to make the leap of faith. We have to risk failure and stark defeat. The cross is central.

Yet the other side of the paradox is also there. God is not a hard taskmaster or a vindictive sovereign. The universe is a universe of law. They that take the sword shall perish by the sword.[19] And on the other hand, "The work of righteousness shall be peace; and the effect of righteousness, quietness and confidence forever."[20] The ordinances of God are true and righteous altogether, and in keeping them there is great reward.[21] Love is the law of life, not of death. If the price of death be exacted of those who follow the way of love and nonviolence as it is exacted of those who take the sword, the former have still chosen by far the better part, for in crucifixion there is redemptive power; suicide whether of people or of nations is sterile.

Thus, in the end, "The individual conscience against the atomic bomb? Yes. There is no other way" becomes, "A dead man on a cross against the atomic bomb? Yes. There is no other way." The atomic bomb is the symbol of the power to destroy and kill raised to demonic proportions. What shall be set over against it? What shall overcome it? A still greater power to destroy and kill? Obviously, there is naught but still more awful destruction in that. In this extremity, is it not at last clear that our sole alternative is the love that absolutely refuses to destroy, will not be tempted to violence and is able and

19. Matthew 26:52.

20. Isaiah 32:17.

21. Psalm 19:9, 11.

willing to die in order that the diabolical chain of evil linked to evil may be broken?

The Nature of the Universe

The awe-inspiring and destructive explosion of the atom is the symbol and the result of the far more terrible disruption that has taken place within the human being and within the human family. It may serve as a warning and a prophecy of the far more catastrophic moral and social disruption that may yet take place. It may serve to remind us, also, of how mighty and how different must be the force that over against these disruptive elements will hold the society of humankind and the universe together. It may serve to convince us that now, when humanity has laid our brains and hands upon the secrets of the physical universe and thus has unleashed the forces which may wipe out humankind and perhaps even shatter its earthly home, we must at last devote ourselves with all the energy we have to searching out the nature of the moral and spiritual universe and that we must, with the passion, single-mindedness, and humility of the scientist and with the patience and ingenuity of the technologist, learn to lay hold upon those forces that can stay the disruptive elements confronting us and can hold the society of humankind and the universe together.

Obviously our age has not yet penetrated to that burning inner core of the spiritual universe where reside those silent and almighty energies that can control the atom and the suns and use them for good and not for evil. We still meddle, fussily and distracted by turns, with time-worn devices, shabby political tricks, the old false or partial solutions that have not availed to ward off disaster. We know that the energies we now have in ourselves and in our national and other social groups are utterly insufficient. We dare not go on thus, repeating the past.

As its central core, the universe is love. As love is the source of creation and joy in the human spirit and in all human life, so is it the source of the infinite creativeness and of all beauty in the universe. As it is love that gives to the human soul whatever unity and direction it has, as it is fellowship by which all human societies are bound together, so is the whole universe bound together by love.

This is the truth about the spiritual realm. God is; and God is Father, is love. In love God created us. We cannot escape from our own nature any more than someone can jump out of their own skin; therefore, we cannot escape the demands of conscience and love. Therefore, also, we cannot escape the consequences of our denial of love, our refusal to be good. Nor can we destroy God. Hence we cannot change the essential character of the universe or defeat God's purpose. But on the other hand, God will not force himself upon us. Love will win its kingdom "by entreaty and not with contention." God is the one whom we can despise and insult. We can waste our substance that he has given us in riotous living. He will wait. He will love. He will suffer crucifixion. He will not compel. He will still be the God "who forgiveth all thine iniquities; who healeth all thy diseases."[22] That is why you live. That is why in spite of all disruptive forces humankind lives. That is the tremendous force that holds the atoms and the suns together.

In the nature of the case, this cannot be proved by intellectual demonstration. That conscience is a response to a moral order you can prove only by making moral decisions and acting conscientiously. If God is indeed love, then you can apprehend him only by loving him and his creatures. If God is the power that binds all life into unity, you find him only if you abide in that unity and do not seek to live in any sense for yourself.

The Venture of Faith

Thus responsibility falls again on the individual, on the person endowed with moral responsibility. "The bell tolls for thee."[23] The fate of humankind rests upon each of us, far more than upon any organization or institution.

As we have pointed out, we have to make the venture of faith. Evil will not overcome evil; violence will not destroy violence. Only by good, by love, can evil be overcome and the world redeemed. We are given no guarantees in advance if we love. We may have to see evil unconquered. We may be simply crucified. Love will not falter or alter because of that. It is simply its nature to love, to give, not to demand, not to bargain.

Yet, paradoxically, in the degree that we give ourselves unreservedly to God and to the love of our fellows because of him, we know indubitably that we have laid hold on infinite power as well as love. Nothing will defeat us. If we are killed in the service of love, we know that all the more power will be released.

We have spoken of the Puritans and of how a new day dawns and a new order comes into being when people apprehend new moral truth and serve it with complete integrity and devotion. But that is nothing compared to the change that takes place in human life when people come to know

22. Psalm 103:3.

23. John Donne, *Devotions upon Emergent Occasions* (London: Thomas Iones, 1624), meditation XVII. See Ernest Hemingway, *For Whom the Bell Tolls* (New York: Charles Scribner's Sons, 1940).

God as love and loving him love their fellows. There was a little company of Christians in the days when the Roman emperor ruled over "the inhabited world." They were unarmed. They "resisted not evil."[24] They adored as Lord one Jesus of Nazareth who had died on a cross. One of their leaders was a man named Paul. He had but recently been one of their fiercest persecutors. Recently he had stood by "consenting" when a young Christian named Stephen was stoned. Stephen had died "crying with a loud voice, 'Lord, lay not this sin to their charge.'"[25] Paul when he himself joined the little company expressed their strongest conviction in the words, "Love beareth all things, believeth all things, hopeth all things, endureth all things. Love never faileth."[26]

Their outlook on life and the future he expressed in the same document in these words: "We preach Christ crucified, unto Jews a stumbling block and unto Gentiles foolishness; but unto them that are called both Jews and Greeks, Christ the power of God and the wisdom of God."[27]

What the Jews saw in that day was the mighty Roman Empire that had conquered and humiliated them. That to them represented power, reality. And over against that when they listened to the Christian preachers they saw only a dead man on a cross, completely discredited at the early age of thirty-three, rejected by the rulers of his people because he would not stop exposing their hypocrisies and rejected by the masses because he would not deliver them in the only way that to them seemed practical. He might indeed have been a great national hero, perhaps even Messiah: "Let him now come down from the Cross and we will believe in him."[28] But he would not save himself and his cause by "practical" measures. And that to the Jews was a stumbling block. What the Greeks saw was also this Roman Empire and its culture, so much of which Rome owed to their own tradition; and that was wisdom. Over against that they, too, saw a dead man on a cross: that to the Greeks was foolishness.

What the Jews and the Greeks and the Romans heard in those days were the disputations in the great universities, and the clank of money on the exchanges, and the laughter in the palaces and the night clubs, and above all—above all—the steady tramp of the Roman soldiers on every road of that world. That surely was real; that was power. Over against that they

24. See Matthew 5:39.

25. Acts 7:60.

26. 1 Corinthians 13:7–8.

27. 1 Corinthians 1:22–24.

28. Matthew 27:32.

did not hear Jesus at all, because of course he was dead. They did not hear his disciples, a discredited little sect of Jewish fanatics.

But what Paul and the early Christians saw was nothing of that sort at all. They saw the great empire tottering and falling. It was built on rotten foundations, not according to the specifications of their Lord. It could not possibly endure. And on the other hand, they saw that crucified Lord "high and lifted up, seated at the right hand of power."[29] He was Lord, not Caesar in Rome yonder. What they heard was not the disputations in the universities, the clank of money on the exchanges, the laughter in the palaces, even the tramp of the Roman soldiery. All that, for them, was already silent in the dust of history. What they did hear were the angelic hosts and the ages to come shouting: "Crown him with many crowns, the Lamb upon his throne."[30] And they were right. They understood the nature of power and they discerned the future.

It seems foolish today that what we have to place against the atomic bomb is conscience and love. But we have to get away from the wisdom and realism that have brought us where we are, very far away from them and very quickly. We have to look in the opposite direction, at that which in its own order is perhaps as invisible to the naked eye, seemingly as devoid of power, as the atom. In the presence of the forces that have been released from the atom and all the material power that is displayed in our time, we must try to understand the profound truth of Paul's observation that God—who seemingly can be so easily overlooked—"chose the foolish things of the world that he might put to shame them that are wise; and God chose the weak things that he might put to shame them that are strong . . . yea, and the things that are not that he might bring to naught the things that are."[31]

We must try to understand the profound wisdom of the early church, which discerned "the *Lamb* in the midst of the *throne*."[32] The Lamb, symbol of meekness, of gentleness, of seeming utter helplessness in the face of evil, of suffering love, which is at the heart of all real power and the secret of every final victory.

29. Isaiah 52:13, Matthew 26:64, Mark 14:62, Luke 22:69.

30. Matthew Bridges, "Crown Him With Many Crowns," 1851.

31. 1 Corinthians 1:27–28.

32. Revelation 7:17.

20

Theology of Despair (1948)

In this open letter, a response to an article of Reinhold Niebuhr's, Muste argues that Niebuhr's emphasis on human depravity created an ideology, not unlike that held by communism, of the inevitability of another world war.[1] *Muste concludes that there is another way: nonviolence as a political strategy and pacifism as a way of life.*

Dear Dr. Niebuhr:

I have just finished reading your editorial, "Amid Encircling Gloom," in *Christianity and Crisis* and the "Editorial Notes" immediately following. The experience has saddened and dismayed me, not alone because of the defeatism and despair that pervade both, but because of the *justification* for despair and even suicide I found there.

1. Muste and Niebuhr knew each other from their involvement with the Fellowship of Reconciliation during the interwar years. First Muste, then Niebuhr became disillusioned with liberal pacifism and left the FOR. While Muste returned to pacifism and the FOR, Niebuhr never did. Over time, they became keen intellectual adversaries. Historian Leilah Danielson has described their exchange well in "Christianity, Dissent, and the Cold War: A. J. Muste's Challenge to Realism and U.S. Empire," *Diplomatic History* 30, no. 4 (September 2006), 645–69.

In the editorial you point out that "our possession of a monopoly in atomic weapons and our fear that the monopoly will run out" in a few years make it possible that Americans may plunge into a "preventative" war against Russia, and certainly make it likely that they will not exercise "the forbearance without which it will be impossible to prevent present tensions from breaking out into overt conflict."[2]

You warn that we shall have to walk the tightrope of avoidance of such a course even while we "defend" ourselves by both military and political weapons—atomic not excluded—against communism, a counsel which is no whit different from that which we may hear from enlightened secular sources! Aside from this, what do you, widely regarded as America's foremost theologian, have to say that might avert the tragedy and lead people out of the "encircling gloom"?

What you offer is a variation on the only text about which you ever preach or write anymore, though there are so many other texts and—I venture to say—more Christian ones, in the Scriptures. If the world is plunged into war, you say, "it would be indeed the final ironic and tragic culmination of the pretensions of modern man."[3] People drawn into war, though not wishing to be, "would merely"—what does that assumption-laden, emotion-ridden word "merely" signify in this context?—"illustrate the human predicament confessed by St. Paul in the words: 'For the good that I would I do not.'"[4]

As befits a Christian prophet, you warn that in these circumstances "we face not merely a Russian or Communist peril but the threat of a divine judgment."[5] But you do not conclude, as did the prophets that were before you, by calling upon your hearers to repent, act, and so flee from that judgment. Instead, you finish with a solemn statement that, I am bound to say, makes little sense if taken at face value: "We are drifting toward a possible calamity in which even the most self-righteous assurance of the justice of our cause will give us no easy conscience."[6]

2. Reinhold Niebuhr, "Amid Encircling Gloom," *Christianity and Crisis* 8, no. 6 (April 12, 1948), 42.

3. Ibid.

4. Ibid.; Romans 7:19. Muste does not use the same wording for the Romans quotation as Niebuhr.

5. Niebuhr, "Amid Encircling Gloom," 42.

6. Ibid.

Moral Paralysis?

Here is an illustration, it seems to me, of your tendency to blur all distinctions, in disregard of your own insistently proclaimed doctrine that there are relative differences that matter. What the sentence just quoted does in the political realm—on the *existential* level, shall we say?—is to convey to people the subtle suggestion that they are paralyzed, under a judgment that they cannot escape, that in the now-so-familiar phrase, "there isn't anything they can do about it." They will feel when they go to war that it is right, necessary, or even holy—and yet they will not have easy consciences! They will not have easy consciences, and yet they will feel self-righteous! That is the human condition.

So there is no true tension, but only *anxiety*, or a pervading sense of futility, for tension in the biblical sense is surely characteristic of a situation where we stand before our God and make a *decision*. Here, no decision is possible anymore. The important decisions have all been made, or are being made, but always by something or somebody else. (I do not mean to say that you deliberately try to convey this subtle suggestion of paralysis and helplessness, but I believe it is the effect of your writing. And a confession on your part that this might be another illustration of how people do the evil which they would not—a confession I well know you are humble enough to make—would not do a thing to mend matters.)

The habit of utterance that seems to me to have grown upon you, and that dismays and disturbs me so, is illustrated again in the editorial note about the Palestine partition question in the same issue. After pointing out that in spite of what the Jews endured at Hitler's hands, they have been grievously wounded again "and not even the Stratton bill has been passed as a balm for those wounds," you conclude: "The whole situation is almost too tragic to contemplate. But the whole world situation has become so tragic that the perplexities of this particular problem only engage a fraction of our conscience." There it is again. The tragic plight of the Jews. What to do? It can "only engage a fraction of our conscience."[7]

The Masaryk Suicide

Sandwiched between these two items is your comment on Jan Masaryk's suicide. It seems to me very revealing. You recall that many people felt that Masaryk's willingness to become foreign secretary of a communist government,

7. Reinhold Niebuhr, "Editorial Notes," *Christianity and Crisis* 8, no. 6 (April 12, 1948), 42.

in spite of his well-known aversion to communism, demonstrated a lack of inner integrity. But, you assert, "he proved himself in possession of a final resource of such integrity by taking his life." You recognize, of course, that "suicide is not an ideal way of coming to terms with the issues of life," but, not being a "perfectionist," you are certain that people cannot attain the ideal anyway. And, having reached the point where the battle against "perfectionists" has become practically your sole occupation, now for the third time with rather obvious avidity you seize the opportunity to emphasize the complete hopelessness of humanity's estate and to pour sarcasm upon "the pretensions of modern man." Young Masaryk "proved his loyalty to his father's political ideas by violating his father's scruples against suicide," and from this you conclude: "That men may be forced into a position in which they can maintain the integrity of their soul *only* by taking their life, points to a dimension of human selfhood which makes nonsense of most modern theories of 'self-realization'!"[8]

I am not suggesting that Jan Masaryk may not indeed have been truer to his father's ideals and to his own attachment to democratic principles by committing suicide—if that is what occurred—than he would have been by continuing to serve in the communist government of Czechoslovakia after the coup. But the assertion that suicide was the "only" way of proving the integrity of his soul is, I think, a very revealing one. So is the fact that every tragedy as it passes in review before you is the occasion for just one comment: that it proves the validity of a theory of human depravity or, more accurately, futility.

The upshot of the business is that Jan Masaryk commits suicide—and it is really the only thing he can do. On the larger scale of world politics the conclusion likewise is that humankind—or at least Western civilization—commits suicide in atomic war. When it comes to a showdown that is the only thing it can do! Surely it is not altogether inappropriate to raise the question whether something like a "death-wish" is not operating here. The one positive element in the situation is that the thesis of humanity's utter futility has been vindicated!

This philosophy of fatalism and "inevitability" has its parallel in the Marxist-Leninist-Stalinist dogma of the "inevitability" of war between "the workers' fatherland" and the capitalist-imperialist world. That dogma also is linked to a low view of human nature and an essentially fatalistic one. It declares that humanity and its history is chiefly, if not entirely, the product of economic forces. According to this view of things, also, the living human beings in Russia, the United States, and elsewhere are essentially spectators

8. Ibid.; Niebuhr, "Amid Encircling Gloom," 42. Emphasis Muste's.

at a tragedy of which they are also, alas, the victims, but which, nevertheless, they have no alternative but to play through to the bloody end.

"Pie in the Sky"

The parallel does not end there. All is happily resolved—in theory—after the "inevitable" catastrophe has taken place. In the Marxist case, the solution is "within history" in the free society that grows out of "the dictatorship of the proletariat." In the other case, the resolution is "beyond history." Actual human beings, living and suffering, killing and being killed, today are offered "pie in the sky" under both systems!

One other observation remains to be made about how your thesis works out in contemporary affairs. In essential matters—support of the Marshall Plan, the need of fighting communism and Russia by both military and "peaceful" means, and so on—your political position today cannot be distinguished from that of John Foster Dulles, who is Thomas E. Dewey's choice for Secretary of State. For you, a socialist who knows how to make use of certain parts of the Marxian analysis, who has been the nemesis not only of conservatives but of liberals for these many years, this conjunction certainly should give pause.[9]

Considered as a political phenomenon it is not an accident that Reinhold Niebuhr, the radical, and John Foster Dulles, the Wall Street attorney and one of the chief architects of the bipartisan foreign policy of the United States, should now be virtually a team. For, if war is "inevitable," whether on the basis of the Marxist class war and materialistic interpretation of history, or on the basis of the theory of human depravity and the necessity of exposing "the pretensions of modern man," in actuality the war will be between Stalinist Russia and imperialist United States, for "communism" on the one hand and "free enterprise" on the other. Let me emphasize that I am not saying that war is "inevitable," only that if there is war, it will be this kind and no other. These are the elements that have an "interest" in making war and that possess the resources with which to make war.

However, in lining up the masses of people for war, these elements must have at least the acquiescence of the church and of Christian leaders, if not their unqualified blessing. They must have in both the conservative and the progressive camps people who are regarded as idealists but who, being practical, know that you have to meet Soviet military might with American military might, including atomic bombs, even while they also use

9. I do not, of course, reflect on Mr. Dulles as a person, in which capacity I consider him both admirable and attractive. (Footnote Muste's.)

other means; "practical" idealists who will not seriously interfere with war preparations; who are, whether conscious of it or not, and despite disclaimers, pretty well convinced in their hearts that war *is* inevitable. Hence the constellation of Niebuhr and Dulles.

Alternative to Suicide

There was open to Jan Masaryk another way than suicide to prove his integrity: open refusal to serve in the post-coup cabinet and the public statement, either in Czechoslovakia or in exile, of the reasons therefore. This probably would have had little immediate or obvious political effect. Many would have regarded it as a foolish gesture, or even as an exhibition of addiction to "perfectionism." He might have lost his life in that case, too. But as it is, his suicide served only to dramatize what the discerning already knew and the American government had already accepted as the basis of its policy, namely, that in the final analysis Soviet totalitarianism will not compromise on essentials. Had he been killed for public repudiation of the Stalinist course, democracy and truth would have had a martyr, Bohemia perhaps another Jan Hus.[10]

The world does not have to go to war and commit suicide, either. But it can escape that calamity only if there are those who do not believe that catastrophe is inevitable; who do not believe that you have to line up with one side or the other in the "cold" war; who are willing to pursue a course that will seem politically ineffective and foolish in the estimation of "the wise of this world"; who will not, indeed, ask for victims or executioners in the name of any cause or theory, but who will be prepared to lay down their own lives if the call comes, since they have learned, from the most authoritative of all teachers, that most infallible and inexorable of all laws: unless the seed falls into the ground and dies, it bears no fruit; but if it dies, it brings forth much fruit.[11]

The Scriptures are not simply an extended commentary on the single text, "Vanity of vanities, all is vanity."[12] We read in them the commandment, "Be ye perfect as your heavenly Father is perfect," and the promise, "Behold, I make all things new."[13] Even Paul declared, "I can do all things in him

10. Jan Hus was a fourteenth-century priest who was burned at the stake for heresy. Although he lived before the Protestant Reformation, he is often considered one of the first Reformers.

11. John 12:24.

12. Ecclesiastes 1:2.

13. Matthew 5:48, Revelation 21:5.

that strengtheneth me."[14] Pacifists verily need to be on guard both against the error of over-simplification and the sin of self-righteousness, but it does not follow that nonviolence as political strategy and pacifism as a way of life are invalidated. For Christian leaders to reject them may be in truth to condemn the church and our age to futility and doom.

14. Philippians 4:13.

21

Pacifism and Perfectionism (1950)

In this series of four articles later published together as a pamphlet, Muste addresses neo-orthodox critiques of pacifism. He acknowledges that there is truth in some of the criticisms of pacifism and admits that pacifists often underestimate the reality of sin, but argues that the gospel nevertheless demands the pursuit of moral perfection. At the same time, he argues that neo-orthodox thought overemphasizes the inescapability of sin and leads people to give up trying to live a moral life.

Part 1: The Doctrine of Perfection

Why has the Christian church not renounced war? Atomic and germ warfare have appalled the church's leaders. No authoritative statement by any major church body attempts any longer to prove that war itself is compatible with the will of God or the teaching and spirit of Christ. The First Assembly of the World Council of Churches at Amsterdam in 1948 expressed deep concern over the inability of the church of Christ to take a unified stand against war, challenged the concept of a just war, and called war a "consequence of the disregard of God."[1] Now the discussion of the hydrogen bomb, with its destructive potentialities a thousand or a million times that of the Hiroshima bomb, has posed the problem still more sharply. Yet still the overwhelming majority of the churches do not declare their irrevocable refusal any longer to sanction or support war, and the numbers of the Christian pacifists increase only microscopically if at all.

Any exploration of the reasons for this must undoubtedly take into account the entanglement of the churches in the existing social and economic order, as well as the fact that vast numbers of church members are Christian only in a superficial sense.

But overshadowing even these is the influence of such men as Karl Barth, Emil Brunner, Reinhold Niebuhr and the large number of unquestionably sincere, learned and devout Christian thinkers and leaders who follow them in an interpretation of the Christian gospel that rules out pacifism, either as a general philosophy of life, or as a practical absolute in the present situation. Though there are considerable divergences of view among them, the basic tendencies they have in common may for purposes of brevity and convenience be grouped under the term neo-orthodoxy. Without attempting to recite neo-orthodoxy's full indictment of liberal and other theologies, its attitude toward Christian pacifism may be summarized briefly as holding that the latter falls into the error of perfectionism in its concept of personal religious experience and the moral life, into the error of utopianism in its concept of human society and the goal of history, and into the errors of sentimentalism and oversimplification in its political strategy.

The impact of the neo-orthodox orientation and mood in Christian thinking and policy today is enormous, especially in the student bodies of theological schools and among the younger ministers. Moreover, quite irrespective of the numbers of adherents it may attract, its criticism merits serious consideration.

Sentimental Pacifism

Pacifists in particular do well to heed neo-orthodoxy's criticism. It is perfectly true that a good many of us have had a soft, sentimental, naïve view of things. Our political analysis often has been superficial. Tending to minimize the power of tyranny and to underestimate the depth and extent of

1. W. A. Visser 'T Hooft, ed. "Report of Section IV: The Church and the International Disorder," in *The First Assembly of the World Council of Churches, Held at Amsterdam August 22nd to September 4th, 1948* (New York: Harper & Brothers, 1949), 88.

depravity in certain persons and systems, we have tended also to assume that there were comparatively cheap and easy solutions for international problems.

Moreover, we pacifists need to take the neo-orthodox criticism to heart in judging ourselves as moral beings and professing Christians, that we may be kept from self-deceit, from pampering ourselves, and from arrogating virtue or moral superiority to ourselves.

I am, however, convinced that in essential respects the neo-orthodox teaching and mood are un-Scriptural, not fully Christian, and a source of the gravest danger to the church and to humankind today; and in this and succeeding articles I wish to deal with these shortcomings, considering in order the doctrine of perfectionism as it relates to personal religious experience, moral life, and ethical standards; then the nature of society and the goal of history; and finally problems connected with the use of love and nonviolence as social and political strategy.

Basic to neo-orthodoxy is a well-known Christian doctrine that has come down through Paul, Augustine, Luther, and Calvin: the doctrine that we are saved by grace through faith and not by our own efforts. Both from a theological and a psychological standpoint this is a sound and extremely useful doctrine, and one that should play a very important part in Christian pacifist thinking.

The person who undertakes to attain perfection in terms of some individual standard invariably finds that the standard is never deep enough. Only a love that does not think primarily of itself, that has the sensitivity to feel the need of others in concrete situations that cannot be blue-printed beforehand, is adequate to human need. To be "perfect" or "whole" is precisely to be unselfconscious, that is, perfectly spontaneous.

Furthermore, there is always an element of competition in this business of keeping the law and striving for individual perfection—"I thank thee that I am not as other men are"—which itself is the deepest kind of violation of the law of life or community.[2]

To make it the aim of life to strive for one's own perfection by one's own power and wisdom involves an assumption of self-sufficiency. But we are creatures, dependent beings, not self-created. We cut ourselves off, therefore, from the source of our being when we consider ourselves self-sufficient. That applies both to our relation to our fellows, and our relation to the universe or God. The idea that individuals, somehow isolated from their fellows and God, can have true merit or even reality, is adjudged completely unsound equally by Christian theology and modern psychology. Modern

2. Luke 18:11.

psychologists and the great Christian mystics agree that the source of evil is the "I," "mine," "me," and that "nothing burns in hell but self-will."[3]

Becoming Integrated

For those who are not accustomed to biblical terms, this doctrine may be expressed as saying that the assumption that we are "saved"—which is to become integrated, or achieve serenity—because we live a good life is true only in a secondary sense. Taken as a primary factor, it is contrary to all human experience. The baby born into a home does not first have to do something to make herself acceptable. For her the great basic fact is that she is accepted. For multitudes of humans born into tolerably normal homes this remains the case right on into their adult lives. Home, as someone said, "is the place where, when you have to go there, they have to take you in," and do.

It is the fact that children are thus accepted, loved, cared for, and trained before they have acquired any merit that makes it possible for them to grow up into acceptable human beings. They are saved by "grace." There is conclusive evidence that the people who grow up to be notably unacceptable and anti-social are those who, in infancy and childhood, suffered deprivation of love. There was no "grace" to accept them for what they were.

Grace

Now the core of Christian evangelical teaching and preaching is just this: "You—no matter who you are—are accepted of God before you make yourself acceptable, and even though you are not acceptable. You always have been; you always will be. 'Like as a father pitieth his children, so the Lord.' . . . Cease, then, from running away from your true home. Stop this agonized striving to be something in yourself. Accept yourself, you have been accepted. Pause to realize the grace available to you, the love that begat you, the energizing spirit that seeks to invade and flow through you; accept it, take it, yield yourself to it. Only believe. God is he who, when you have to go there, has to take you in, and has all the time been waiting to take you in, as the parable of the Prodigal Son portrays."[4]

Certainly the New Testament offers no way of salvation save this of simple trust in the everlasting mercy and unmerited grace of God.

3. This comes from the *Theologia Germanica*, a fourteenth-century mystical writing.

4. See Psalm 103:13, Luke 15:11–32.

Exacting Ethic

But it is equally certain that the New Testament never so much as hints that this implies any lowering or compromising of the standard to which we are called to conform or that God's grace is not equal to enabling us to live according to the will of God!

The true evangelical position is surely that stated so admirably by Karl Holl:

> It is all the more astonishing that on the basis of such a conception of God, which seemed to dissolve all morality, Jesus nevertheless built up an ethic, and the most exacting ethic conceivable at that. . . . The meaning is clear: pardoning grace overcomes, because at the same time it encourages and humbles. It creates an inner affection, a feeling of gratitude which must find expression, and for which the highest is not too much to do. . . . From this follows the most splendid feature of the ethic of Jesus, namely, the naturalness, the spontaneous character of the action, which he supposes even in things most difficult and self-denying. . . . God takes the initiative: with his forgiveness he creates something quite new, out of which arises at once a real, close, and warm relationship to God, and with it at the same time a morality which ventures to take even God himself as its model.[5]

Let us dwell for a moment on these crucial items in Christian experience. First of all, the demand made upon us is the utmost, as Holl remarks, namely that people saved by grace shall take even God himself as their model. "Be ye perfect, as your Heavenly Father is perfect." "If anyone would be my disciple, let him take up his own cross and come after me."[6]

And how steadfastly there runs throughout the New Testament the note of joy, elation, confidence, achievement, victory. It is a triumph song of the accepted sinner who becomes acceptable. "Beloved, now are we the children of God and it is not yet made manifest what we shall be. . . . Everyone that hath this hope set on him purifieth himself even as he is pure. . . . Whosoever is begotten of God doeth no sin, because his seed abideth in him: and he cannot sin because he is begotten of God."[7]

5. Karl Holl, *Distinctive Elements in Christianity*, trans. Norman V. Hope (Edinburgh: T & T Clark, 1937), 21–23. This quotation differs insignificantly from the original.

6. Matthew 16:24, Mark 8:34, Luke 9:23.

7. 1 John 3:2–3, 9.

True, we love only because Christ first loved us; but we do love, and thus we have passed out of death into life. What a difference between the feeling we get from these and other typical New Testament passages and that derived from so much in the neo-orthodox writings, which sometimes impress one as all based on a single text: "The good that I would I do not; the evil that I would not, that I practice. . . . Wretched man that I am, who shall deliver me?"[8]

For in this very passage the apostle does not end with the cry of despair, "Who shall deliver me?" but with the cry of gratitude and victory, "I thank God through Jesus Christ our Lord."[9] And he makes it plain that the victory has, among other things, its revolutionary and transforming moral results and would have to be dismissed as spurious and not fully Christian if it failed to bear such fruit. "The ordinance of the law" is to be "fulfilled in us." If we still "mind the things of the flesh" then we are not Christ's. "We are debtors, not to the flesh, to live after the flesh; for if ye live after the flesh, ye must die." Only "if by the Spirit ye put to death the deeds of the body, shall ye live."[10]

The moral life is a paradox truly enough and we are greatly in the debt of neo-orthodox theologians for having brought the paradox back into the focus of our thinking and preaching. But they get their paradoxes twisted around, I think. It is true, as they insist, that even where grace abounds, sin still also persists. (They seem to me sometimes to come very close to saying that where grace abounds, sin abounds much more!) But this is not the Christian last word; it is the statement of the paradox in its negative, non-creative form. The Christian, scriptural, creative statement of the paradox is ever: *"Where sin abounds, grace much more abounds."*[11]

The negative and essentially non-Christian version of the paradox runs: "When I am strong, or think I am, I am weak and do not realize how weak I am. Truly, 'even the youths shall faint and be weary and the young men shall utterly fall.'[12] When I am pure, then I am impure. When I am wise, or think I am, then my mind is closed to knowledge and wisdom. When I love, I hate in subtle ways. When I seek life, or think I have it, I lose it."

8. Romans 7:19, 24.

9. Romans 7:24–25.

10. Romans 8:4, 6–7, 12–13.

11. Romans 5:20.

12. Isaiah 40:30.

The Gift of Grace

Most of us fail to dwell sufficiently on this truth, but we fail equally to dwell on the positive and creative statement of life's experience. "When at last I know I am weak, I am strong. Then I find myself the channel of the spirit of the one who 'giveth power to the faint and increaseth strength to him that hath no might.' When at last I know how impure I am and no longer seek to evade or escape the humiliating and bitter realization of that, then I am purified 'even as he is pure.' When I no longer regard truth as an achievement or possession of mine and am no longer defensive about my opinions and ideas, then my mind is liberated and truth can enter its open door. When I recognize in what subtle ways I am tempted to seek my own and to hate others, then I cease to hate and do accept and love my fellows. When I lose my life, I find it."[13]

All of this is so clearly the Christian message of redemption that for all his pessimism Niebuhr cannot avoid pointing to it. Thus in his latest book he says that the New Testament "promises a new beginning in the life of any man, nation or culture which recognizes the persistence and depth of man's defiance."[14]

Daniel Day Williams, in his book *God's Grace and Man's Hope*, in similar vein declares: "God does transform rebellious and self-sufficient men into persons who can begin to love their fellows"; and he adds the very important observation: "The Power which works this transformation is *released in the depths of the personal life just at the point where man finds his own self-righteousness shattered*."[15]

Thus Christian humility, the abandonment of human "pretension" to which Niebuhr summons us, is the "moment" in which we experience the transforming power of God and are born anew of his spirit. It is not the moment in which we experience as final or decisive our own helplessness and corruption. When we become obsessed with human helplessness and corruption instead of being caught up in transcending them by the grace of God, we are still preoccupied with self, still self-centered and, therefore, still self-righteous. That heart that is "deceitful above all things" arrogates virtue to itself because it "knows," as "other men" do not, how self-righteous we are.[16] If we do not end with the experience of the grace and power of

13. 2 Corinthians 12:10, Isaiah 40:29, 1 John 3:3, Matthew 10:39.

14. Reinhold Niebuhr, *Faith and History* (New York: C. Scribner's Sons, 1949), 140. The punctuation of this quotation differs from that of the original.

15. Daniel Day Williams, *God's Grace and Man's Hope* (New York: Harper and Brothers, 1949), 58. Emphasis Muste's.

16. Jeremiah 17:9.

God as that which overcomes and blots out our preoccupation with our sinful selves, we are but giving another demonstration of the pretension and corruption of humanity.

Part 2: Hope and Free Will

Not only in its presentation of the nature of the Christian experience of salvation is the neo-orthodox position open to important criticisms, but also in its teaching with respect to the moral life and experience: what people ought to do and can do.[17]

The opening sentences of Dr. Williams' *God's Grace and Man's Hope* read: "The Christian religion has always created hope in the human spirit. It has produced men who live in the world of affairs with a unique expectancy."[18] He proceeds then to criticize Reinhold Niebuhr and certain other theologians for cutting this "nerve of hope." Similarly, the neo-orthodox orientation and mood tend to cut the nerve of moral action in the individual, largely as a result of what it has to say about sin.

As they use it, "sin" appears to refer to two different things: the ordinary, garden variety of sin, which is the failure of human beings to do what they ought to do; and a sort of primal curse that rests upon people and history and binds them with a chain of evil, quite apart from any choices of good and evil on the part of individual human beings or groups.

Dr. H. D. Lewis of the University of Wales has stated one type of criticism of the neo-orthodox presentation of sin as a "mysterious cosmic disaster" so effectively that it would be foolish to attempt to improve upon it and unfortunate to paraphrase rather than quote him:

> A sinfulness which is as much that of the race as of the individual, which depends on a freedom quite different from the power to choose between good and ill, which is "introduced into the human situation," and made inevitable by a "force of evil prior to any human action," is devoid of relevance to the conduct of individual lives; and for that reason alone it must stand discredited at the bar of ethics.[19]

To this Dr. Lewis adds:

17. I ask the reader to keep in mind, however, what has already been said about the religious experience: what God does for humanity, and the source of the dynamic for moral action. (Footnote Muste's.)

18. Williams, *God's Grace and Man's Hope*, 17.

19. H. D. Lewis, *Morals and the New Theology* (London: Victor Gollancz, 1947), 68.

> The upshot of Niebuhr's doctrine is the presentation of sin, as many are only too prone to regard it today, as some mysterious cosmic disaster, some vague blot upon the universe which we just cannot conjure away, something also on account of which we must all bow our heads in shame, and, in particular, something towards which we should adopt certain religious attitudes and about which theological doctrines have to be formed. The preacher must stand in his pulpit at appointed times to pronounce himself "agin it," and to announce the way of salvation. But none of this appears to touch the individual in the conduct of his life, and however much he may be induced to give formal assent to his own involvement in the sins of the world, he remains fundamentally serene in the assurance that it does not really concern him for the simple reason that there was nothing he could have done about it.[20]

To agree with this criticism is not to say that humanity's lot is not in certain aspects a tragic one. We are finite creatures whose days are as grass. We cannot transcend our finiteness. The circumstances of our lives are often desperate, our social environment depressing and corrupting. Suffering of many kinds is likely to fall to our lot. But the issue of the moral life is not whether we can overcome our limitations and escape suffering: it is how we meet suffering (and pleasure as well), and whether we can and do fulfill the will of God for humanity, equipped and situated as we are.

In dealing on the plane of moral conduct with the very real problem of human sin in its proper sense, the extreme neo-orthodox emphasis on human impotence and corruption is a dangerous distortion.

Thus, if we are to acknowledge the existence of such a thing as moral life and moral responsibilities, then we must have some genuine freedom of choice. If in fact we cannot choose to do the right thing, then we are not free, not any more than we would be if we had no power to choose the wrong. Either humanity cannot be so impotent as many neo-orthodox utterances make us out to be, or we are not morally responsible beings.

Similarly, this overemphasis on human impotence and corruption is irreconcilable with the basic character of the moral consciousness itself: what happens in the "moment" when we experience the "sense of ought," the feeling that one "must" do this or that. To quote Mr. Lewis again: "As deep rooted an assurance of the moral consciousness as any" is that "the 'sense of ought' carries with it the assumption that I can, not that I cannot."[21] Moral responsibility becomes a fantasy if we say in effect that the moral

20. Ibid., 68–69.

21. Ibid., 31.

consciousness means: "You ought to do this, because—or although—you cannot." If I cannot, that is the end of it.

People may and do have questions about what is right. They may choose wrongly in some instances, by mistake.[22] But moments come that require a moral decision, and we find ourselves confronted with an inexorable "ought," the will of God made known to us. In such a moment we know perfectly well the difference between telling the truth or a lie, accepting a responsibility or dodging it, dwelling upon an impure thought or facing it for what it is and rejecting it. No amount of sophistry enables us, if we choose the evil, to say later, "I could not help it." The categorical imperative is precisely: "You could help it."

This is so indubitably the case that Niebuhr, for example, on occasion clearly supports this position. "The chain of evil," he declares, "is not an absolute historical fate."[23] And he asserts that the "self is always sufficiently emancipated of natural necessity not to be compelled to follow the course dictated by self-interest. If it does so nevertheless, it is held culpable both in the court of public opinion and in the secret of its own heart."[24]

Negative Use of Facts

But this is not the prevailing impression left by the Niebuhrian pronouncements. Instead, there is here another striking instance of Niebuhr putting his finger on a very sore spot, an important psychological and spiritual fact, but using it on the whole in a negative and defeatist rather than a positive and creative way.

Thus he points out correctly how in simple subtle ways we delude ourselves as a result of social and class bias and the like, and his castigation of liberals and pacifists is largely merited. But, clearly, if self-deceit is an incurable defect of the human mind and spirit, then the neo-orthodox theologians themselves are also subject to it. Consequently, their criticism of others can be dismissed on the grounds either that it is an expression of self-deceit or that there is nothing anybody can do about it in any case. If, on the other hand, the criticism has validity and point, it is precisely because the possibility of rising above it exists and people ought, therefore, to accept and utilize the criticism. But it is the self-deceit the neo-orthodox theoreticians tend to emphasize rather than the fact that in some sense the

22. There are serious difficulties at this point, and with some of the problems of "compromise" and the like that will be dealt with in a later section. (Footnote Muste's.)

23. Niebuhr, *Faith and History*, 28.

24. Ibid., 93–94. The punctuation of this quotation differs from that of the original.

human spirit sees through its own devious ways; the self-deceit rather than the "grace" that prevents us from resting comfortably in it.

We live in a time when the individual is in danger of becoming a cipher. We are overwhelmed by the vast and intricate technological machinery around which our working lives are organized, by the high-powered propaganda to which we are incessantly subjected, and by the State-machine on which we are increasingly dependent and by which we are increasingly regimented in peace and war.

In the face of such circumstances the individual *must* be able to believe in our own essential dignity and in our ability somehow to assert it. Instead, the neo-orthodox position has the effect, to use Dr. Lewis' vivid formulation once again, of drying up "the very springs of individual responsibility . . . in an apathetic surrender to oppressive doctrinal fictions."[25] The neo-orthodox version of the religious experience of grace and justification, the extreme alienation of humanity from God so as to "veil the nature of God altogether from the eyes of man" and to make the Christian revelation wholly mysterious, "an insoluble enigma expressible only in paradox and antimony," also supports this contemptuous view of humanity and human powers that gives support to the most dangerous trend of our times.[26]

Moreover, by making the process of salvation a wholly irrational one, it gives support to the idea that one must find salvation in the irrational. This is the notion that was used so effectively by the Nazis and is embraced by all reactionary movements, and that appears in a somewhat different form in the worship of the monolithic party, and the immolation to it of the individual's reason and conscience, which we encounter in communism.[27]

Having said all this, however, it is important also to take some of the central admonitions of neo-orthodoxy humbly and seriously to heart. A

25. Lewis, *Morals and the New Theology*, 70–71.

26. Ibid., 108–9.

27. We cannot restore the Russians to sanity except by recovering our own; we can overcome materialism only by renouncing it, and practicing brotherhood. Only the nonviolent can apply therapy to the violent.

But to ask a nation like the United States at the peak of its wealth to be willing to become poor, or at least poorer, so that others may cease to be poor, or at the peak of its power to renounce its power, is to ask a miracle comparable to that of atomic fission. Human experience suggests that such a new order can come only if there comes into being first a fellowship of persons who in themselves and through their fellowship embody the new order and who become its completely committed witnesses to all the world.

The communists have in their International such an instrument, and every day bears fresh and startling witness to its effectiveness on a world scale. Obviously an International of Love and Nonviolence is needed, and this is what the Christian church in principle is and in practice ought to be. (Footnote Muste's.)

discussion of the experience of grace and the demands of the moral law necessarily must issue in personal application. Intellectual speculation upon these matters may help, but it cannot take the place of decisions taken in "real life," on the "existential" level. The great sin is not in the intellectual distortions that may characterize speculations about these matters, but in the practical distortions of life as God meant it to be—the failure even to will the good, much less to do it—of which we are guilty. Here each of us must be our own critic and no one else's. The only real "answer" to what neo-orthodox theology has to say about human corruption and moral impotence has to be given by our lives, individual and corporate, by the church of Christ and by the members of that church. And who is equal to that challenge? As someone remarked recently, at the close of a long discussion when a feeling of deep humility had settled on the group, "That's where Niebuhr has us!"

What do we who contend that Christian theology cannot dispense with a doctrine of perfection have to say at this point?

In the nature of the case perfection can never be a claim. To claim perfection for oneself except in a society of the perfected would be to set up an ego that arrogates virtue to itself, the very root of imperfection. Moreover, the possibility of perfection arises precisely in the moment of true humility, when one has yielded oneself to God, and has ceased to make any claim for oneself.

The question as to whether in fact perfection can be achieved is one of those questions that should not be asked because it cannot be answered. The question cannot be answered in the negative because perfection is what God asks of us and we cannot place limits upon what "his grace made perfect in weakness" can accomplish.[28] On the other hand, as soon as we begin to talk about perfection as an achievement of actuality, all the difficulties already stated emerge.

Perfection Demanded

Nevertheless, perfection as the demand God makes upon us cannot be ruled out. "If ye keep my commandments," said Jesus, in the solemn closing hours of his life, "ye shall abide in my love, even as I have kept my Father's commandments and abide in his love. . . . I am the vine, ye are the branches; he that abideth in me and I in him, the same beareth much fruit. . . . Verily, verily, I say unto you, he that believeth on me, the works that I do shall he do also; and greater works than these shall he do."[29]

28. See 2 Corinthians 12:9.

29. John 15:10, 5; 14:12.

As the neo-orthodox theologians point out, the revelation in Christ stands in judgment over our achievements as well as our failures, and even in our righteousnesses, which are "as filthy rags," we stand in need of forgiveness.[30] But we stand under judgment precisely because we should and could have done what we failed to do. And the word of forgiveness is necessarily accompanied by the charge, "Go and sin no more."[31] Forgiveness in its most basic aspect means this: that God will not let us drop out of the moral universe; he will not free us from the requirement that we be his children reborn in Christ.

In every important sphere of life the passion for perfection is the indispensable binding and transfiguring element. What would our intellectual life and science be like but for the insatiable effort to wrest from the universe its innermost secrets? Suppose scientists, instead of sitting down austerely before some phenomenon, trying a hundred "solutions" if necessary and discarding in the process some of their oldest and most cherished ideas, were to tell themselves, "Well, people are but poor, fallible creatures. I am bound to deceive myself anyway." Clearly it is the passion for perfection, expressed in the iron determination not to be deceived, which alone makes science possible.

The same is true of the artist's desperate, agonizing effort really to "see" a landscape or a human face and transfer it to canvas; of the composer's straining to hear the exact harmonies of her symphony; and of the poet's longing for the word, the phrase, the sonnet that expresses his soul. And as with the artist, so with the artisan. Many have commented upon the frustration suffered by multitudes of human beings because the world seems no longer to need their craftsmanship.

So it is with human relations. How accurately the child senses whether there is genuine integrity in the relations of grown-ups to him or her and to each other! How desperately we need truth in all group relationships and how swiftly and surely the lack of it produces tension and frustration! How deeply each of us feels the need of giving and receiving love from parent, child, wife, husband, friend! And when all has been said that can be said by modern theologians or psychologists about our ambivalent and self-deceiving egos, we still long to give and to receive love and not any substitute. And we actually have experienced enough love to know that it has to be genuine and whole; that, as in Tennyson's homely yet perceptive lines, "In love, if love be love, if love be ours, faith and unfaith can ne'er be equal powers"; and

30. Isaiah 64:6.

31. John 8:11.

that we cannot tolerate even "the little rift within the lute that by-and-bye will make the music mute."[32]

Moral Standards Blurred

A civilization that has blurred the ideas of obligation to the highest moral standards and accountability to God has no bond to hold it together. A generation that believes itself condemned to moral impotence is doomed to moral impotence and to disintegration.

So it is, finally, in the deepest and innermost realm of all, that of religious experience, that the human soul thirsts for God, not for a lesser being, and will not rest until it finds its rest in him.[33] "My soul thirsteth for God; yea, e'en for the living God."[34] Even *my* soul . . . for the *living God*.

There it is, as it was yesterday and will be forever. That "thirst" and its quenching in the water of life that proceeds from God and becomes in us as a well of water springing up into eternal life is what religion and all our theologies are about. Nothing else finally is worth writing about. There would be no human life if this binding element of the thirst for perfection and its satisfaction were not in it.

There is, of course, a better keyword to use here than the term "perfection." The keyword is "commitment" or "surrender." It is the purity of heart, the integrity, of which Jesus spoke. It is Kierkegaard's concept, "Purity of heart is to will one thing."[35]

When our theological discussions are ended as when they began, the one overarching question remains: Are we willing to make this unconditional surrender to the will of God as it is revealed? Are we willing to make the unequivocal and complete commitment of all we have and are to his service? Christ stands before each of us and says: "Will you take up your cross and follow me?"[36]

And the first and gravest difficulty is simply that we will not say yes to that question, as Tertullian suggests in a notable passage: "The state of faith does not admit of necessities. No necessity of sinning have they, whose one

32. Alfred Tennyson, "Merlin and Vivian," in *Idylls of the King* (New Haven: Yale University Press, 1983), lines 385–86, 388–89.

33. See Augustine, *Confessions*, 1.1.1.

34. Psalm 42:2.

35. Søren Kierkegaard, *Purity of Heart is to Will One Thing: Spiritual Preparation for the Feast of Confession*, trans. Douglas V. Steer (New York: Harper & Brothers, 1938).

36. Matthew 16:24, Luke 9:23.

necessity is that of not sinning. . . . For (otherwise) *even inclination can be pleaded (as a) necessity having of course an element of compulsion in it*."[37]

We are warranted, therefore, in humbly asking those of our fellow Christians who frame, or accept, elaborate and distorted doctrines about humanity's general inability to do the will of God and adhere to the ethic of the gospel whether they are in this way rationalizing their own disinclination to obey the gospel at some very specific point—in not renouncing war, for example, when deep in their hearts they know there is no longer any way in which it can be reconciled with the gospel. Yet who among us is not stricken with shame by the knowledge that we, too, are holding back part of the price of complete commitment that God asks? What is there for us to do in face of the ghastly need of our age and the disaster that threatens it but pray unitedly for the spirit of repentance and faith, knowing that all things are possible to those who believe and are willing to submit to the baptism of the Holy Spirit?

Part 3: Utopianism in Christianity

The doctrine of utopianism holds a key position in scriptural and Christian teaching about the nature and goal of society or history. Unless there is a strong reaffirmation of the revolutionary Christian hope of God's kingdom on earth, the battle against war and communism cannot be effectively waged and a democratic world order achieved.

There is general agreement that the Judeo-Christian faith is a dynamic one. It emphasizes the concepts of purpose and goal both for the individual and for humankind or society. It is, as has often been remarked, an historical religion. It is in history that God is incarnated and reveals himself. His will is worked out in the history of his people and of humankind.

As the Genesis account of Abraham and the commentary upon it in the eleventh chapter of Hebrews reminds us, the important thing in the biblical worldview is always the city that still lies ahead, which has truer and more divine foundations than the city where one now is. The decisive thing about any person or society is not the city to which it is bound because of what has happened before, but the city to which it is called by God.

The concept of freedom for the individual and of a free society, which is of such vital importance in the Western tradition, derives largely from this biblical teaching. Clearly under that teaching no existing "city"—institution,

37. Tertullian, *De Corona Militis*; quoted in C. J. Cadoux, *The Early Christian Attitude to War* (London: Headley, 1919), 112. Parentheses Cadoux's. This quotation differs insignificantly from the original.

state, church, economic order—has an absolute right over the individual or an absolute claim upon one's allegiance.

Furthermore, this prophetic view of history is revolutionary in the most drastic sense. When we argue, as do the Niebuhrians, that the city that is to be stands in judgment over every existing city or society, *we* take this to mean that God demands of every society that it meet the divine specifications.

To proclaim *this* society, in which people shall live as sisters and brothers in God and the will of the Father be done on earth as in heaven, is ever the task of the true church. This is what it means to be salt that has not lost its savor, leaven that has not ceased to ferment, a light that is not hid under a bushel, a voice that speaks to people in the name of God and does not simply repeat what they tell each other.

That it is the will of God that the society of righteousness, brotherhood, and peace be established on earth seems to me impossible to dispute on scriptural or Christian grounds. I do not see how the purpose of God, as revealed in Jesus, could well be anything else, and it cannot logically be held that God's purpose is incapable of realization.

Judgment for What?

The repeated neo-orthodox assertion that every human social achievement stands under the "judgment" of God and of God's holy and perfect purpose for humankind makes no sense whatever unless humankind actually is called to conform to that purpose, and it obviously is not so called if it knows in advance that it cannot so conform. But indeed humankind, for all its confusion and corruption, will not give up its quest for that "city which hath foundations," for as surely as the human being was made for God and turns to him, so surely was humanity made to live in that community of love, and in no other.[38]

I do not believe that the neo-orthodox theologians succeed in resolving the enigma of life and history by asserting that we apprehend by faith that the love that is revealed in Christ and that "is defeated in the actual course of history," will ultimately "beyond history resolve life's ambiguities."[39] What we learn from the essential prophetic and Christian worldview is that God does incarnate himself in history; that humanity's historic task is to serve this God and to build a community in which people live as kings and priests

38. Hebrews 11:10.

39. Niebuhr, *Faith and History*, see 135–36. These are not direct quotations.

to God;[40] and that God in Christ is forever working redemptively in history, demonstrating that in this community and in nothing else or less is the meaning of the existence of the human race on earth, and waiting to bestow upon people the power to realize that meaning. It is our experience of this inexorable purpose and limitless grace of God in our own lives and in the history of humankind—our experience in history of the power of love and the cross to resolve contradictions and overcome evil—that provides us with our sole basis for any real knowledge of or faith in the divine power beyond history. The argument, "We see the weakness of love demonstrated in history, therefore we shall see its power demonstrated beyond history" is logically a non sequitur and practically, as Marx charged, "opiate of the people," reactionary and counter-revolutionary in its effect.[41]

The Niebuhrian treatment of the cross is also unsatisfactory in this connection. It is time that the "weakness" of a Messiah "without a sword," (to use Machiavelli's phrase); a revolutionary who will not build his kingdom on violence, is displayed on the cross for all to behold. To leave it there, however, is certainly not scriptural or Christian, nor is it in accord with the simple facts of history. Divine power was released into history in that event. It is not the cross in the context in which the neo-orthodox theologians constantly speak of it that either in fact or in the Christian worldview stands in isolation at the center—or "on the border"—of history. It is the incarnation, the life of Jesus, the cross, the resurrection, the church, and the world which for two thousand years has not been able to take its eyes off the man who hung upon the cross. The Lamb that was slain is in the midst of the throne.[42] God has not abandoned this "history" in which you and I live to Hitler or Stalin, to Russia or to the United States. He has not abandoned it to any secular or merely human forces. He maintains his purpose and covenant of old to make "the kingdoms of this world . . . become the kingdoms of our Lord and of his Christ."[43] It is still the mission of his church to proclaim this divine purpose, and not something other or less.

40. See Revelation 1:6, 5:10.

41. The first quotation does not appear to be a direct quotation. For "opiate of the people," see Karl Marx, "Contribution to the Critique of Hegel's Philosophy of Law," in *Karl Marx, Frederick Engels: Collected Works* (New York: International Publishers, 1975), 3:175.

42. See Revelation 5:6.

43. Revelation 11:15.

Not "The End"

Amsterdam is right: "The world is in God's hands. His purpose may be thwarted and delayed, but it cannot be finally frustrated. This is the meaning of history which forbids despair or surrender to the fascinating belief in power as a solvent of human trouble. . . . Nothing is impossible with God. . . . We are laborers together with God, who in Christ gives us the way of overcoming demonic forces in history."[44]

Nor do I believe that the apocalyptic passages in the Gospels and in Revelation leave room only for the Niebuhrian interpretation. In the passages referred to, the titanic conflicts in "the last days" do not constitute "the end." The end is not the battle but the victory of the Lamb and of those who have taken up their cross and followed him. "They reign upon the earth."[45]

It is true that when seers, either in the Old Testament or the New, steeped in the prophetic worldview, contemplate the historic situation, they pronounce judgment and doom upon it. But precisely because the city of stagnation and corruption is falling to pieces, new and revolutionary possibilities open up again.

So the cry of judgment and doom issues as it were from one side of the prophet's mouth while the cry of hope, "The kingdom of God is at hand!" issues out of the other.[46] There is no hope because of your sin and there is infinite hope if you will but repent and believe, because there is the infinite grace of God and his majestic and unalterable purpose—this is the prophetic and apocalyptic message.

Choice Between Absolutes

Any culture or civilization that does not have this vision of sin, judgment, and righteousness will be a very different one from the Christian civilization—imperfect as it has been—that we have known. It will be like the nightmare George Orwell pictures in his novel *1984*.[47] The choice today, whatever may have been the case in the past, is indubitably between a civilization Christian in its very essence or a totalitarianism that is no longer human in any sense known to us. Social scientists, philosophers, and theologians may still discuss, as they do, whether the world community in which people live

44. Visser 'T Hooft, "Report of Section IV," 88. This quotation differs insignificantly from the original.

45. Revelation 5:10.

46. Mark 1:15.

47. George Orwell, *1984* (New York: Signet Classics, 1950).

together in truth and love as children of God is "the goal of history" and whether humanity can achieve that goal. In the meantime the scientists who have unlocked the secret of the atom have already created the situation that means we have to choose, not among relativities that leave us at ease and free to guess again another day, but between "absolutes." People who hold in their hands the awful powers we now have or presently shall, either rise spiritually to the stature of the children of God who know how to renounce power for themselves or for any doubtful end, or they will perish.

One of the most serious criticisms to be made of neo-orthodox theology is that for all its emphasis on sin and judgment its effect is to blur this concept of the seriousness and absoluteness of the issues of history. It is true that somewhere, according to this theology, God's purpose stands in judgment over all. But it is far away, not here. It is then—"beyond history"—not now. Here and now it is a matter of "relativities and ambiguities," not a decision for Christ or Satan. This is taught us because if we regard what we have built as absolute, then we shall be self-righteous, arrogant, unmerciful.

Other Temptations

This last is true and we need to take it to heart. But we are subjected to more than one temptation, and the temptation to absolutize our own achievements may not be the most serious or pervasive. That temptation may be rather not to see that it is God with whom we have to reckon, his absolute and eternal purpose for humankind that we are bidden to forward, and that the judgment that will overtake us if we strive for a lesser purpose will not be relative and ambiguous but, as our fathers believed, concrete and total.

Was it "relativities and ambiguities" that people were choosing between when they rejected and crucified Christ or chose to leave all and follow him? It was not so then; and it is not so now. Any individual or church that concentrates even for a moment on the absolute nature of the decision that now confronts our world will either be plunged into complete despair and consequent impotence or will experience the agonies of true repentance and then realize at last that there is no hope save in *hoping all things* from God.

Consider now the bearing of what we have been saying about the Christian concept of humanity's historic task and the goal of history on the present situation. The Judaeo-Christian concept of the city that is to be—the concept that people by the grace of God can control their own destinies, are not bound to their past or an inexorable fate and have limitless possibilities—has played a role it would be difficult to exaggerate in shaping Western civilization, and thus increasingly the whole of humankind.

So unmistakable and central is this vision in the Scriptures and so obvious and crucial has its role been that Niebuhr himself from time to time gives expression to it in terms that even the most unbridled liberal of an earlier day might have hesitated to use. Thus, alluding to a quaint phrase from one of the sixteenth-century sectarians, Niebuhr writes: "There are no limits to be set in history for the achievement of a more universal brotherhood, for the development of more perfect and more inclusive human relations. *All the characteristic hopes and aspirations of the Renaissance and Enlightenment, of both secular and religious liberalism*, are right at least in this, that they understand the side of Christian doctrine which regards the *agape* of the kingdom of God as a resource for *infinite developments toward a more perfect brotherhood* in history."[48]

In a period of crisis people are not able to rouse themselves to the herculean effort required to break through to a radically new order of life, without such a hope in the possibility of infinite development toward a more perfect brotherhood in history. They cannot make the terrible sacrifices required unless they believe that they are making them in a supreme cause and for the highest good. We stand today at perhaps the most critical moment in the history of humankind, and it is appalling to realize that the Christian churches and religious teachers of Europe and America are not proclaiming the great Hope and in its name summoning people to revolutionary action.

Yesterday it was the liberals in the churches and the socialists, in and out of the churches, who offered that hope. Today it is the communists. There is no space to discuss in what respects they were or are in error; but it is not in holding before people the vision and hope of a liberated and redeemed humanity.

Why is it that theologians and Christian leaders who can make such ringing declarations of Christian hope and prophetic utopianism can nevertheless place their main emphasis on extremely pessimistic views of history and present possibilities? How is it that they insist that the best we can do is deal with "relativities and ambiguities," and nearly always in the crucial moment support the "relativities and ambiguities" for which their respective nations go to war? The Orthodox Church does that in Russia and most of the churches in the Atlantic Pact countries do about the same. Why is it that

48. Reinhold Niebuhr, *Nature and Destiny of Man*, vol. 2, *Human Destiny* (New York: Charles Scribner's Sons, 1943), 85. Emphasis Muste's. This quotation differs from the original, including having "religious liberalism" where the original has "Christian liberalism."

Christian leaders, instead of being engaged in the daring and revolutionary action so obviously needed, are politically mainly identified with the same positions as the non-Christian, secular liberals, and have no distinctive, Christian program to offer?

Here it is legitimate to remind some of our physicians of their own prescription, though it is necessary to do so in love and with restraint. Teachers who are in the condition just described might rationalize their own impotence and that of the society to which they belong by means of a philosophy that argues humanity's general inability to solve the problems of its history. They might even suggest that humanity's attempt to master its historical task would be an evidence of self-sufficiency, pride, and "pretension."

Crisis of Our Age

I think something of this sort is happening because the historical crisis of the atomic age cannot be dealt with effectively by Christian leaders or churches that do not break unequivocally with war. These are, therefore, bound to be pessimistic and to attempt to rationalize "the relativities and ambiguities" in which they are enmeshed. There are two chief reasons why this is so.

In the first place, it has become impossible for Christian leaders or churches to drift toward atomic and biological war with any feeling of satisfaction and hope. If Christian teachers are not going to draw the line at atomic and biological war, they are obviously not going to draw the line at all. Under these circumstances no responsible Christian teacher can be easy at heart. I am sure none is. But until the break has been made, such people are bound to be pessimistic, to regard history as essentially tragic, and to verge on fatalism.

Secondly, it is Western civilization and the Western nations that these Christians wish to save. That is the meaning of the policy of the Atlantic Pact and the national programs of the Western nations.[49] But in its historic or present form this Western society cannot be saved. Colonialism cannot be saved. The American economy, based on having the United States as rich as the rest of the world put together, cannot be saved. Democratic nations that embark on atomic and biological war cannot be saved, at least not as democratic nations.

49. The Atlantic Pact established the North Atlantic Treaty Organization (NATO).

Human Self-Will

Those who identify themselves with a dying order have to develop a pessimistic philosophy. They cannot speak persuasively of infinite historic possibilities. And again, they cannot be easy at heart. For the question must surely be raised whether the most stupendous example of human self-will and "pretension" may not be given by those who still think that the Western world as it is today can be saved, or who at any rate try to save it, and can contemplate using atomic and biological war for the purpose.

The communists look upon the same world as the rest of us and they are not pessimistic. They believe they can solve the problem of history. They may be wrong, but they can believe it because they are not trying to save the existing order. They can hope, and no one will dispute that it gives them a tremendous advantage.

The early Christians were not pessimists either, and one decisive reason was that they did not identify themselves, their own future, or that of the church, with the Roman political order of the day or with the Hellenistic culture. They knew that these were not based on the specifications of their Lord and therefore could not endure. There would be a new heaven and a new earth.[50]

This is the perennial Christian hope. That the church should proclaim it again is the desperate need of our age. It is also the condition on which the church itself can experience another Pentecost. For this reason Daniel Day Williams' recent defense of Christian utopianism is an important and encouraging portent, the more so because this critique of certain aspects of neo-orthodoxy comes from a non-pacifist source. Says Dr. Williams: "Utopianism in the Christian hope. . . . is the willingness to let the old order be shaken to pieces and to believe that a better is possible under God who is forever making 'a new heaven and a new earth.'"[51]

Once again, however, if we are to be found faithful and are not to fall under "the greater condemnation," we must end on the note of confession. We have charged that certain of our Christian leaders are pessimists and defeatists and fail to sound the note of revolutionary Christian hope because they are driven to rationalize their continued attempt to save an order that cannot and ought not to be saved. That charge is, I firmly believe, warranted. But who are the greater sinners, these, or we who make this charge and profess to see how desperately the world needs a reaffirmation of the Christian hope for society and belief in the kingdom of God, and who nevertheless

50. See Isaiah 65:17, 66:22; 2 Peter 3:13; Revelation 21:1.

51. Williams, *God's Grace and Man's Hope*, 162. The ellipsis has been added where Muste omits material.

also still cling to the existing order, its comforts and its privileges, and are not ready to leave all and follow him?

Part 4: Love in Action

The failure of the nonpacifist theologians to make room in their political strategy for a creative application of love and nonviolence to power situations stems in part from a secularist and nationalist sentimentalism of their own. Because he excludes a return to the simplicity of the New Testament ethic, Niebuhr has no means of extricating himself from the position he now occupies of providing a pseudo-Christian cover for the sterile sophistication of power-politics, a moralistic screen for the Churchill-Luce-Truman line.[52]

The recent case of Klaus Fuchs, the brilliant and idealistic nuclear physicist, who during seven years of employment by the British government supplied atomic weapons information to the Soviets, furnishes an apt starting point for an analysis of this point. An ardent anti-Nazi, Fuchs believed that the Russian regime and the communist movement were offering the only really effective opposition to Nazism. Explaining how he came to "betray" the nation that employed him, he said: "I used my Marxian philosophy to conceal my thoughts in two separate compartments. One side was the man I wanted to be. I could be free and easy and happy with other people without fear of disclosing myself because I knew the other compartment would step in if I reached a danger point."[53]

One side of him was "the man I wanted to be"—simple, decent, loyal, friendly. But this side was dominated by the other compartment of his thought and life, in which, for the sake of a political end in which he believed, he violated the very standards he observed in the first compartment.

This phenomenon of human beings doing their thinking and acting in separate compartments is a familiar one. We observe it in any society

52. This presumably refers to Henry Luce, a politically conservative influential magazine publisher. Luce started and controlled *Time*, *Life*, *Fortune*, *Sports Illustrated*, and other major magazines. Less likely is that it refers to his wife, Clare Boothe Luce, who was a Republican member of the US House of Representatives and was often critical of Roosevelt and Truman.

53. This excerpt of Fuchs's confession was read by the prosecutor during his trial and was widely quoted in newspapers. It also is quoted in Joint Committee on Atomic Energy, *Soviet Atomic Espionage* (Washington, United States Government Printing Office, April 1951), 16. The wording differs significantly from the more recently released full statement, available at http://www.pbs.org/wgbh/amex/bomb/filmmore/reference/primary/fuchsstatement.html.

with a dominant and a subject group. Under the slave economy in the South the members of the dominant white group often were intensely religious people. Many of them were exceptionally sensitive and fine-grained people. Fairly often their simple human affection spilled over on members of the black group, as in the case of the white child and the black nurse, but always provided that this did not endanger the basic social pattern. According to that social pattern, the black had to be "kept in his place," which was not that of a human being among human beings. If harsh measures were necessary to maintain the pattern, that "could not be helped." (So President Truman, according to most Americans, "had no choice" when he made the H-bomb decision.) As in the case of Klaus Fuchs, the rigid social pattern could be trusted to keep the members of the dominant group from "forgetting themselves" and letting their impulse to be decent and affectionate toward human beings, regardless of color, endanger the social pattern.

The people today who condemn everything in American foreign policy but condone or even approve all Soviet actions, including forced labor camps, and who so sorely irritate a lot of Americans, are another illustration of the two-compartment, double standard behavior.

Surely the most startling and tragic instance of such behavior in the contemporary world is seen in the attitude of multitudes of people toward war. Twelve top nuclear physicists, meeting a couple of days after Truman's H-bomb decision, declared: "We believe that no nation has the right to use such a bomb, no matter how righteous its cause. This bomb is no longer a weapon of war but a means of extermination of whole populations. Its use would be a betrayal of all standards of morality and of Christian civilization itself."[54]

It would seem that no one could have laid down a moral absolute more clearly and emphatically than these scientists did. Somewhere a line had to be drawn: the means had become so outrageous that no end could justify them. One would suppose that these scientists, having drawn the line, would then have gone on to say that the nation must not make H-bombs, and that in any case they would have no part in making them. But when a reporter raised this question, their spokesman, Dr. Allison of the University of Chicago, "jumped to his feet" and said: "There is no one here who will not obey the President's directive."[55]

54. S. K. Allison et al., "Let Us Pledge Not To Use the H-Bomb First!" *The Bulletin of Atomic Scientists* 6, no. 3 (March 1950), 75.

55. William L. Laurence, "12 Physicists Ask U.S. Not to Be First to Use Super Bomb," *New York Times* (February 5, 1950), 1. This may not be the same report Muste read.

The great majority of Christians are apparently in the same position as these scientists. They profess belief in Christ's way, in love, forgiveness, outgoing good will, the cross. In some areas of life they live largely this way, and certainly feel bound to try. At the same time they can justify or accept war, including atomic and "super-atomic" war. They acquiesce in having their sons taught to control any impulse to spare the babies and women under a plane carrying an H-bomb, any impulse to fraternize with the enemy, to see and to treat them as human beings.

Compartments for Morals

In Compartment One we are in direct contact with other human beings. We try to be simple, human, affectionate. It is precisely these relationships between husband and wife, child and parent, brother and sister, friend and friend, that we find the deepest satisfactions and realize the greatest values. Here we are "the people we want to be."

In Compartment Two, on the other hand, we are usually most concerned, not with means and with human relationships, but with vast and complicated ends: the Russians and communists with the achievement of the Bolshevik revolution to liberate humankind; we with the defense of the democratic and Christian way of life, the survival of the American nation. When we are thus preoccupied with these "ends," we persuade ourselves that the means, abhorrent though they may appear, are justified because the end we expect to achieve is so great and good.

The great religious teachers, including Jesus and Gandhi, have always taught that it is this schizophrenia that is perhaps the chief source of confusion, evil, and corruption in human life—the schizophrenia not of "abnormal" people whom we put into institutions, but of the "normal," good, religious people, which makes an insane asylum out of a civilization such as ours today.

The great religious teachers have also all in one way or another agreed upon the cure. "Except ye become as little children," said Jesus, "ye cannot enter into the Kingdom of God."[56] We have to become simple, direct, and human again, the kind of people we "want to be"; and we have to be "whole" or integrated. That is to say, we must cease using one set of standards in one sphere of life and an entirely different set when we are dealing with complex social and political objectives like the communist revolution or the "defense of the democratic way of life."

56. Matthew 18:3.

Regard the Means

These teachers have always called upon people, caught in the complexities of a great crisis, to take their eyes off the distant and imposing *ends* and to fix them close at home upon the *means* they are using. They have raised questions about whether we really can control results, and whether, in corrupting our means and ourselves in order to secure certain results, we do not presently find that we have lost all along the line. They ask in what moral scales people weigh, let us say, the survival of the United States as a nation against the wiping out of another nation by hydrogen bombs.

Thus Søren Kierkegaard, the Danish theologian held in such high regard by the neo-orthodox school, in a notable passage toward the end of *Purity of Heart is to Will One Thing* asks whether "the means are as important to you as the end, wholly as important? Otherwise it is impossible for you to will only one thing, for in that case the irresponsible, the frivolous, the self-seeking and the heterogeneous means would flow in between in confusing and corrupting fashion."[57] At another point he asks, "Have your thoughts become giddy until the greatness of the goal made you look upon illicit means as of negligible importance? Alas, this state of giddiness is found least of all in eternity," i.e., in the thought of God.[58]

He points out that a person may fail to reach a goal through circumstances over which he has no control, and so be blameless. "He might even have been prevented from reaching the goal just by being unwilling to use any other means than those which the judgment of eternity permits. In which case by his very renunciation of the impatience of passion and the inventions of cleverness, he is even worthy of praise."[59]

We need to come back, then, to some simple moral decisions and then start anew from there to tackle our social and political problems—the decision, for example, that it is simply not human, decent, or moral for a nation to use hydrogen bombs, "no matter how righteous its cause." Failing this, we are indeed caught, as Kierkegaard suggests, in "the inventions of cleverness" to which we give priority over the purity of our means. In the practical realm Christian theologians, as well as secular teachers and leaders, hold that we must reckon with the "realities of power"; the question is not, they argue, "the naked question"—to use a phrase of David Lilienthal's—of making or not making H-bombs, but of the "responsible use" of the power

57. Kierkegaard, *Purity of Heart is to Will One Thing*, 187.

58. Ibid., 189.

59. Ibid., 187–88.

it represents.[60] We must not become Utopian but must shape our course according to what is expedient and politically attainable. The practical (sic) result of this reasoning is that we have landed in political disaster and the totally inexpedient—imminent destruction of civilization, if not the extinction of the race! In the moral realm, in our effort to defend "all the moral values of Western and Christian civilization," we are violating and destroying just those same values. It has remained for a secular commentator, Max Lerner, rather than one of our Christian leaders, to make the simple declaration: "The naked question about the H-bomb is a moral one . . . You cannot drape enough garments of expediency around the problem to hide its moral nakedness."[61]

To insist upon this return to moral superiority and directness as the only safe starting point for our political programs and strategy is not, as some critics of pacifism contend, to be indifferent to, or naive about, the political results of our actions. To be "child-like" in the sense in which the great religious teachers have constantly exhorted people to be is not at all the same as being "childish." The simple-minded person is not a simpleton.

For one thing, the pacifist bases his action in large measure upon the indubitable fact that the means do enter into the end, and therefore people will be balked in achieving good ends, as they have repeatedly been, by the impurity of the means they use. "The law of the means," which Jesus taught and exemplified in his own life, is clear and inexorable: Satan will not cast out Satan for you; violence will not overcome violence; evil will not put an end to evil. Evil can be overcome only by good.[62] The ethical, the divine element has to be injected into politics or disaster will overtake society. The word the church utters must be God's word; not the version of any well-meaning politician. Always in the ultimate crisis that word of God will in some sense say to people that they have to be prepared to "lose the whole world," to sacrifice the seemingly promising "results" of compromise, rather than "lose their souls."[63]

The Niebuhrians themselves have to recognize this in theory or in the abstract, or they could not remain on Christian ground. Thus one of them recently described Niebuhr's position as that of "a consistently pragmatic ethic

60. David Lilienthal was the chair of the Atomic Energy Commission. This phrase was reported in various newspapers. See "Balanced Defense," *Schenectady, NY Gazette* (February 1, 1950), 12.

61. The source of this quotation is unknown. Maxwell Lerner was a professor known for his frequent contributions to publications including *The Nation*, *New York Post*, *The Atlantic*, and *The New Republic*.

62. See Matthew 12:26; Mark 3:23; Romans 12:17, 21.

63. See Matthew 16:26, Mark 8:36, Luke 9:25.

on, of course, a *dogmatic* base, *absolute loyalties* and pragmatic politics."[64] I surmise that most pacifists—certainly those who engage in any kind of political activity—would have little difficulty in accepting that formula. They take it to mean that the "dogmatic base," the "absolute loyalty" to God and to the Christian law of love, must always play a decisive part in the means we use in every sphere of life. They hold that it forbids the kind of rigid compartmentalization that is implied in the familiar phrase, "Moral man and immoral society."[65]

Redemptive Love

The creative application of the element of redemptive love in politics is indeed far from easy or simple. The solution is not the one proposed by people who say that "if only everybody would get religion and be loving, then all would be well and we would not have to do anything about these economic and political problems—they would solve themselves." Insofar as pacifists have tended in that direction they have merited the trenchant Niebuhrian criticism.

The trouble with the Niebuhrians is, as I see it, that in practice they keep the "dogmatic base" and the "absolute loyalty" completely separated from "pragmatic politics." The demand of love remains, it is true, as a "judgment" standing over our political activities and pronouncing them inadequate, "pretentious," and corrupt; but love is never applied directly to those political activities—as salt or leaven—to make them less inadequate, pretentious and corrupt. It is not used to "spiritualize politics" save in the most limited degree.

No New Moral Issue

The disastrous results are now apparent. Each time a new and more destructive weapon such as the H-bomb is introduced, we are told that this "does not raise any essentially new moral issue." In one sense this is true enough, but either one takes this to mean that the evil that was all the time inherent in war and violence has now been made unmistakably clear, or one fails to draw any moral line, ever. Even Amsterdam may declare that the entire doctrine of "just war" is now "challenged" by the utter indiscriminateness of the weapons employed, but in practice Christian theologians and the churches

64. The source of this quotation is unknown.

65. This phrase is the title of one of Reinhold Niebuhr's most famous books.

still do not make a clean break with war, in spite of the fact that on what might be called "purely pragmatic" grounds these weapons might well be rejected as suicidal.[66]

To the theologian as to the statesman who bases their action essentially on what seems politically expedient and feasible at the moment, and who will not allow for an element that breaks up the old pattern, that lifts the conflict to another level, it always seems that the next step grows inevitably out of the preceding one. We "have no choice" in view of what the Russians are doing, and so on. That despairing phrase is as a matter of fact a true and revealing description of the situation into which the philosophy we are criticizing leads people and nations. If we do not begin and continue with the recognition that we are first of all responsible for making the simple moral choice between love and hate or indifference, then of course having deprived ourselves of the hard obligation to choose we presently "have no choice."

Thus it is that the Niebuhrians supply a pseudo-Christian cover for the Churchill-Luce-Truman line. The churches continue to support, though mildly criticizing, the current government policy. They do so because they are the victims of "nationalist sentimentalism." In dealing with political problems, that is to say, they look at things primarily from the American national standpoint rather than from the universal Christian one. Probably the emotional roots of most Americans go much deeper down in the soil of nationalism than in the soil of Christianity. The flag stirs a deeper loyalty than the cross. The former can conscript; the latter cannot.

Space permits only the briefest reference to the kind of program the nation would venture upon if it were persuaded to inject a distinctively Christian element into its international relationships.

1. The American people would resolutely practice democracy, especially in race relationships. Then the colored masses of Asia and Africa once again might think of "democracy" rather than communism as their ideal and hope. That might well constitute more "security" than all the atomic weapons in the world.

2. They would develop an adequate program along the lines of Point IV and the "McMahon proposal," and would refuse to divert their money and moral "steam" into military armaments.[67] There is never enough left

66. Visser 'T Hooft, ed., "Report of Section IV," 89.

67. The Point Four Program was a United States technical assistance program for foreign nations started by President Truman. It was the fourth foreign policy objective in his inaugural address. US senator Brien McMahon's proposal was for the US to set aside two-thirds of its arms budget for five years for peaceful economic aid to be distributed by the United Nations. This offer was to be conditional on the agreement

when a huge armaments program has been paid for to do an adequate job of feeding the world's hungry and rehabilitating its shaky economies.

3. They would, if it were necessary—and it probably would be—take unilateral initiative in laying down their arms, pulling out of the armaments race and thus starting a *dis*armament race.

4. They would prepare to offer nonviolent resistance and non-cooperation to aggression, if it should occur in spite of the shift from a foreign policy of power and defensiveness to a policy of outgoing and unconditional good will.

The means by which the nation might be brought to the spiritual revival that would make such revolutionary action possible on the political level would be people who would constitute what might be called a "peace army" or a "new missionary enterprise." They would be men and women, especially youth, who would accept the Christian, nonviolent way of life that we have set forth and who would be totally committed, utterly expendable, for it. They would go all over the world, with a special mission to communists and people who now come under their influence. They would go, not as Christians in effect now do, with Point Fours, Marshall Plans, good will and generosity in one hand and H-bombs in the other; but with readiness to help in any kind of suffering, leadership in the struggle for social justice, reconciliation in conflict situations in one hand, and the Gospel of Christ, of the divine-human society, the Kingdom of God, in the other. They would be "defenseless" as those early Christians who penetrated the Roman world.

As it is now, it is the communists who penetrate everywhere and carry on an immense and often highly successful propaganda. The Christian and "democratic" message has little or no appeal to them or the masses whom they reach. The current could be reversed, the Gospel of love and freedom made to penetrate among all countries, even into Russia, only in such terms as we have indicated and by people who were as ready to die for their faith as communists are for theirs, or soldiers have been for the cause in which they believed.

A New Spiritual Dynamic

Whenever in a desperate crisis in human history groups of this kind have come forth, a new spiritual dynamic has been released. That applies to the "remnant" called forth in Israel by the prophets, to Jesus, the early Christians, St. Francis, the early Quakers, Gandhi. It is the only hope for human

---

of all other nations to do the same and the establishment of international control of atomic weaponry.

civilization today. For if we wage the battle for democratic and Christian values on the communist level and with the same kind of weapons as the Kremlin, either general chaos will result, or else general totalitarianization and mechanization of life—the kind of nightmare George Orwell painted in *1984*. In either case Christian values will disappear, and a truly human civilization in which the individual still has dignity and worth will be out of the question. The fantastic power now in the hands of people who trust in power and despise love will annihilate or dehumanize humanity.

If the Christian churches were soon to make a clean break with war and rally their youth in such a crusade as we are calling for, it might be possible to avert the catastrophe of a third world war. The Quakers have for a few decades done something of this sort on a small scale and with a not too well-developed philosophy or truly global strategy. The main drive has been much more remedial than nonviolently revolutionary, but even so the results are quite amazing. They are about the only Americans who can even talk to Russian leaders. Suppose the great Christian denominations had been following some such program in the past thirty or forty years instead of doing what they have been doing!

The "Remnant"

Even if, however, the "peace army" was not able to avert the catastrophe—and such groups must always be willing to seem politically impotent and irrelevant at the outset—it is still the case that without such a "remnant" the Christian church and human civilization will perish. The salt, become savorless, will be trodden under foot.[68]

It is possible that pacifists and nonpacifists in the Christian community might, though not reaching theological uniformity, unite on a common strategy along some such lines as we have suggested. In so abysmal a crisis as this that possibility must be earnestly explored. Niebuhrians could, on essentially pragmatic grounds, such as the uncontrollability of modern war and the impossibility of salvaging any semblance of democracy in an atomic armaments race, arrive at the conclusion that war must be ruled out. They might also agree that nonviolent resistance, non-cooperation, was the pragmatically feasible (non-Utopian) way to apply as much love in the situation as is possible in history.

On the other hand, pacifists also could join in the development of nonviolent resistance either on the ground that nonviolence is the expression of love in society, the means to avoid "double-standard" and

68. See Matthew 5:13.

"compartmentalizing" ethics; or in the case of those pacifists who accept a good part of neo-orthodoxy, on the ground that nonviolence is as near as people can come to injecting the "salt" and the "leaven" of love into the power-situation, to "spiritualizing politics." If a nation were prepared, under such an ethical drive, to devote to the development of nonviolent science and strategy of resistance one-tenth of the money, energy, and brains that is now spent on the obsolete "science" of war, it would surely be arguable that the chances were that this would provide much more "security" than any nation now has.

22

A Prayer for Peace (1950)

Muste wrote this prayer for the Conference on the Church and War, held in Detroit, Michigan in May 1950. The conference's main theme was calling churches to devote themselves to working against the social, economic, and moral causes of war. Church Peace Mission, one of the many organizations Muste helped lead, was founded as a means of sharing the work started at the conference.

LORD, Thou hast been our dwelling-place in all generations; before the mountains were brought forth or ever Thou hadst formed the earth and the world, even from everlasting to everlasting Thou art God.[1]

We come to Thee in a day of confusion and anguish; in a time when terror walks at night about the earth and destruction wastes at noon-day.[2]

Nevertheless, we are not dismayed or as those who have no hope.[3] For we know that we and our fellows throughout the world grope in darkness because we have trusted in our own wisdom and now it has been turned

1. Psalm 90:1.
2. Psalm 91:6
3. See 1 Thessalonians 4:13.

into foolishness.[4] We are stricken because we have not lived according to Thy laws. We are impotent to do even the good that we would, because we have relied upon our own strength.[5] Even while we fathom the secrets of the physical universe and exercise power almost akin to Thine, people and nations are wasting their heritage and destroying themselves, because we have forgotten that without love all this is nothing, and have not sought first the Kingdom of God and his righteousness.[6]

Now we confess that without Thee we are nothing, and in so confessing receive the blessed assurance that with Thee all things are possible.[7]

Grant to us and all people that we may become again as little children willing and able to receive Thy truth for our guidance.[8] Remove all barriers of self-centeredness, self-will and fear which prevent us from submitting and committing our wills to Thine.

Pour out Thy spirit upon Thy church in order that its divisions may be healed; that it may proclaim the everlasting gospel of love to the world with a single voice and with new power; and that in the name of Christ it may take the weapons of the flesh out of the hands of its sons, forbid war, and proclaim the peace of Christ to the nations.

And incline the peoples everywhere and those who are in authority over them to heed this call, that they may at last enter into the heritage which Thou hast prepared for them, beat their swords into plough-shares, and their spears into pruning hooks, and learn war no more.[9]

And unto Thee, Eternal Father, who hast promised, "Behold, I make all things new," shall be praise and dominion, now and ever more, through Jesus Christ, our Lord, who taught us when we pray to say: Our Father, Who art in Heaven, hallowed be Thy name; Thy kingdom come; Thy will be done on earth as it is in Heaven. Give us this day our daily bread, and forgive us our trespasses as we forgive them who trespass against us. And lead us not into temptation, but deliver us from evil, for Thine is the Kingdom, and the power, and the glory, forever. Amen.[10]

4. See Job 12:25, 1 Corinthians 1:20.
5. See Romans 7:15, Zechariah 4:6.
6. See Matthew 6:33.
7. See Matthew 19:26; Mark 9:23, 10:27, 14:36.
8. See Matthew 18:3.
9. See Isaiah 2:4, Micah 4:3.
10. See Revelation 21:5, Matthew 6:9–13.

23

I Believe (1950)

In this speech, given at his sixty-fifth birthday party, Muste speaks of the things that shaped him: his belief in God, love of nature, thirst for knowledge, conviction that every human being is to be loved equally, and his view that we work for causes we believe in not because we are guaranteed success, but because it is right. He also shares how his belief in the possibility of the kingdom of God informs his advocacy of nonviolence.[1]

First of all, I believe in God. I think it is possible to build a reasoned argument for the existence of God, though there are serious dangers connected with the effort. It is not on that account, however, that I believe in God but simply because I cannot not believe in him. He is given in my experience and as the ground of all my experience as surely—more surely—than this hand that I raise before my eyes, this desk that I grasp.

1. Muste's introductory remarks that preceded this speech, which were not included in the published version and are not included here, can be found along with the original manuscript at the Swarthmore College Peace Collection, A. J. Muste Papers, later accessions box 2.

This does not mean that I behave consistently, as this belief requires. God had always been to me at least as much the Demand from which we try to escape—I suppose my Calvinist upbringing may account for that—as he is the Everlasting Rock upon whom we rest, the Redeemer who makes no conditions when we return to him after having tried everything else—to whom we do never turn until we have tried everything else.

Secondly, there is a noble line in the creation story in Genesis on which I have dwelt repeatedly during the years: "And God saw everything that he had made, and behold, it was very good. And there was evening and there was morning, the sixth day."[2] I do not think there has been a day in my conscious life when I have not had some moments in which I have been shaken and renewed and transported by some aspect of the ineffable beauty of creation. There are many days when the revelation of beauty in the face of a child or an old man, in the deep blue sky, in a poem, a dance, in the leafy tracery of a tree, is almost continuous. Some of you will know A. E. Housman's poem about cherry blossoms:

> Loveliest of trees, the cherry now
> Is hung with bloom along the bough,
> And stands about the woodland ride
> Wearing white for Eastertide.
> Now, of my threescore years and ten,
> Twenty will not come again,
> And take from seventy springs a score,
> It only leaves me fifty more.
> And since to look at things in bloom
> Fifty springs are little room,
> About the woodlands I will go
> To see the cherry hung with snow.[3]

So I felt about spring blossoms when I was twenty and there were still innumerable years left. So I feel about them now at sixty-five when according to Housman's reckoning, which I do not accept, there are only five years left.

The Pursuit of Truth

Thirdly, I believe in the pursuit of knowledge, of truth, wherever it may lead. The fact that scientists prostitute their knowledge, imagination and skill to make atomic bombs and biological weapons causes no greater revulsion

2. Genesis 1:31.

3. A. E. Housman, "Loveliest of Trees, the Cherry Now," in *A Shropshire Lad: Poems By A.E. Housman* (New York: Heritage, 1951), 13.

in me than the suggestion that therefore there should be a moratorium on science, that "there are some things that the human mind should not pry into." No safety or peace in any sphere of life is ever purchased by an evasion, a slurring over, a trembling at fact or truth. There are few things for which I am more grateful than for the fact that at sixty-five my curiosity is as unslaked as it was at six or sixteen. I pray God that the human mind may never lose its insatiable curiosity—which is the courage of the mind—or have it even a little dulled. The remedy for the risks which that involves is not that some ecclesiastical authority or politbureau should place a clamp upon the human mind but that humanity should develop a conscience to match its mind.

Fourthly, I believe that every human being is to be loved equally—and is equally worthy of love. One of the greatest sentences ever uttered in all human history is the familiar one: "Fourscore and seven years ago our fathers brought forth upon this continent a new nation, conceived in liberty and dedicated to the proposition that all men are created equal."[4] I think I can honestly say that I try very hard to keep this truth—this fact—that all people are to be loved equally in clear focus before my mind's eye.

This is not to say that human beings do not perform many unlovable actions. It is not to say that every one has an equally good mind, any more than that every one's nose is as big as mine. The law that all human beings are to share equally the love we have to give springs, for one thing, from the fact that love does not ask merit in advance from the object of its love. It is by being accepted that human beings can become acceptable, not the other way round. To every one of us the word of the apostle applies in the profoundest sense: "Ye are not your own, ye were bought with a price" by parents, friends, the patient generations who have gone before us and who served us before ever we had proven to be meritorious.[5] And the law that we must love all our fellows equally springs, in the second place, from the fact that when we see ourselves truly we know there is no one below us, no one whom we have any right to shut out.

The special love which we receive from and give to parents, lovers, children, had for its purpose to reveal the nature of love to us, its richness, the possibility of the including attitude toward others. If it fails to do this and becomes exclusive it is terribly corrupting so that in such a case Jesus can say: "If a man hate not father, mother, wife, child . . . he cannot be my disciple."[6]

4. Abraham Lincoln, "The Gettysburg Address."

5. 1 Corinthians 6:19–20.

6. Luke 14:26.

Fifthly, God does not issue blank checks. Life does not guarantee us results. We have to work for the causes in which we believe as if everything depended upon it, not because we shall then be successful but because it is right. One way to express this law of life is of course to say that you cannot eliminate the cross from life and history. Another way to say it is that there is an element of tragedy in life and that in us, therefore, an element of hardihood and toughness is needed.

I want to bring in part of another Housman poem here, which I probably read more than once at Brookwood Labor College graduations. After referring to those who unavailingly resort to drink to meet life's intractable and tragic aspects, he gives his own counsel:

Therefore, since the world has still
Much good, but much less good than ill,
And while the sun and moon endure
Luck's a chance, but trouble's sure,
I'd face it as a wise man would,
And train for ill and not for good.
'Tis true, the stuff I bring for sale
Is not so brisk a brew as ale:
Out of a stem that scored the hand
I wrung it in a weary land.
But take it: if the smack is sour,
The better for the embittered hour;
It should do good to heart and head
When your soul is in my soul's stead;
And I will friend you, if I may
In the dark and cloudy day.
There was a king reigned in the East:
There, when kings will sit to feast,
They get their fill before they think
With poisoned meat and poisoned drink.
He gathered all that springs to birth
From the many-venomed earth;
First a little, thence to more,
He sampled all her killing store;
And easy, smiling, seasoned sound,
Sate the king when healths went round.
They put arsenic in his meat
And stared aghast to watch him eat;
They poured strychnine in his cup
And shook to see him drink it up:
They shook, they stared as white's their shirt:

Them it was their poison hurt.
—I tell the tale that I heard told.
Mithridates, he died old.[7]

The Coming of the Kingdom

Finally, I believe nevertheless in the coming of the kingdom of God on earth, in the achievement of the revolution which will bring to pass a brotherly and peaceful human society. It is a paradoxical thing to say this after what I have just been saying; and certainly that heavenly kingdom will not come if we will work for it only on condition that its coming is guaranteed. It may seem utterly mad to assert this hope in a day when cynicism has become synonymous with sophistication and profundity, and hope is esteemed a vice rather than a virtue. Nevertheless, I do so believe.

Now my recent observation and experience in India have greatly strengthened my conviction that this true revolution can only be achieved nonviolently.

There is perhaps just one thing on which all the people who come to such a gathering as this, and whose respective primary interests are in the fields of labor, adult education, religion, civil liberties, independence of subject peoples, internationalism, or pacifism, would agree: that is the thing we call democracy—the way of life which gives a central place to respect for the human personality, its rights over against the state or any other institution, and the freedoms of speech, press, assemblage, association and religion which the development of free spirits require.

Therefore, we are also united in regarding totalitarian communism as a menace, and in believing that it is of crucial importance to find a way to combat and stop it.

I am more than ever convinced that the future of all the causes for which we are working depends now upon immediate and unconditional abandonment of a policy of war to stop Russia, or violence to "contain" communism. If the future is one of war and civil strife, no semblance of a free economy will remain, and labor will be enslaved to the war-making state. Civil liberties will not survive the militarization of life. Subject peoples will throw off one yoke, only to have a more galling one placed upon them.

War, together with economic disruption and the social unrest which it entails, plays into the hands of the Kremlin. The communist doctrine that

7. A. E. Housman, "Terence, this is Stupid Stuff," in *A Shropshire Lad: Poems By A.E. Housman* (New York: Heritage, 1951), 131–33.

the goal of history can only be achieved by violence, will not be disproved but validated by counter-violence. Violence and totalitarianism are twins: so are nonviolence and democracy.

Gandhi demonstrated on a grand scale in one situation, that of India, that nonviolence is capable of scientific application to social problems. The Gandhian science of nonviolence must now be developed and applied on a world scale.

Stalin or Gandhi

The choice before us is between Stalin and Gandhi. World-shaking events, such as the communist conquest of China, occur almost daily, to drive home for those who have eyes to see the lesson that there is no other choice.

Now to say that the nonviolent revolution, the divine-human society, can be realized on earth is to assert the possibility of miracle. That is precisely what I mean to assert. The universe, life, history are ultimately miraculous, in the sense that they can never be fully explained as effects of causes in the past. Something new emerges, is born—born in the life of individuals and of humanity out of decisions people make, out of a response they make to something ahead rather than to a shove from behind.

The ancestor from whom my first name derives, Abraham, is the great symbol here. It is said of him that he "went out not knowing whither he went."[8] The great eleventh chapter of Hebrews makes it clear, however, that if Abraham and men and women like him could not define their goal precisely, they did have a direction. They were seeking a city, and not the city from which they had come. If it had been they could have returned to it as, alas, most of those who leave it tentatively and do not simply remain rooted in that which is, do.

Abraham is then the living symbol of the great historical, revolutionary, creative law that the important thing about any person, people, age, is not their past but their future—not the city from which they came but the city to which they go, by which they are irresistibly drawn, for the sake of reaching which they do not shrink from fire and sword, destitution and affliction, bonds, imprisonment, or death.

They run the risk, it is true, of getting lost, for in the nature of the case that city which they seek is not yet to be found on any map. They and their fellows have by God's grace to bring it into being. And they may dream erratic dreams or build carelessly. But it is they alone who have a chance to

8. Hebrews 11:8.

find that city—who ultimately shall find, for it is written that "God himself is not ashamed of them, to be called their God."[9]

Thus Abraham. And if in some small measure I may continue in the years ahead to symbolize and be faithful to the mad, relentless, joyous search for that city which is to be—the city of which all true workers, all true educators throughout the ages, all true revolutionists, all true democrats, and all true people of faith have dreamed—I shall be more than content.

9. Hebrews 11:16.

24

Jesus and the Way to Peace (1954)

In this pamphlet, Muste draws upon Jesus' life to argue that Christians should embrace a pacifist position. He explains that Jesus chose God's method, the way of the cross, instead of the violent methods of Caesar. This is because God is love and "does not resort to the sort of thing people call power." Muste applies this to the United States' increasing trust in military might and calls the church to lead the nation in ceasing to "depend upon these Satanic weapons."

Jesus was born under a dictatorship. He knew what it meant to live in a period when naked power seemed to prevail; like people of our day, he faced the problem of how to deal with this evil.

Convinced that he was God's chosen instrument to deliver his people from the domination of the Roman conqueror, he declared: "The Kingdom of God is at hand: repent and believe the good news."[1] To the Jews that meant: "The revolution is here, the day when there will be an end of tyranny and people will live in freedom and security." That was the vision of a life lived in obedience to God's laws that the prophets had held before Israel.

1. Mark 1:15.

The Temptations of Jesus in the Wilderness

When a young person feels divinely called to a great mission, they are sure to be brought up sharp by the question: "That is a fine ideal but how are you going to realize it in this practical world?" It was that question Jesus faced in the temptations. As we try to make that picture real to ourselves, we can understand what an awful problem Jesus felt it to be.

The story of the temptations must have come to his disciples from Jesus himself. It was as though Satan himself drove him into the wilderness, he told them. For forty days and forty nights he went without food as he wrestled with his problem.[2]

What was that problem? The briefest and simplest way, perhaps, for us to understand it is to think of the third and climactic temptation. He seemed to stand on a high mountain and "all the kingdoms of the world and the glory of them" lay there before him. And Satan said: "Yes, this is the great world which you are to purge of dictatorship, oppression and war, and make into God's world. But of course you will need power to accomplish this. Great power. The kind of power that Caesar has, sitting on the throne of the world in Rome."

"Of course," Satan would have gone on, "you will not abuse your power as Caesar does. You will use it solely for good ends. With it you will save the world and make it over again."

A moment's pause and then the voice of Satan again as Jesus faced the greatest decision of his life: "You are wondering how you can get all that power. How can you, a carpenter from Nazareth, make your way to Caesar's throne, so that you may free your people?

"Well, there is only one way to do it. These kingdoms are mine. To have power over them, you have to fall down and worship me. You may be a little shocked to hear it put so bluntly, but a person who is going to become great must not be a dreamer. You have to take the world as it is. You have to get influence in the way in which influence is acquired in this world.

"Without political and military power you will be impotent. With them you will bring the reign of evil on earth to an end at last. When you are on the throne in Rome, you will not be like the other Caesars the world has known. You are God's anointed, the Messiah whom your people await. You will mount the throne and bring order, righteousness and peace to the world."

It was at this point, it would seem, that all questioning in Jesus' mind ended. He was sure that he saw God's will and God's way to the goal. He said

2. The story of Jesus' temptation appears in Matthew 4:1–11, Mark 1:12–13, and Luke 4:1–13.

to that figure at his elbow: "Get thee behind me, Satan."[3] This suggestion that had just been made to him he thrust aside as satanic, the ultimate temptation that comes to the one who seeks to do God's will on earth.

God the Father, Not the Dictator

Why did he judge this temptation to be so utterly satanic?

For one thing, Satan's suggestion implied a conception of God totally opposed to Jesus' conception. The whole foundation of Jesus' faith was the conviction that God is love, the Father of all people. Humankind is, therefore, God's family—brothers and sisters. Keep hold of this truth and live by it—"love the Lord thy God and thy neighbor as thyself"—and you can solve all problems. Let go this truth, and all will be confusion and woe.[4]

The very worst thing is to think of God as a dictator reigning over his subjects. "God, our Father," we can imagine Jesus exclaiming, "numbers the hairs of your heads. Without him not a sparrow falls to the ground. And you degrade him into a monarch lording it over slaves, a warrior trampling his enemies into the dust! To think of the Father in these terms is blasphemy; it is satanism!"[5]

In one of the most beautiful of the parables Jesus said in effect: "Think of God as a very simple father, who had a no-good son. The son asked for his share of the inheritance and without a word of protest the father gave it to him, after which the son promptly went away and squandered it. When there was nothing else left for him to do, he went back home. And what did his father do about this wastrel? He had been looking and longing for him all the time, so he saw him afar off, and ran as fast as he could to meet him, and embraced him, and called on everybody to celebrate with him. The older son did not understand it. But that is how it is, and you had better understand it if you want to know what life means and how in this sad and tumultuous world things are to be set right again."[6]

God Loves

God does not resort to this thing people call power. Power can produce subjects for a monarch, but not sons and daughters who freely love each other

3. See Matthew 4:10, 16:21–23.
4. Matthew 22:37–38, Mark 12:30–31, Luke 10:27.
5. See Matthew 10:29–30, Luke 12:6–7.
6. This story, known as the parable of the Prodigal Son, is recorded in Luke 15:11–32.

and the common Father. When sin and evil arise, God keeps on loving. He would hardly be God, Jesus suggests, if he did not. Even sinners love those that love them. God is God because he loves sinners, and suffers with them and for them.

God cannot be found, therefore, where the big noise is heard and the great guns are going off. There was an Old Testament prophet who had to learn that lesson. There was the wind, and the earthquake, and the fire that devastated the mountainside—and God was not in any of them. Then there was a still, small voice that anybody might have failed to notice. And that was God.[7]

When things go wrong, and there is "trouble" in this God's world, it means that there are children who must be reconciled to each other and to God. It means that family ties that have been torn must be knit together again. That is the problem, and anyone who would bring good in place of evil must use means that are appropriate in dealing with such a problem.

That brings us back to Jesus standing on the mountaintop. If God was the kind of God whom we have described, then no armed Caesar could serve as his instrument and revelation. The Father could only be revealed by one to whom all people were brothers and sisters. He, too would have to love the evil as well as the good—especially the evil, for their need was greater! Like the Father he would keep on loving people no matter how they might revile and oppose him, and no matter what it cost. Since his mission was to knit together again the sundered family of humankind, and to kindle love in the hearts of his sisters and brothers in place of indifference and hate, his methods could not be those of rulers and warriors. His ultimate weapon would have to be a cross, not a sword.

Love that Accepts Suffering

We may put the meaning of that third temptation and Jesus' rejection of it in still another way.

Suppose he had sought to take Caesar's place and used the means that would be necessary to accomplish that end. By the time he got there, he would be like Caesar. The devil was a liar from the beginning, and never more so than when he said to Jesus, as he constantly says to good men and women: *"If you will bow down before me, then you can do God's will. If you do evil good will come of it. Through violence you will establish peace. You are the exception, so you will be able to use Caesar's methods to overcome Caesar and yet be utterly unlike the other Caesars when you get to the top."*

7. This story about Elijah is found in 1 Kings 19:11–13.

It was this suggestion that Jesus rejected as satanic, because it is the last, most subtle temptation that assails the good person who is filled with a desire to save humankind. Such people are not subject to the ordinary temptations to be lazy, to steal money, to indulge the flesh. But just because they are not seeking their own selfish advantage, they feel: "this evil is so monstrous that it must not be permitted to triumph. What if I, Jesus, have to kill some Romans in order to free Israel and other oppressed peoples? The alternative is to run the risk that this tyranny may continue; surely that cannot be God's will. What if we, Christian Americans, have to drop atom bombs on Japanese cities? Does it not stop the war more quickly and end Japanese militarism? What if we kill a quarter of a million human beings in Dresden in one night? Don't you have to use any means in order to stop the Nazi hordes? What if we must use hydrogen bombs on every Russian city? Is it not God's will that we defeat godless communism?"

Suppose Jesus had yielded to such suggestions and had become the Warrior-Messiah his people expected God would send them? Whether he had succeeded or failed in his effort to liberate them from Roman rule, the world would have had another great national hero to admire. But there would have been nothing distinctive about that. There would have been no Christ. There would have been no cross. There would have been no Christian church, no Christian faith. *All these, with all they mean for humankind, we have because Jesus did not yield to the suggestion that evil can overcome evil. He clung resolutely to the conviction that love is the only force that can overcome evil and redeem evil people, though he knew that in the end it would mean the defeat and the ignominy of the cross.*

Love that accepts suffering on behalf of evildoers is Godlike. It is the ultimate expression of the divine nature. The idea that good can be accomplished and God's will be done by inflicting suffering on others is satanic. It is the ultimate source of evil in the world.

At another crucial turning point, when Peter had exclaimed, "Thou art the Christ," Jesus again emphatically pointed out that this did not mean conquest and the paraphernalia of power.[8]

The Garden of Gethsemane

At the very end, in the Garden, the agony was almost more than Jesus could bear. Defeat and death stared him in the face. All his work was about to be undone. His disciples were about to run away. Nothing would remain. And he was God's chosen instrument to deliver his people. Surely God did not

8. See Matthew 16:15–25.

want this to happen! At any rate, it need not happen. "Even now I could call and there would be legions at my command. Father, if it be possible, let this cup pass from me."[9]

But no sooner had he looked away from himself and from the surroundings into the face of the Father than the old conviction came back. God was the Father. He had no weapon against his rebellious children but a Father's unwavering love. Jesus, if he was indeed to be the Father's son, must do the Father's bidding in his Father's way. There might be some question as to what his exhausted flesh and torn spirit wanted in that awful moment, but he could not question what the Father willed. Therefore—"nevertheless, not as *I* will, but as *Thou* wilt."[10]

Once again, what if Jesus had made another decision? There would have been no Christ, no cross, no Christian church, no Christian religion. That is sure.

So when Jesus returned from the temptations and began to speak to his oppressed people, he said something like this: "Do not hate these Romans. Love them. You say they are oppressors. They are, but so are you, O Pharisees. And it is worse for you, because yours are the law and the prophets. You should have set a higher standard. Repent of your own sin, instead of indulging in the pleasant pastime of repenting of the Romans' sins.

"If you will give up the notion of overcoming Caesar by Caesar's methods and thus behaving like him in your turn, you will introduce a new, spiritual element into this vast edifice the Romans have built. You will be salt, leaven. You will lose your life, it is true, as one power-state among many. But thus you will break the eternal, tragic circle of evil leading to evil, and in losing your life, you will save it and save this civilization as well. And then I will be your king—a new kind of king who comes meek, and riding upon an ass.[11]

"If not, if you attempt by the world's old methods to achieve liberation, you will perish. There shall not be left here one stone upon another that shall not be torn down.[12] And because the salt that should have preserved this civilization will have lost its savor—because you will have become just like everybody else—this civilization also will perish.[13] And me you will crucify.

"But," said Jesus, "that will not be the end. After three days, I will rise again. Why should you think that you can kill or stop God from loving

9. Matthew 26:39, 53.

10. Matthew 26:39.

11. See Zechariah 9:9, Matthew 21:5.

12. Matthew 24:2, Mark 13:2, Luke 21:6.

13. See Matthew 5:13, Mark 9:50, Luke 14:34.

his children? Why should you think that you can get rid of me out of your thoughts or that you can keep my spirit from working in the world? Over and over again people will have to face the question as to whether they will try other ways—build on sand—or whether at last they will heed these words of mine and do them, and so build human society on the rock."[14]

The Verdict of History

What is the verdict of history in the matter? Paul, only a few years later, was sure he knew. "We preach Christ crucified," he said exultingly, "to the Jews a stumbling block and to the Gentiles foolishness, but to them that are called, both Jews and Greeks, Christ the power of God and the wisdom of God."[15]

What the Jews and Greeks saw in that day was the mighty Empire of Rome. That was reality; that would last. Over against that they saw only a dead man on a cross. What they heard were the disputations in the great universities of that day, and the clank of the money on its exchanges, and the laughter in the palaces and the night clubs, and above all, the tramp of the Roman soldiers on every road of that world. Surely there was reality, there was power.

What Paul and the early Christians saw and heard was nothing of that sort at all. For them, all that was already silent in the dust of history. What they saw was their crucified Lord "seated on the right hand of power on high."[16] The creed of that early church was, "Jesus is Lord!"—not that man yonder in Rome. What they heard were the angelic hosts and devout souls in the ages to come, shouting: "Crown him with many crowns, the Lamb upon his throne."[17]

What is Your Decision?

Were these early Christians right or wrong? Is it Caesar who lives, or Christ?

We are living in the supreme crisis in our own and the world's history. Never has a nation possessed such a vast enginery of military power as the United States in this hour: the most highly mechanized army in the world, a navy greater than all others put together, the greatest air force in the world, a stockpile of atomic and hydrogen bombs, stores of biological weapons. Yet

14. See Matthew 7:24–27, Luke 6:47–49.

15. 1 Corinthians 1:23–24.

16. Mark 14:62.

17. Matthew Bridges, "Crown Him With Many Crowns," 1851.

it is not enough. We are not secure. We are more afraid than we have been before.

What are we going to do? Continue to pile up arms, to seek security in material power and military might? Or will the church of Jesus at last lead the nation in ceasing to depend upon these satanic weapons? That can only happen if the churches that name the name of Jesus, themselves renounce war and dare to rely on the power of goodwill, of faith in God, of sacrificial love, to overcome evil.

What the churches do depends in turn on the decision that individual Christians make. What is your own decision? Can you reconcile participation in atomic war with the teachings and spirit of Jesus? If not, will you refuse henceforth any voluntary participation in war and war preparations, and join with others in seeking to demonstrate that sacrificial love, such as seen preeminently in Jesus, is indeed the one effective force for overcoming evil and transforming our confused and divided society into a creative fellowship?

25

The Sound of the Trumpet (1960)

This article is yet another of Muste's critiques of Reinhold Niebuhr's theological "realism." Muste adds to his early arguments against Niebuhr by examining the impact of three decades of the popularity of Niebuhr's thought. Muste argues that by divorcing ethics from the kingdom of God, Niebuhr's ideas serve to discourage people from seeking to change "immoral society." Niebuhr's realism, despite its focus on sin, has not led to an attitude of self-examination or repentance, but has instead desensitized the national conscience. It has done nothing to challenge those who see themselves and their nation as relatively good.

One of the comments about pacifists we have heard most frequently for many years is that they have a sentimental view of human nature. In the field of religion this attitude toward pacifism has found notable expression in our time among writers of the neo-orthodox persuasion. Pacifists are, with rare exceptions, characterized by these writers as addicted to a liberal theology with no real conception of the corruption and depravity of humanity. Consequently, pacifists are supposed to have unrealistic and romantic notions about the power structures in society and the extent to which moral standards, and especially the Christian ethic of love, are relevant to corporate and natural life.

The pacifist reply to these criticisms has taken various forms. There is no space to deal with this now, and in a sense it has become irrelevant. The scene has shifted. Events are, so to speak, taking the offensive against the neo-orthodox theologians. They and we are now confronted with a paradoxical development. Three decades of emphasis on our involvement in the sins of the society to which we belong, of the need of forgiveness, of repentance, have not resulted in a national spirit characterized by humility, or an awareness that we must repent and mend our ways. By and large it is just the opposite.

It should surely give pause to teachers of Christian theology and ethics that among the suburbanites and exurbanites who now swell the records of American church membership and attendance, there is no evidence of a more widespread and deep conviction of sin and thirst for forgiveness than marked their forefathers. The emphasis on such matters may have made an impact in the seminaries, among the younger and middle-aged clergy and in the higher echelons of the Student Christian Movement, but surely not in the general run of church members. Churchgoers of today are not for the most part a "peculiar people" but are, on the contrary, essentially assimilated to the prevailing culture, which no one thinks of characterizing as profoundly religious or Christian.

As for the American people in their relation to the rest of the world and the problem of peace, the prevailing mood is that, as nations go, we have not behaved so badly, and in fact in some cases very well. The depravity and need for repentance and all that, we saw in the Nazis and fascists and Japanese militarists a couple of decades ago; subsequently and even now we see them in the communist world.

It is true that neo-orthodox ethical teaching has said that *all* social and especially national behavior is marred by lust for power, violence, self-righteousness and in time of war by increasing moral blindness.

Amoral Ethics are Unbiblical

But at this point the concept of "the lesser evil," of relative distinctions, takes over. Here in the United States at any rate the influence has always been that the relative difference is in our favor. We are far from perfect—but, for practical purposes, in this present crisis, we are decisively less imperfect than the adversary, and hence justice requires that our cause be preserved. I am not arguing now that there are not relative distinctions. I am simply pointing out what seems to me to be the effect of the hammering away at this concept on the mood of the people and the government of this country.

Furthermore, the effect of much neo-orthodox ethical theorizing has been to remove political issues from the sphere of morals to that of amoral power structures and relationships. In the familiar phrase, "moral man and immoral society," the tendency has been to place the emphasis on the, by definition, immoral society that operates according to its own laws and drastically circumscribes if it does not immobilize the moral in people, rather than emphasizing what moral people might conceivably do to an immoral social or political order.[1]

All this has little resemblance to the biblical teaching regarding sin, forgiveness, and repentance. This teaching is always specific, challenging just *this* person, *this* nation, not generalized. Each is called upon to repent of our own and not our neighbor's or adversary's sin. In fact, pointing the finger at the mote in another's eye is perhaps the cardinal psychological error and the ultimate sin for individual or nation.[2] In the biblical teaching there is no such thing as a nation that is an autonomous power structure operative to preserve and extend itself according to its own laws. Rather all people and all their societies are subject to the law of God. People are to live and to build their societies according to the divine pattern, not to bend the divine pattern to their desires and the exigencies of their nations.

By contrast with the biblical view, Americans think of themselves and their Western allies as the (relatively) good, civilized, Christian people who are threatened and have to defend the citadel of virtue and democracy against the rest of the world—against the masses of colored people who won't stay put any longer and especially against the atheistic and barbaric communist world. There is virtually no general awareness of the fact, which Martin Niemöller has often pointed out in recent years, that it was the Western nations that in recent centuries dominated the situation and overran the earth. It was the Western, Christian nations that fought the two most destructive wars in all history. If the world now is an avenging one, if it will not leave us alone, if it is terrifying, if war has become a monster which threatens to devour us, *this is the world which the West made. This is war which the West, not least the United States, "perfected." This world that will not leave us alone is the world that we would not leave alone: witness our missionaries, movies, commercial travelers, military bases and Polaris submarines all over the world.*

1. *Moral Man and Immoral Society* is the title of one of Reinhold Niebuhr's most famous books.

2. See Matthew 7:1–5, Luke 6:41–42.

There is surely something to be repented of here and it would make some difference in our national attitudes and even policies perhaps if we understood this. But the idea of a nation that has been and is in its way aggressive and in need of repentance does not fit the self-image that Americans have. It is not the image that is drawn for them by most Christian preachers and ethical teachers.

The United States committed a crowning atrocity in Hiroshima and Nagasaki in 1945. This was a major technological and political event in human history. It was a sin. It should be repented of. It never has been. Americans generally, and even, I suspect, multitudes of church members, still regard it as a comparatively minor event, the necessity for which was regrettable but which nevertheless saved a lot of American and even Japanese lives. What few understand is that the dropping of those bombs had an effect on the image of America in the minds of the peoples of Asia and Africa—an effect that damages our power position and gives an incalculable advantage to the Russians, who ever since can say they are only doing what "Christian" America did before them and against which they naturally must have a defense and deterrent.

Interestingly enough, the neo-orthodox and politically "realist" theologians agreed that those first atomic bombings were evil. Speaking of the so-called obliteration bombings of German and Japanese cities in the later stages of the War as well as of the atomic bombings, a Study Commission of the National Council of Churches chaired by Robert C. Calhoun but predominantly composed of nonpacifists, including Reinhold Niebuhr, said in 1946 that "we have sinned against God, and the people of Germany and Japan," and needed to repent.[3] But this judgment and this call to repentance were not made a major element in Christian teaching. Leading theologians were inhibited by their own approach to the problem from making it such. In that very Report they said that while "in the circumstances" that existed in 1944–45 the bombings had been sinful, this did not mean that the bombs should be done away with.[4] A couple of years later, the inference that there might even be "circumstances" where their use would be permissible was made explicit in the Dun Report.[5] The consequences of this attitude is that

3. Robert Calhoun et al., *Atomic Warfare and the Christian Faith: Report of the Commission on the Relation of the Church to the War in the Light of the Christian Faith, Appointed by the Federal Council of the Churches of Christ in America* (New York: Social Action Magazine, 1946), 12. This is not a direct quotation.

4. Ibid., 13n.

5. *The Christian Conscience and Weapons of Mass Destruction: Report of a Special Commission Appointed by the Federal Council of the Churches of Christ in America* (New York: Federal Council of the Churches of Christ in America, Department of

these Christian teachers did not protest against the obliteration bombings when they were perpetrated and did not present any effective opposition to the subsequent development of the H-bomb, ICBM missiles, and biological weapons. You can characterize an action in this field as sinful only when it is past and you have had a chance to know the "circumstances" under which it was done. You are inhibited from using, or at least trying to use, the moral imperative, the "normative principle," as Martin Buber puts it—the divine "Thou shalt not"—as a means to determine what "circumstances" shall or shall not be permitted to arise.[6] The moral trumpet habitually gives out an uncertain sound, because the trumpeter has their eye on a political score and a political conductor.

"Nuclear Pacifism"

In the past couple of years a considerable number of Christian theologians have reached the conclusion that nuclear war faces the Christian conscience with a problem that can only be resolved by an unequivocal renunciation and, to paraphrase George F. Kennan, throwing ourselves on God's mercy.[7] A group of leading theologians in the Boston area, in the main nonpacifists in the traditional sense, in an as yet unpublished study recently stated their conclusion that "a Christian rational for war is no longer tenable."[8] Quite independently and, I think, without any significant contact with any Christian pacifist agencies, a group of seven faculty members of the Theological Seminary of Dubuque University, Dubuque, Iowa, in January issued a statement in which they conclude that "there is no conceivable end" which justifies nuclear war. They draw very specific conclusions:

> All men and nations who follow the policy of war by mass extermination provoke the wrath of God and His just retribution, whether they deny Him or profess to worship Him.
> We therefore confess our sin and the sin of our people to Almighty God and to the survivors of those whom we have wantonly destroyed. We further confess that we as Christians have been shamefully weak and tardy in this our confession of guilt.

International Justice and Goodwill, 1950).

6. Martin Buber was a famous Jewish philosopher. The source of this quotation is unknown.

7. George F. Kennan, "Foreign Policy and Christian Conscience," *The Atlantic* 203, no. 5 (May 1959), 48.

8. The source of this quotation is unknown.

> As "fruit that benefits repentance" we declare that we can no longer support the government's policy of *the threat and exercise* of the means of mass extermination, whether nuclear, chemical or biological. We cannot sanction the *production, testing and application* of the means of mass extermination, nor can we approve of any military service that involves the use of such instruments of warfare.[9]

The contemporary situation has called forth this declaration from people who in these matters have been largely in agreement with Reinhold Niebuhr for many years. By contrast, a statement recently made by the latter seems to me to provide a tragic illustration of the seeming inability of a brilliant and deeply committed Christian to extricate himself from a philosophy of the relation between the Christian ethical imperative and the Christian hope, on the one hand, and political "realism," on the other hand. Even when it filled a useful purpose, Niebuhr's philosophy was too one-sided and schematic to be truly "realistic" and now, in the field of the nuclear power struggle, it is irrelevant. It may, indeed, even contribute to that tragic dénouement of Western civilization, or simply civilization, which political realism sought to avoid. Niebuhr writes: "It is argued rightly that if we use these instruments we will annihilate ourselves not only physically but morally. *If the bomb were ever used, I hope it would kill me*, because the moral situation would be something that I could not contemplate. At the same time *you cannot disavow its use absolutely prematurely without bowing yourself out of responsibility for the whole generation*."[10]

This means that we must continue to *threaten* to use the H-bomb and biological weapons. Is this consonant with Christian ethics? If it were, when—short of the ultimate catastrophe, i.e., of their actual use—does it cease to be "premature" to disavow their use? In practice, there is in Niebuhr's concept of politics no point at which the divine prohibition against evil is to be heeded against political calculations. The result is a state of political impotence from which there is no escape, because, in practice, there is no faith that repentance and Christian obedience might introduce a new dynamic into political life.

9. David I. Berger et al., "A Statement Concerning the Use of the Means of Mass Extermination in the Waging of War," January 12, 1960; quoted in *Presbyterian Outlook* 142, no. 9 (February 29, 1960), 5. Emphasis Muste's. This quotation differs insignificantly from the original.

10. Reinhold Niebuhr et al., "A Discussion," in *Foreign Policy and the Free Society* (New York: The Fund for the Republic and Oceana Publications, 1958), 67. Emphasis Muste's.

Niebuhr is well aware that nuclear war may occur through accident or otherwise. One can understand a person in a moment of human anguish expressing the hope that he would not be alive to witness the suffering that would occur or face the problem of trying to survive. But apparently this is not such an instinctive outcry, since it is the "moral" situation that would be intolerable. Does he mean then, as the preceding sentence in his statement seems to suggest, that, if the bomb were used, he would have annihilated himself morally? That he would have been implicated in an ultimate moral transgression? If so, then how is it a lesser evil not to disavow now an act that would mean annihilating oneself morally? Instead of being apprehensive that disapproval might be premature, one would surely dread that it might already be too late. Suppose one felt that such disavowal, even on the part of so influential a political and religious voice as Niebuhr's, would have little effect on the nation's course. This could not constitute a *moral* reason for not doing it. No Christian would suggest that we have a right to risk destroying ourselves morally, because other people would so destroy themselves anyway. Nor can the argument of the "lesser evil" be introduced here in the form that a communist nation might subdue us or even bomb us, for if Niebuhr means what he seems to mean when he asks for death if the bomb is used, then using it *is* the ultimate evil.

Symptomatic of a considerably different approach, yet also an illustration of the tug of the ethico-political philosophy that we have been discussing, is the most recent available printed statement by John C. Bennett, Niebuhr's colleague at Union Seminary. In the December 1959 issue of *Social Action*, published by the Council for Christian Social Action of the United Church of Christ, Bennett writes: "I do not see how Christians can sanction the use of megaton weapons. . . . It may be inconvenient to say this now because it may reduce the deterrent value of the possession of such weapons, but *we cannot go on for many more years being chiefly guided by strategic considerations on so basic a moral decision.*" To do so would "distort the public conscience and reduce our moral sensitivity. *For such assumptions to go unchallenged within the Church is for the Church to go against its essential nature.*"[11]

Bennett follows this clear analysis, however, by permitting the moral challenge to be muted by a minor strategic consideration: "What I am saying does not necessarily imply a form of pacifism, for *it might lead to a greater emphasis on conventional weapons.*"[12]

11. John C. Bennett, "Preventing Nuclear War," *Social Action* 26, no. 4 (December 1959), 8. Emphasis Muste's. The punctuation of this quotation differs from that of the original.

12. Ibid. Emphasis Muste's. The punctuation of this quotation differs from that of

But he immediately returns to the moral indictment of nuclear war, concluding with this warning: "A nation that does not recognize any limits to the evil which it may perpetrate for a political purpose is in no position to pass moral judgment on Communism."[13]

The United States is at a critical point in relation to nuclear war. There are indications that the leaders of both the great powers are aware of the suicidal and irrational character of nuclear war and hope things will not get completely out of hand. Some awareness of the menace is growing on the general public. But the arms race has not in any degree been abated. There are admittedly elements in the Pentagon and elsewhere that do not even want testing stopped and have demonstrated that they command plenty of ingenuity and political power. France, in defiance of the UN, forces its way into the nuclear club. German rearmament proceeds apace. And so on and on.

Conscience and Rational Fear

In this situation of stalemate, what can get us off dead center? What is the nerve that can be touched to move the masses into action? Nowhere in the world now are there political parties or labor unions that are solidly anti-war. Even progressive American unions run to the Defense Department for orders to fend off unemployment tomorrow rather than acting to save themselves and their children from possible nuclear annihilation next year. One nerve that might be conceivably touched is fear—not a general or diffused anxiety but a straight facing of the facts of what nuclear annihilation would mean, that it might actually happen to us. But whether mass action will develop out of this form of rational fear is problematic and in any event it is not enough by itself. So the question arises whether the nerve of *conscience* or *moral outrage* could be galvanized. Is it out of the question that the ultimate sense of decency in most people, the humane and to some degree Christian heritage of our culture, should bring the American people to the point where they could cry out: "No, we will not under any circumstances perpetrate mass extermination of another people"?

I think it is not necessarily out of the question; but it will not happen unless there is a great moral leadership whose trumpet sounds a clear and persistent challenge, inspires faith and enables the people to draw upon new springs of spiritual energy. I do not know where in our society to look for such leadership, if not to its religious institutions and in particular the

the original.

13. Ibid. This quotation differs insignificantly from the original.

Christian churches. But it will not come from them if they are shackled by a philosophy that is confused—at least at the point of nuclear war preparation—about the priority of morality over strategy.

Beyond "Simple Moralism"

Nor is it only a matter of avoiding war by enunciating a moral scruple about weapons. If war is to be averted, then the West must win the minds and hearts of the people in communist and uncommitted countries. As it is, the West does not have a coherent and positive sense of purpose. It does not have an alternative way of life, a goal for global human effort in the nuclear age to hold forth confidently to humankind. The West is essentially on the defensive, seeking to hold on to what it has. The United States is clear about a race with the Russians for missiles or for journeys into space, but not about anything else.

Neo-orthodox philosophy, by divorcing ethics from the kingdom of God, has contributed to this situation. It has emasculated the ancient prophetic vision of a "new heaven *and a new earth*, wherein righteousness dwelleth" and people shall "learn war no more."[14] Instead it has tended to serve to desensitize the national conscience to war at the very time war technology broke through all restraints.

A quarter of a century ago, Jacques Maritain defined the problem and the task in terms which can hardly be improved upon: "To absent oneself from history is to seek death. Eternity does not vacate time; but possesses it from on high. Our duty is to act on history to the limit of our power, God being first served."[15]

14. 2 Peter 3:13, Isaiah 2:4.

15. Jacques Maritain, *Freedom in the Modern World*, trans. Richard O'Sullivan (London: Sheed & Ward, 1935), 88.

26

Saints for this Age (1962)

This pamphlet is based on a lecture on "Springs of Religious Living in Our Age" that Muste gave to a Quaker audience in 1961. In it, he enlists the early church as a model for the present day and pleads with his audience to boldly pursue the kingdom of God together, while not underestimating the difficulty of the task. Muste was active in Quaker circles for most of his life, after first joining a Quaker meeting in 1918. He greatly respected Quakers' pacifism and work for social change.

"To all that be in Rome, beloved of God, called to be saints."[1]

I spend a good deal of time these days among those who are regarded as unbelievers, and my thoughts constantly shuttle back and forth between the conviction that many of these are the true believers, and the wish that I might be able to give them an account of the faith that is in me, and which in some sense they do not have, in language which is comprehensible to them. For many of us also, religion, or the living of the religious life, is a problem in this age. So beside us who say, "Lord, I believe, help thou mine unbelief,"[2]

1. Romans 1:7.
2. Mark 9:24.

stand those others whose heart's cry, if it could be uttered, might be, "Lord, I do not believe; help me to recognize that nevertheless I do believe."

To put it another way: our age is an age of crisis, and in the final analysis the crisis is religious. It has to do with ultimates, with what it is to be human, with the presuppositions by which people live, with the nature of the resources upon which we draw in extremity, the quality of life people seek, the values that they embrace, the drums by which they march, the commands they dare not disobey. It is essential that we should think about these things.

During the past week, my mind has repeatedly turned to those words of the Apostle Paul, who opened his Letter to the Romans: "To all that be in Rome, beloved of God, called to be saints."[3] This salutation tells us three things about the people to whom Paul addressed his Epistle. They were in Rome, not in heaven or the desert of the Sahara; they were beloved of God; they were called to be saints. They lived in Rome, a big city, a metropolis, the center of government and in considerable measure of culture. Most early Christians were city dwellers, as we are. In that Mediterranean world geographical and cultural boundaries that once had tended to isolate city-states and kingdoms from each other had been wiped out. This was partly because roads had been built, ship routes developed, communication speeded up; partly because the common Hellenistic culture had spread; partly because the Roman Republic and the Empire which had recently succeeded it had established its rule and a relative peace throughout that world.

In the old sense, the tribes or families, the city-states or villages constituting close communities in which people were born, lived, and died, no longer existed. People were in motion. They were sucked into the cities, especially into great Rome—slaves, merchants, adventurers, sophisticates, evangelists, intellectuals. Concurrently, the tribal and local or regional religions that had related their devotees to a realm beyond the immediately tangible and visible had lost their power and relevance. An assortment of philosophies that intrigued or even fed the mind but did not nourish the heart was offered. Materially, life was easier in that era of an expanding economy. But people were now individuals, on their own, rootless, fragmented. They were individuals, but not persons. The sensitive ones among them who could not live on the surface of life, nor find satisfaction in intellectual cynicism, nor in the moral heroism of the Stoics, experienced spiritual agonies in the search of release from guilt, escape from the bleak prison of the self, release from the terror of death: that is, the nightmare of the meaninglessness of a

3. Romans 1:7.

life which consisted of the passage of time, of working to keep alive, and of distractions. They suffered agonies in the search for identity and salvation.

It is important to add that the operative religion, to which all were expected to adhere, was the religion of the Emperor, or of the State. It was a prudential, and hence a spurious, religion, which was quite content with outward observance, but very suspicious of dissent, intolerant of divided allegiance, even on the part of people who lived the most exemplary and useful and inoffensive lives. Christians and Jews had a God who claimed a higher allegiance than Caesar; they had an experience that they regarded as richer than citizenship in the Empire. Consequently they were regarded as atheists, godless. The State cult had to be enforced and at the same time it had to demand unquestioning obedience, because something had to hold things together in a world where there were individuals but where natural and traditional communities had been dissolved and new ones not yet delivered from the womb of time, not yet revealed by the Creator. Meanwhile the steady tramp of Rome's soldiers was heard in every road of that ancient world.

The Early Church

In addressing the Christians living in that city in those days Paul could use the term "beloved of God" and be sure they would recognize its applicability to themselves. Let me try to state very briefly and sketchily some things in Christian experience to which that phrase points.

To begin with, these people were not first saints and then and therefore beloved of God. In a way it was just the opposite. It was because they were not saints, because they had looked steadily and deeply enough into themselves to realize that they were not saints, that there was some subtle corruption within, an ultimate inability to lift oneself to true virtue and pure, understanding love by one's own bootstraps, that in the moment of ultimate despair and self-abasement they had found—not the abyss, not eternal darkness, not the Enemy of the Soul, but God, pure grace, possibility. The experience was mediated to them by the figure on the cross. No doubt they cried out in much the same language as the medieval hymn writer:

> O sacred head, now wounded . . .
> with thorns thine only crown
>
> Mine, mine was the transgression,
> and thine the deadly pain.[4]

4. James Waddel Alexander, trans., "O Sacred Head Now Wounded," 1830.

I suppose the experience is somewhat analogous to what takes place in psychoanalysis: when the self has been confronted, when the hidden has been brought to the surface, the perhaps paradoxical result is not horror and paralysis—they come when the hidden has not yet been faced—but release and a new birth.

Secondly, there was ecstasy for these uprooted and inwardly torn individuals in the realization that they were "beloved," but it was not the essentially sentimental feeling that sometimes passes for religious experience, of being a father's favorite child. It was not the feeling "God loves me, though everybody else hates me," which really means that I hate everybody else—individuals were saved but not *as individuals*. They were baptized into the church, that is, they were saved by finding that a true community existed, a community of love, and by finding themselves a part of it. "By this we *know* that we have passed from death into life, because we love the brethren."[5] There is no such thing as being forgiven but unforgiving. On the other hand, people who do not have the experience of being forgiven, that is, have not been able to accept themselves, cannot be forgiving either, cannot accept others for what they are.

In the third place, then, the crucial development was the emergence of a Christian community, a fellowship, a family that embraced all of humanity.

The State sensed a threat in this fellowship that meant more to its members than the civic order and their citizenship in that. It sensed a threat in a fellowship that was somehow set apart from "the world," though its members were in their external behavior good citizens, law-abiding. To understand the real situation it is necessary to look at it from the other side, from *within* the church. The fact that to its members this "Society of Friends" was profoundly satisfying, real and permanent—"the gates of Hell shall not prevail against it"—meant that "the world" in which they existed was seen by them as deeply lacking, as unreal, impermanent, bound to pass away.[6] Augustine in a later century was to say of the seemingly powerful and indestructible "world," the civic order: "The kingdoms of the world seem able to dominate and destroy everything; but they are themselves dominated and destroyed by their own lust for power."[7] He might have said: by their own will to exist as they are, to arrogate to themselves a substantiality which never belongs to what is, but only to what may be.

5. 1 John 3:14.

6. Matthew 16:18.

7. Augustine makes this argument in *The City of God*. This does not appear to be a direct quotation.

The practical result of their feeling of the unreality and inadequacy of "the world" was that the early Christians had broken loose from it, from its allurements but even more, since it is not too uncommon for people to resist superficial allurements, from its rewards, its threats, its standards, and its version of what constitutes security. They knew in their bones that all this was perishing, "there shall not be left here one stone upon another that shall not be torn down."[8] Consequently, their faces were turned toward the future, a future already present in some profound sense; to the *new* kingdom, of which Christ was king, the *new* society in which all were his sisters and brothers and hence each other's. They were not merely, like their uprooted contemporaries, in movement; they were in movement toward a goal.

History as Movement Toward a Goal

The concept of history as movement toward a goal is deeply imbedded in Western thinking. Its source is primarily Hebraic. Abraham is not only the progenitor of Israel but "the father of many peoples." He stands at the beginning of both profane and sacred history because in obedience to divine command he left the city of his ancestors. Unquestionably, this represents a great turning point in human history. It is in one sense the greatest revolution of all, since it is the father of revolutions and of the revolutionary concept of history as the expression of God at work. History and the daily life of humanity are, therefore, real and not illusory. If God is to be found at all, God must be found here. People become co-workers, co-creators, and they are in movement toward a goal.

There had, of course, been nomadic wanderings before Abraham. But they were essentially movements of a geographical character. The tribe moved as a tribe and fought as a tribe, for the immediate purpose of obtaining forage for the flocks. When people settled down, cultivated land, and built cities, they conceived of their society as having been founded by the gods of the place or by divine ancestors. The pattern of life was fixed, as if in the nature of things. Individuals could hardly conceive of themselves or be conceived of by others as having an existence outside this pattern. Their destiny and duty was to remain in the city of their birth so that their children after them could inherit this same fixed and sacred pattern.

But with Abraham the divine command becomes radically different. What makes a person the true servant of the Most High is that they do not remain in the place of their birth. It has its sacredness and importance, but as a point of departure. Through Abraham people in the Hebraic tradition

8. Matthew 24:2, Mark 13:2, Luke 21:6.

came to know that their destiny and their God are not ties that bind and confine them. They are ahead of them and are drawing them outward and onward. The crucial thing about people, or societies, is not where they came from but where they are going.

What is of even more significance about Abraham than the fact that he emigrated from Ur of the Chaldees is that there was no city, no society or community for him to move into. Had his journey been simply a geographical one, to another Ur with another name, it would have constituted no part of the source of dynamic Western civilization.

The fact is that Abraham "went out, not knowing whither he went."[9] He was a fool and a gambler. But he was not a little fool; rather he was a big one, whose foolishness consisted in taking on a herculean task. He gambled for stakes of such a nature that the gambling itself became the pattern of human history. It created Western society and is still its lifeblood and its reason for existence.

Abraham went out looking for a city that existed—and yet had to be brought into existence. It was the perfect and holy city—which had to be built and whose "builder and maker is God."[10] Precisely because it was God who built the city, it could be built only by Abraham's faith and labor.

The creative movement in history is not from any city-that-is to another city-that-is. The reality is not what people tend to call the real. Insofar as it is fixed and has a fixating or binding effect on people or societies, it is already becoming unreal and insubstantial. What matters is the movement from the unreal, because unrealized, city-that-is to the city-that-is-to-be, which is more real because the potentiality of realization and completion remains.

Looking Toward a New Age

The experience of having broken loose, of being through with an illusory reality and related instead to the real, was indicated for, and habitually expressed by, the first Christians in the concept of the second coming of Christ. This is a concept about which there has been enormous controversy. It is certain that the early Christian response to the idea was not that of certain groups who become convinced that Christ is going to return on a certain date and hour and who leave ordinary work and ties to wait on some hilltop to greet him. Nothing is made clear more repeatedly in the New

9. Hebrews 11:8.

10. Hebrews 11:10.

Testament than that the second coming would be a surprise. "Of the day and the hour no man knoweth."[11]

What the concept meant to the early Christians in life, as distinct from dogma or verbal formulation, was that to them Christ whom the world deemed foolish, weak, defeated, dead, was in fact the wisdom of God, the power of God. He was alive, here, and always about to come in power and glory. The divine was always about to break into history.

There was continuity, it is true, but there was also discontinuity. The past did not simply grind out the future through the sieve of the present. The reality was the *new* age, the new fellowship of love. Consequently, change and possibility were the operative concepts with which they worked.

As we look back and reflect on these things, we do so, of course, from our own standing ground in the perspective of the whole history of the church, of the Western world, the vast stream that issued from those tiny, hidden springs in Rome. The early Christians could not look from this perspective.

We know also that what came about in many respects did not resemble their dreams. It never does. Corruption was mingled with the glory. It always is. Nevertheless, there is no doubt that these believers "in Rome, beloved of God," this fellowship, represents a great movement in history, in the dialogue between God and humanity, in the unfolding of the divine-human society.

Joy and Experimentation

The third idea in Paul's salutation, "called to be saints," did not mean that they were all or always extremely virtuous, ascetic, saintly in the usual sense of the word. Paul's Letters to the Corinthians suggests that there was quite a variety of saints, not all saintly.

What is clear, for one thing, is that they got a great kick out of being saints, that is, Christians. Joy was an outstanding characteristic of them. On the face of it, you cannot command Christians to be joyous, as if it were a duty. But the apostle could perpetuate the paradox and shout: "*Rejoice*, and again I say, Rejoice."[12] It was simply inconceivable that the experience of fellowship with one another and with Christ should not produce effervescence. Personally, I always have a certain suspicion of alleged saintliness that lacks this tone of buoyancy and effervescence.

11. Matthew 24:36, Mark 13:32.

12. Philippians 4:4.

Saintliness expressed itself in *experimentation*, growing out of and demanded by the experience of love and of release, of having cut loose. Experimentation took place in relation to violence: the early Christians did not serve in Caesar's armies—"Our Lord in disarming Peter disarmed every soldier."[13] It took place in economic life, in a religious communism of consumption, though not of production. Such experimentation seemed to follow naturally from their altered view of the nature of history.

Community

Religious people in such a time see apocalyptic visions and embrace an apocalyptic view of history. I surmise that some form of apocalypticism is a conscious or unconscious part of the mentality of those who are drawn into intentional communities, whether they are religious or not. In our own day, many people are attracted to the Jehovah's Witnesses and Seventh Day Adventists. They are growing. I think it must be granted that as dissenters from the prevailing culture they are pretty effective. There is no question that their members find an intense and deeply satisfying fellowship in their movement. It is also true that in these denominations there are standards regarding the use of income, and a degree of economic sharing that one does not find in the more respectable churches. But these people do not live in communities of the kind we usually associate with that term. They live much more in the mainstream of urban or rural life, and mingle more constantly with people than communitarians generally do.

The same thing may be said of the early Christians, and it will certainly not be contended that they were not effective or that they did not achieve *koinonia* of a remarkable kind, even though they did not live in some Middle Eastern or Italian Rifton or Primavera settlement, but rather in a second- or third-century equivalent of London, Paris, or New York.[14] "See how these Christians love one another," their neighbors used to remark.[15] In the field of social relationships, perhaps the most amazing thing about these men and women, who also lived in an age of deep cleavages in society, is that they could say, not as a mere form of words, not as an ideal perhaps partially

13. Tertullian, *On Idolatry*, chapter 19. Muste's quotation has been corrected. It originally read: "Our Lord is disarming, Peter disarmed every soldier."

14. The Woodcrest (Rifton, New York) and Primavera (Asunción, Paraguay) settlements are part of the Bruderhof communities, intentional communities similar in orientation to the Hutterites (an Anabaptist sect). They practice common ownership and plain dress and are pacifists.

15. Tertullian, *The Apology*, chapter 39.

achieved, but as a fact of their life: "In Christ Jesus"—here in this fellowship of love—"there is neither Jew nor Greek, barbarian, Scythian, slave, free."[16] It is about as if in a Baptist Church in the Deep South whites and blacks worshipped together—as of course they should—and if attacked for that by the heathen were to shout joyously together: "In Christ Jesus there is neither black nor white, neither North nor South."

We Are In Rome

Let me now try to relate some of the facts about the condition and the response of the "saints in Rome" to our own condition and response, being mindful of the danger in pressing historical analogies in a mechanical fashion.

It is obvious that there are indeed many resemblances. Even the members of the so-called historic peace churches are today largely city-dwellers. The world is becoming urbanized in the twentieth century.

Old boundaries are being wiped out. The reality at this point is to some extent obscured, for one thing, by the deep East-West cleavage and also by the intense upsurge of nationalism. But the East-West conflict is itself the result of One World coming into being, and evidence that any important development is now a global one. The eruption of nationalism takes place in the larger and dominant context of worldwide communication, industrialization, and nuclear technology.

It is a world in which the old faiths are no longer dominant factors. This is true both in the sense that religious institutions are not decisive in fashioning culture or shaping national policy, and in the sense that religious practices do not, for the most part, deeply satisfy churchgoers.

Human beings are physically in motion again. Psychologically and spiritually they are rootless. Old traditions and ties have been loosened, new ones not yet formed. It may be said that individuals are emancipated *from* many things, but they are not *persons*, and hence free for living. As the common phrase goes, they are fragmented and alienated. Political discussion and action tends toward taking opinion polls. Life, like much diplomacy, becomes an elaborate minuet performed by puppets.

Another contributing factor is the threat of nuclear annihilation. Those of us who are engaged in "peace work" may feel frustrated because we do not seem to be able to penetrate a thick crust of indifference and to make the mass of citizens aware of the threat. But a closer look makes it clear that this element that shuts out the future, that places the survival of humankind in

16. Colossians 3:11.

jeopardy, is having a subtle, corrosive effect in many fields and in the depths of the human spirit.

One more thing has to be noted, namely that in our time as in Rome of the first Christian centuries, the operative religion, the one in which people actually believe or to which in any case they submit, is that of the State. It is a prudential religion. And as is always the case where there is not a deep inner religion, external enforcement tends to prevail and increase. You have to have the effects of loyalty in human society; if, therefore, human beings *are* not loyal, you have to force them to be. This phenomenon exists both in the communist and in the non-communist world, though in different forms and perhaps in somewhat different degrees.

After all this it is no surprise that we can add that the tramp of soldiers is heard on every road of our world as in the ancient Roman one, or, since soldiers tend perhaps to become obsolete, that the missiles and other machines of war multiply, and in this case too, on both sides of the so-called "Iron Curtain." We are indeed in Rome.

In some sense also we know ourselves to be "beloved of God." We belong to the Society of Friends, a community of love, a family of persons. Insofar as we are not just another "denomination," we know also that the salvation of our age is in our keeping; that is, that it lies in the divine-human society which is "rooted and grounded in love."[17] This is the unity that alone can make one world out of "one world," and not one nightmare, one hell, one burned-out cinder.

We know also and in a way we respond to the fact that we have a mission, we are "called to be saints."

Yet we have not, let me put it, experienced Pentecost. The Spirit has not invaded the houses where we meet. We are not on fire. How then wait for the Spirit? How open the door?

Spiritual Agony

First let us recall what we said about the spiritual agony of the early Christians, the confrontation of a person with their own corruption, weakness, alone-ness; and the finding God, love, truth, precisely at that moment of genuine despair. Do we perhaps sometimes tend to obscure this aspect, this spring of religious living by our focusing exclusively on the idea that people are "naturally good," that there is "that of God" in every person? I do not mean to deny the truth to which such phrases point, but we always have our

17. Ephesians 3:17.

"treasure in earthen vessels," do we not?[18] In fixing our eyes on one aspect of truth we inevitably shut out or blur another.

It was surely by the hard road of spiritual agony that people like George Fox and James Naylor arrived at clarity, power and serenity.[19] I am suggesting that we shall achieve confidence and power only in the degree that we do not deceive ourselves about ourselves. This experience of self-examination and repentance is not something that takes place once and for all. It is a state rather than an event.

This is an experience I came to understand when in 1915 as a young pastor I had to face—not academically but existentially—the question of whether I could reconcile what I had been preaching out of the Gospels, and passages like 1 Corinthians 13 from the Epistles, with participation in the war which had already begun in Europe and in which it was clear the United States would eventually become involved. The problem, as it presented itself to me, was simply one for the Christian conscience. It was a problem that I could not evade because I had been brought up to take religion, specifically the biblical teaching and gospel ethic, seriously, and to abhor the sham that enables people to preach what they do not try desperately to practice. Moreover, my upbringing had given me a definite attitude regarding the struggle that goes on perpetually in the human spirit and in society as to whether the gospel demand shall be adjusted to the outward circumstances or the recalcitrant reality shall be made to conform to the high ethical demand. I did not believe that there is a pat rule that one can find in a proof text and apply to a complicated situation, thereby achieving perfection. I had received too solid a dose of Calvinism not to have a strong conviction about human frailty and corruption. It was this that had made me aware, long before Freud was more than a name to me, that when we are sure that we are honest, we deceive ourselves; when we imagine ourselves to be pure, we are impure; and when we bask in the glow of the feeling that we love, the fact is that in subtle ways we hate.

In each psychological "moment" of our lives, in each moment of decision it is necessary for us to know this. It is in the moment when we know how foolish we can be that we begin to be wise. It is when we are aware of our impurity that we are pure. It is when we are aware in what subtle ways hate can express itself that we learn to love.

It is salutary, I suggest, that we who are Quakers apply this test to our social activities. We think that in our practice of silence, in avoiding ballots and decision by majority, in depending on "the sense of the meeting" we

18. 2 Corinthians 4:7.

19. Fox and Naylor were two of the founders of Quakerism.

have a way of overcoming the artificiality, the evasions, the power plays, the rivalries of conventional "political" behavior and struggle. In a measure we do. But it would be fatal to feel complacent and self-satisfied at this point. Evasion, indirection, the play of ambition, the thirst for power, are not absent from our quarterly and yearly meetings, our committee work, the staffs of service committees, and so on. It will help to nourish a religious life in our midst if we think of such insights as are represented in the "sense of the meeting" concept, not as ripened fruit we have produced, but as seed that has been providentially planted within us, which has by no means come to full growth and for which we often furnish dry or even sour soil.

The Gospel Demand

But this does not alter the nature of the demand the gospel places upon us. The poet who does not agonize to translate the vision they see truly and exactly into their poem is not a poet. The person who does not passionately strive to be honest, pure and loving is not a person. The temptation to pride and self-righteousness is real and pervasive, but the temptation to adapt the gospel demand to circumstances and to abandon the hard effort to mold one's own life and the world according to that imperious demand is no less subtle and pervasive.

G. K. Chesterton, in a beautiful passage in the volume *Alarums and Discussions*, has stated his version of this law of life:

> Bows are beautiful when they bend only because they try to remain rigid, and sword blades can curl like silver only because they are certain to spring straight again. . . . The foil may curve in the lunge, but there is nothing beautiful about beginning the battle with a crooked foil. So the strict aim, the strong doctrine, may give a little in the actual fight with facts; but that is no reason for beginning with a weak doctrine or a twisted aim . . . Do not try to bend, any more than trees try to bend. Try to grow straight, and life will bend you.[20]

We cannot extricate ourselves from the human condition, which means both that we do not lose the capacity for self-deception and hence the need for self-examination; and that we fail, like the apostle, to do the good that

20. G.K. Chesterton, "The Furrows," in *Alarums and Discussions* (New York: Dodd, Mead, 1911), 86–87.

we would. But we can be safely grateful that it is, nevertheless, the good that we will, and that we, too, can do all things in Christ who strengtheneth us.[21]

Facing the Evil in the World

In the next place, as a true religious life depends on facing ourselves, probing deeply into ourselves, it also depends upon and is nourished by facing our world, our age. We are called to be Saints "in Rome." One thing this implies is that we must face the evil in other people and in the various social patterns which constitute "the world."

Consider Eichmann and his trial in Israel.[22] There are people who perpetrate monstrous evil. There are regimes that permit or even breed monstrous evil. People habitually deal with such situations as if they themselves were good and therefore entitled to sit in judgment and to cast these criminals into hell or blast these regimes off the face of the earth, and to all such the gospel says: "Have you seen that monster in yourself?"

But there is also a perverse way of using that admonition into which we sometimes fall. Subconsciously we argue that after all *we* are not so bad, not "that bad," and accordingly this person is not so bad, this regime is not so bad either. But this really means that we have not yet faced the hater and killer in ourselves. And it will be in the degree that we are sensitive in this area and do not equate love with sentimentality, and child-likeness with childishness, and reconciliation with glossing over and suppressing reality, that our faith in "that of God" in people will be pure and hence efficacious.

The same kind of counsel applies to our dealing with the "realities of power and the power struggle" in the world. Ultimately, as Augustine declared in the passage we have already quoted, the power structure is not permanent, not real. It is the house built on sand. Yet in its way the Roman Empire was real enough. So is the United States, the Soviet Union, the H-bomb, the Polaris missile, the arms race. We have to function in relation to such realities and as Martin Buber said in a profound utterance: "It is difficult, terribly difficult, to drive the plowshare of the normative principle into the hard soil of political reality."[23]

21. Romans 7:18–20, Philippians 4:13.

22. Adolf Eichmann was one of the major organizers of the Holocaust, in charge of organizing transportation logistics. He was captured in 1960 in Argentina by agents of the Mossad, Israel's intelligence agency. After a highly publicized trial, he was executed by Israel in 1962.

23. Martin Buber, *At the Turning: Three Addresses on Judaism* (New York: Farrar, Straus and Young, 1952), 24. This quotation differs from the original.

We and some of our fellow Christians are continually at cross-purposes, it seems to me, because they tend to say: "There is no normative principle, or at any rate it doesn't apply here; the realm of power is autonomous, it develops according to its own laws." We, on the other hand, tend to fall into sentimentalism. We don't realize that the soil *is* hard, that it *is* "terribly difficult" and complicated to make love operative in politics. To a very considerable extent, I surmise the answer to the question whether we can have in our day a Christianity that "speaks to power" authoritatively and yet in love depends on whether we can resist our respective temptations and come together to agonize our way to a common program.

Another thing I have in mind when I refer to realistically facing our world is something quite different, on which I have really no light to throw. Yet it is something we must at least be aware of. I refer to science, both physical and social-psychological, the runaway technology, the "wisdom" of our age. These things represent a great danger—apart from the threat of nuclear annihilation. The inner life of humanity may be neglected, starved, fragmented, shattered under these pressures. It has even been suggested that humanity may be threatened with a new fall, now that it seems to be fathoming the secrets of the universe.

We tend to regard these developments as simply evil or completely mysterious, or to ignore them. But if we do try to evade and escape from the findings and the challenge of the new knowledge, it means that we are afraid, we have not yet experienced "the love which casteth out fear."[24] Being afraid and evasive, we shall also be ineffective and futile in trying to bring to the Greeks of our age a wisdom—a "foolishness"—which is indeed wiser than their own.

Commitment and Creativity

My last and, I feel, most important observation relates to what I had in mind when I spoke of the early Christians as having "broken loose." They understood that for all its size, seeming stability and power, the "world," the "age," in which they lived was ephemeral, weak, doomed. It was not built on sound foundations. They had, therefore, turned their backs on it in the sense that they were not placing their bets on it, did not give it their ultimate allegiance, were not intimidated by what it could do to them, and did not seek satisfaction and security within its structure, under its standards. They were loose—not tied to "business as usual."

24. 1 John 4:18.

I wrote at the beginning of this essay of my present experience among those who are considered "unbelievers." Some of my fellow-Christians are unable to understand why so much of my life has been spent among such persons and groups, and more particularly why, at one period, I counted myself among them. Perhaps it is in this area of "looseness" that one can find the key to this experience . . . it was on the Left—and here the communists of the period cannot be excluded—that one found people who were truly "religious" in the sense that they were virtually completely committed, they were betting their lives on the cause they embraced. Often they gave up ordinary comforts, security, life itself, with a burning devotion, which few Christians display toward the Christ whom they profess as Lord and the incarnation of God. Later I was to mourn the wastage of so much youthful devotion, and its corruption among communists and others, which I had witnessed from the inside. Yet the beauty and attractive power of commitment to that which we profess to believe remains—and it plays a considerable part in the contemporary world struggle.

Besides, the Left had the vision, the dream, of a classless and warless world, as the hackneyed phrase goes. This also was a strong factor in making me feel that here, in a sense, was the true church. Here was the fellowship drawn together and drawn forward by the Judaeo-Christian prophetic vision of a "new earth in which righteousness dwelleth."[25] The now generally despised Christian liberals had had this vision. As neo-orthodoxy took over, that vision was scorned as naive and utopian. The "kingdom" was something to be realized "beyond history." And again, the communists are those who are today able to convince vast multitudes that they do cherish the ancient dream of brotherhood realized on earth and have the determination to make it come true. This is a measure of the fall of what is called the Free World. The liberal Christians were never, in my opinion, wrong in cherishing the vision. Their mistake, and in a sense, their crime, was not to see that it was revolutionary in character and demanded revolutionary living and action of those who claimed to be its votaries.

The other aspect of the experience of the early Christians was that they *did* feel the reality, the authority, of the fellowship which they had found. It had the keys to the future. They lived in *this* world and by its power. Perforce, therefore, they were *experimentalists*, seeking to live out the implications of the love they had experienced, of that "love of God and not of self" to which they were joyously committed.

This quality of looseness from the world-that-is, of experimentation, creativeness, characterizes all the great periods of religious history. This is

25. 2 Peter 3:13.

certainly true of early Quakerism. It is from this same spring that our religious life will have to be nourished.

Become a New Humanity or Perish

There is no doubt that our world is doomed. I do not mean by this that I think nuclear war and resultant nuclear annihilation are inevitable. It would be even more risky, I think, to assert that they will not happen. But I am not here making a political judgment or calculation. In a much profounder sense, the world we have known is passing. The uncovering of nuclear secrets, other developments we might mention, make this certain. Humankind *has* to find the way into a radically new world. Humankind has to become a "new humanity" or perish.

If we are true at such a juncture to the seed of love that is in us, that light of faith that neither inner nor outer storms have put out, then we shall be loose and experimental. We shall set less and less store by the world's gifts of money, success, respectability, comfort. Most of all, we shall then truly live *in* the Society of Friends, the fellowship of love, shall truly believe that the divine-human society is real, is the future. We shall be aware that we stand at the end of an era, but much more basically that we stand before a new beginning.

It is surely in this context very significant how many Friends experienced a refreshing, a nourishing of the inner life of the Spirit when recently a thousand of them "cut loose" and "experimented," standing in silent vigil around the Pentagon.

By grace, if we continue in this way we shall daily love more deeply. Daily, in the freedom of the Spirit, we shall build in our homes, neighborhoods, cities, the city that is to be, whose builder and maker is God.

We shall do it not because we are wise, strong, politically astute, but because the Spirit dwells in our hearts and the Lord is coming, will reveal himself. His kingdom is *ever* at hand.

For us all is as yet unbegun; but where the Spirit of the Lord is, there is liberty and possibility.

All this was movingly stated some ten years ago by an American poet, Muriel Rukeyser, who did not come at the matter primarily from a Christian approach. In a volume entitled *The Life of Poetry* she said: "Now again we see that all is unbegun. The only danger is in not going far enough. . . . If we go deep enough, we reach the common life, the shared experience of man, the world of possibility. If we do not go deep enough, if we live and write halfway, there are obscurity, vulgarity, the slang of fashion, and several kinds of death."[26] Let us mark the dangers if we do not go far enough: "obscurity," confusion as to our goals; "vulgarity," the resort to clever and evil means to achieve our ends; "the slang of fashion," such as succumbing to the ways of "Madison Avenue." For us, too, no doubt "several kinds of death" will be available if we do not realize how clean the break must be, how loose of the "world" we must be, how thoroughly experimental, how profoundly convinced of possibility—if, that is to say, we do not go far enough.

26. Muriel Rukeyser, *The Life of Poetry* (New York: Current Books, 1949), 201.

Bibliography

"Admonitions for War Time." Script of a sermon broadcast on the Church of the Air Program, Columbia Broadcasting System. March 3, 1940. Swarthmore College Peace Collection, A. J. Muste Papers, box 5 (microfilm reel 89.3).

Christianity, the Only Hope of the World. Philadelphia: Book Association of Friends, 1918.

The Church's Responsibility for Peace: A Matter of Life and Death. An Address Delivered to the General Synod of the Reformed Church in America. June 7, 1937. Committee on International Justice and Goodwill, Reformed Church in America, [1937].

"Church's Witness to Her Faith." *The Intelligencer-Leader* 5, no. 19 (September 2, 1938): 4–5, 20.

"Evangelism and the Industrial Workers." Manuscript. c. 1937–39. Swarthmore College Peace Collection, A. J. Muste Papers, box 13 (microfilm reel 89.5).

Fellowship and Class Struggle. New York: Fellowship of Reconciliation, 1930. Reprint from *World Unity* 6, nos. 1–2 (April–May, 1930): 7–17, 115–23.

"Fragment of Autobiography." *Christendom* 4, no. 3 (Summer 1939): 329–40.

"Glad to Be Alive and a Christian in 1918: Sermon Preached by Rev. A. J. Muste at the Ordination and Installation of Harold Linson Stratton, Harvard Congregational Church, Dorchester, Massachusetts, January 10, 1918." Informally published pamphlet. Swarthmore College Peace Collection, Fellowship of Reconciliation records, section II, series C, box 3.

"I Believe." *Fellowship* 16, no. 2 (February 1950): 3–7.

Jesus and the Way to Peace. New York: Fellowship of Reconciliation, 1954. Swarthmore College Peace Collection.

"The Knowledge of God." Handwritten sermon notes. November 1936. Swarthmore College Peace Collection, A. J. Muste Papers, box 5 (microfilm reel 89.3).

"The Man on the Cross Against the Atomic Bomb." Chapter 5 of *Not By Might: Christianity, the Way to Human Decency*. New York: Harper & Brothers, 1947.

"Of What Shall We Be Afraid." In *Tracts for These Times*, 3–15. Boston: Geo. H. Ellis, 1915. Swarthmore College Peace Collection, Congregational and Christian Church subject file.

Pacifism and Perfectionism: A Discussion of Some Neo-Orthodox Criticism of Pacifism. New York: Fellowship of Reconciliation, n.d.

This pamphlet combined:[1]

1. The version of this piece that appeared in Nat Hentoff's *The Essays of A. J. Muste* included only the first two articles and incorrectly gave the date as 1948.

"The Doctrine of Perfection I." *Fellowship* 16, no. 3 (March 1950): 7–11.
"The Doctrine of Perfection II." *Fellowship* 16, no. 4 (April 1950): 13–18.
"Utopianism in Christianity." *Fellowship* 16, no. 5 (May 1950): 11–16, 32.
"Love in Action." *Fellowship* 16, no. 6 (June 1950): 7–13, 32.

"A Prayer for Peace." *The Presbyterian Tribune* 65, no. 10 (July–August, 1950): 23.[2]

"Questions from the Left." In *Labor Speaks for Itself on Religion; A Symposium of Labor Leaders Throughout the World*, edited by Jerome Davis, 97–107. New York: Macmillan, 1929.

"Return to Pacifism." *The Christian Century* 53, no. 49 (December 2, 1936): 1603–6.

Saints for This Age. Wallingford, PA: Pendle Hill, 1962.

"The Sound of the Trumpet." *Fellowship* 26, no. 9 (May 1, 1960): 11–16.

"Surfeit and Famine." *World Tomorrow* 1, no. 10 (October 1918): 253–55.

"Theology of Despair: An Open Letter to Reinhold Niebuhr." *Fellowship* 14, no. 8 (September 1948): 4–8.

"The True International: Eighteenth Article in the Series, 'How My Mind Has Changed in This Decade.'" *The Christian Century* 56, no. 21 (May 24, 1939): 667–69.

"Unable and Unwilling to Conform." Originally appeared as: "April 27—A Message to the Fellowship." *Fellowship* 8, no. 5 (May 1942): 75–76.

"Unity in Crisis: Sermon to First Presbyterian Church of Brooklyn, N.Y." Manuscript. July 27, 1941. Swarthmore College Peace Collection, A. J. Muste Papers, box 5 (microfilm reel 89.3).

"The Way of the Cross." *The Christian Century* 55, no. 50 (December 14, 1938): 1541–43.

What the Bible Teaches About Freedom: A Message to the Negro Churches. New York: Fellowship of Reconciliation, 1943.

2. A version of the prayer was printed in the program for the May 1950 Detroit Conference on the Church and War and was read in unison by the participants. The program and drafts of the prayer can be found at the Swarthmore College Peace Collection, Fellowship of Reconciliation records, section II, series F, box 1. A report to the Fellowship of Reconciliation membership about the conference can be found in series A-5, box 3.

Recommended Reading

Commins, Gary. *Spiritual People, Radical Lives: Dorothy Day, Martin Luther King, Jr., Thomas Merton, A. J. Muste*. San Francisco: Freedom Voices, 2000.

This book is notable for its examination of Muste's spirituality. It was previously published as *Spiritual People, Radical Lives: Spirituality and Justice in Four 20th Century American Lives*. San Francisco: International Scholars Publications, 1996.

Danielson, Leilah. *American Gandhi: A. J. Muste and the History of Radicalism in the Twentieth Century*. Philadelphia: University of Pennsylvania Press, 2014.

Danielson is perhaps the foremost living authority on Muste. This biography is especially detailed in describing Muste's involvement in the labor movement.

———. "Christianity, Dissent, and the Cold War: A. J. Muste's Challenge to Realism and U.S. Empire." *Diplomatic History* 30, no. 4 (September 2006): 645–69.

This article is a well-researched look at Muste's critique of US foreign policy and his debate with Reinhold Niebuhr over "Christian realism."

———. "'It Is a Day of Judgment': The Peacemakers, Religion, and Radicalism in Cold War America." *Religion & American Culture* 18, no. 2 (Summer 2008): 215–48.

In this article, Danielson explores the connection between Muste's faith and activism.

Hentoff, Nat. *Peace Agitator: The Story of A. J. Muste*. New York: Macmillan, 1963.

This is an early non-scholarly biography of Muste.

Kosek, Joseph Kip. *Acts of Conscience: Christian Nonviolence and Modern American Democracy*. New York: Columbia University Press, 2009.

Kosek looks at the impact of Muste and other radical Christian pacifists on US democracy. Beginning with World War I and ending with the civil rights movement, this book is an important history of the US pacifist movement.

Muste, Abraham Johannes. *The Essays of A. J. Muste*. Edited by Nat Hentoff. Indianapolis: Bobbs-Merrill, 1967.

The first collection of Muste's writings, this is essential reading for anyone interested in Muste.

———. *Non-Violence in an Aggressive World*. New York: Harper & Brothers, 1940.

This is Muste's first book and a good source of his thinking during the late 1930s.

———. *Not By Might: Christianity, the Way to Human Decency*. New York: Harper & Brothers, 1947.

Muste's second of two books, this is the main source of his thought immediately following the conclusion of World War II. A number of the chapters are deeply theological.

Robinson, Jo Ann Ooiman. *Abraham Went Out: A Biography of A. J. Muste*. Philadelphia: Temple University Press, 1981.

This well-researched biography is comparable in importance to Danielson's.

Subject Index

Scripture Index

Isaiah (*continued*)

Jeremiah

Daniel

Hosea

Micah

Zechariah

Matthew

Mark

Luke

John

Acts

Romans

1 Corinthians

2 Corinthians

Galatians

Ephesians

Philippians

Colossians

1 Thessalonians

Hebrews

James

2 Peter

1 John

Revelation